Judicial Review in New Democracies
Constitutional Courts in Asian Cases

In recent decades, new democracies around the world have adopted constitutional courts to oversee the operation of democratic politics. Where does judicial power come from, how does it develop in the early stages of democratic liberalization, and what political conditions support its expansion? This book answers these questions through an examination of three constitutional courts in Asia: Taiwan, Korea, and Mongolia. In a region where law has traditionally been viewed as a tool of authoritarian rulers, constitutional courts in these three societies are becoming a real constraint on government. In contrast with conventional culturalist accounts, this book argues that the design and function of constitutional review are largely a function of politics and interests. Judicial review – the power of judges to rule an act of a legislature or executive unconstitutional – is a solution to the problem of uncertainty in constitutional design. By providing "insurance" to prospective electoral losers, judicial review can facilitate democracy.

Professor Tom Ginsburg is Assistant Professor of Law and Political Science and Director of the Program on Asian Law, Politics, and Society at the University of Illinois. He holds B.A., J.D., and Ph.D. degrees from the University of California, Berkeley. He has worked extensively in Asia on legal reform and democracy programs, spent a year lecturing at Kyushu University, Japan, and worked at the Iran-U.S. Claims Tribunal in The Hague. He has authored numerous articles on comparative law and international arbitration.

Judicial Review in New Democracies

Constitutional Courts in Asian Cases

TOM GINSBURG

University of Illinois

CAMBRIDGE UNIVERSITY PRESS
Cambridge, New York, Melbourne, Madrid, Cape Town, Singapore, São Paulo

Cambridge University Press
The Edinburgh Building, Cambridge CB2 2RU, UK

Published in the United States of America by Cambridge University Press, New York

www.cambridge.org
Information on this title: www.cambridge.org/9780521817158

© Cambridge University Press 2003

First published 2003

A catalogue record for this publication is available from the British Library

Library of Congress Cataloguing in Publication data

Ginsburg, Thomas, 1967–
Judicial review in new democracies : constitutional courts in Asian cases /
Thomas Ginsburg.
p. cm.
Includes bibliographical references and index.
ISBN 0-521-81715-3 – ISBN 0-521-52039-8 (pbk.)
1. Constitutional courts – East Asia. 2. Judicial review – East Asia.
3. Judicial power – East Asia. 4. Democratization – East Asia. I. Title.
KNC608 .G56 2003
347.5′035–dc21   2002041004

ISBN-13 978-0-521-81715-8 hardback
ISBN-10 0-521-81715-3 hardback

ISBN-13 978-0-521-52039-3 paperback
ISBN-10 0-521-52039-8 paperback

Transferred to digital printing 2006

To Amber

"...in the mysterious East as in the pellucid West, constitutions, however detailed, are no better than the institutions they are written into."

– Clifford Geertz, *Local Knowledge* (1983), p. 204

"Every judge who judges truly becomes, so to speak, an associate of the almighty in the creation of his World."

– Talmud Shabbat 10a

Contents

Acknowledgments

I have incurred many debts in writing this book. Martin Shapiro has been a generous advisor before, during, and after my graduate work in the Jurisprudence and Social Policy Program at Berkeley. Robert Kagan was crucial in shaping the research strategy and provided superb comments on the entire manuscript. Robert Cooter has been an extraordinary model of theoretical creativity. Bob Berring, Neil Devins, Malcolm Feeley, Sam Ginsburg, Thomas Gold, James Lindgren, Richard McAdams, Eric Posner, Mark Ramseyer, Eric Rasmusen, Tom Ulen, Stefan Voigt, and Omri Yadlin provided helpful comments on all or portions of the manuscript or related projects. In Seoul, Mr. Park Tae-jin and Ms. Lee Kyong-sook of The Asia Foundation kindly arranged my visits. Dean Ahn Kyong-whan of Seoul National University and Judge Kwon O-gon, then of the Constitutional Court staff, provided invaluable help. Professor Rex Wang in Taipei was kind enough to share his vast experience and network of friends. In Ulaanbaatar, Ms. B. Tsenderkhuu and Ms. Z. Batuya of the Constitutional Court staff and G. Ganzorig, then of the Supreme Court, were extremely helpful. The Law Faculty of Kyushu University in Japan served as host for the research and drafting, and my thanks go to Professors Shinichi Ago and Masaru Yanagihara there. Research assistance at various points was provided by Claudia Acosta, Nykhana Chambers, Jessica Yu-jen Chen, Irene Hubicki, Dorothy Koontz, Joy Hsiu-yi Lin, Liu Cheng-lin, Allison Marshall, and Rebecca Shieh. Jane Williams of the University of Illinois College of Law Library provided extraordinary research assistance on this and many other projects. Susan Mart edited an early version of the manuscript and made this a better book. Diane Valk-Schwab of The Hague and Joetta Morgan of the University of Illinois

College of Law helped work on the draft, and Jeanette Sayre of Boalt
Hall rendered invaluable assistance at a key moment. I thank you all and
indemnify you from blame for errors in the text or thought behind it.
Thanks also to my parents for great patience and care, to my children
for being themselves, and to Amber, to whom this book is dedicated, for
everything.

Chapter 2 is an expanded version of an article that appeared as "Economic Analysis and the Design of Constitutional Courts" 3 *Theoretical
Inquiries in Law* 49–85 (January 2002). Chapters 5 and 6 include some
material from "Confucian Constitutionalism?" 27 *Law and Social Inquiry*
763–800 (2002). Thanks to these journals for allowing me to use this
material in this book.

Notes on Usage

Chinese and Korean names appear throughout the text and notes with family names first. For consistency, the anglicization of Korean names has been made uniform, with personal names hyphenated and the second syllable in lower case. I apologize should this deviate from preferred usage. Japanese names appear mainly in the references and are presented in western format with personal name first.

Judicial Review in New Democracies

Constitutional Courts in Asian Cases

Introduction

The Decline and Fall of Parliamentary Sovereignty

THE DECLINE OF PARLIAMENTARY SOVEREIGNTY

The idea of the sovereignty of Parliament was long seen as the core of democratic practice. The superior position of the popularly elected legislature and its corollary of majority rule have been central principles for democratic revolutionaries since the notion was appended to the unwritten English constitution.[1] At that time, the threat to liberty was monarchical power, and the subjugation of monarchical power to popular control was the primary goal. The resulting doctrine was that Parliament had "the right to make or unmake any law whatever; and further, that no person or body is recognized by the law of England as having a right to override or set aside the legislation of Parliament."[2]

In the continental tradition, the intellectual underpinning of parliamentary sovereignty was provided by the Rousseauian concept of the general will. The people were supreme, and their general will as expressed through their republican representatives could not be challenged. This theory, combined with the regressive position of the judicial *parlements* in the French Revolution, led to a long tradition of distrust of judges in

---

[1] The original focus in England during the Glorious Revolution was on control of the crown rather than the rule of the people per se, because the democratic franchise was quite restricted. Jeffrey Goldsworthy, *The Sovereignty of Parliament: History and Philosophy* (1999). Rakove distinguishes the supremacy of Parliament from the idea that representative bodies were primarily designed to be law-making bodies. Jack Rakove, "The Origins of Judicial Review: A Plea for New Contexts, 49 *Stan. L. Rev.* 1031, 1052 (1997).

[2] Albert V. Dicey, *The Law of the Constitution* 3–4 (8th ed., 1915).

France.[3] The *government du juges* replaced the crown as the primary threat to popular will in French political thought.[4]

It was natural that the early proponents of democracy supported parliamentary sovereignty. They saw threats to liberty from the traditional sources: the *ancien régime*, the monarchy, and the church. Once these formidable obstacles to popular power had been overcome, theorists could hardly justify limitations on the people's will, the sole legitimate source of power. As democratic practice spread, however, new threats emerged. In particular, Europe's experience under democratically elected fascist regimes in World War II led many new democracies to recognize a new, internal threat to the *demos*. No political institution, even a democratically legitimate one, ought to be able to suppress basic liberties. Postwar constitutional drafting efforts focused on two concerns: first, the enunciation of basic rights to delimit a zone of autonomy for individuals, which the state should not be allowed to abridge; and second, the establishment of special constitutional courts to safeguard and protect these rights. These courts were seen as protecting democracy from its own excesses and were adopted precisely because they could be countermajoritarian, able to protect the *substantive* values of democracy from procedurally legitimate elected bodies.

The ideal of limited government, or constitutionalism, is in conflict with the idea of parliamentary sovereignty.[5] This tension is particularly apparent where constitutionalism is safeguarded through judicial review. One governmental body, unelected by the people, tells an elected body that its will is incompatible with fundamental aspirations of the people. This is at the root of the "countermajoritarian difficulty," which has been

---

[3] Jeremy Jennings, "From 'Imperial State to l'Etat de Droit': Benjamin Constant, Blandine Kriegel and the Reform of the French Constitution," in *Constitutionalism in Transformation: European and Theoretical Perspectives* 76, 78 (Richard Bellamy and Dario Castiglione, eds., 1996). The *parlements* had engaged in a kind of judicial review themselves. Mauro Cappelletti, *Judicial Review in the Contemporary World* 33–34 (1971). The activation of the *Conseil Constitutionnel* in the Fifth Republic, especially because it unilaterally read the preamble of the constitution as being legally binding in 1971, has radically changed French practice in this regard. See Alec Stone, *The Birth of Judicial Politics in France* (1992).

[4] This distrust of a judicial role in governance, beyond applying legislation, led the French to create a special system of administrative courts in 1872. This system of special courts applying a separate law for the government led Dicey to argue that the French *droit administratif* was less protective of individual liberties than the English institutional manifestation of the rule of law. Dicey, *supra* note 2, 220–21, 266.

[5] Paul W. Kahn, *The Reign of Law*: Marbury v. Madison *and the Construction of America* 215 (1997).

the central concern of normative scholarship on judicial review for the past three decades.[6]

Although the postwar constitutional drafting choices in Europe dealt parliamentary sovereignty a blow, the idea retained force in terms of political practice. More often than not, the idea was used by undemocratic regimes. Marxist theory was naturally compatible with parliamentary sovereignty and incompatible with notions of constitutional, limited government. Similarly, new nations in Africa and Asia reacting to colonialism often dressed their regimes in the clothes of popular sovereignty, though oligarchy or autocracy were more often the result.

Today, in the wake of a global "wave" of democratization, parliamentary sovereignty is a waning idea, battered by the legacy of its affiliation with illiberalism. Judicial review has expanded beyond its homeland in the United States and has made strong inroads in those systems where it was previously alleged to be anathema. From France to South Africa to Israel, parliamentary sovereignty has faded away. We are in the midst of a "global expansion of judicial power," and the most visible and important power of judges is that of judicial review.[7]

Even in Britain, the homeland of parliamentary sovereignty and the birthplace of constitutional government, there have been significant incursions into parliamentary rule. There have been two chief mechanisms, one international and the other domestic. The first mechanism is the integration of Britain into the Council of Europe and the European Union (EU), which has meant that supranational law courts are now regularly reviewing British legislation for compatibility with international obligations. The domestic subordination of legislation of the British Parliament to European law was established when the House of Lords disapplied a parliamentary statute in response to the European Court of Justice's (ECJ) *Factortame* decision of 1991.[8] More recently, the incorporation of

---

[6] The term, and the terrain of the debate, were laid out by Alexander Bickel, *The Least Dangerous Branch: The Supreme Court at the Bar of American Politics* (2d ed., 1986).

[7] Neal Tate and Thorsten Vallinder, eds., *The Global Expansion of Judicial Power* (1995).

[8] *R. v. Secretary of State for Transport, ex parte Factortame Ltd (No. 2)* [1991] 1 A.C. 603. The case concerned parliamentary legislation aimed at preventing primarily Spanish-owned but British-registered ships from operating in particular quota areas. This violated various EU law principles of nondiscrimination. The House of Lords asked the ECJ whether it could issue a preliminary injunction against an act of Parliament and was told that it had an obligation to do so where legislation violated EU treaty rights. For a detailed discussion of the case, see Josef Drexl, "Was Sir Francis Drake a Dutchman? – British Supremacy of Parliament after Factortame," 41 *Am. J. Comp. L.* 551 (1993).

the European Convention of Human Rights into United Kingdom domestic law by the Human Rights Act 1998 has led to greater involvement of courts in considering the "constitutionality" of parliamentary statutes (and administrative actions) under the guise of examining compatibility with Convention requirements.[9] Although as a matter of domestic law the Human Rights Act attempts to preserve parliamentary sovereignty in that it allows an explicit parliamentary derogation from the convention, it has not been wholly successful. The Parliament now tends to scrutinize legislation for conformity with the convention, and this is a source of constraint; furthermore, even explicit parliamentary derogrations may still lead to a finding by the European Court of Human Rights that Britain has violated its obligations. Thus, it cannot really be said that the Parliament is truly sovereign in Dicey's sense of being unchecked by other bodies.

The second mechanism is the growth of domestic judicial review as shown by an expanding body of administrative law. According to many observers, United Kingdom (UK) courts are exhibiting growing activism in checking the government, especially since the 1980s.[10] This administrative law jurisprudence has grown in recent years. The practice of international courts reviewing British legislation no doubt played a role in undermining the primary objection to domestic judicial review. The British objection to domestic courts exercising judicial review was *not* that judges were incapable of it or that the rule of law was a secondary goal. Indeed, it was the assertion that government was subject to ordinary law applied by ordinary judges that was at the heart of Dicey's celebration of the English constitution. Rather, the traditional objection to judicial review was that the people acting through Parliament possess complete sovereignty. This argument has now lost force. If the will of the Queen in Parliament is already being constrained by a group of European law professors sitting in Strasbourg, then the objection to constraint by British judges is much less potent.

---

[9] See, for example, Ian Leigh, "Taking Rights Proportionately: Judicial Review, the Human Rights Act and Strasbourg," *Public Law* 265–87 (2002), and David Feldman, "Parliamentary Scrutiny of Legislation and Human Rights," *Public Law* 323–48 (2002).

[10] See, for example, Jerold L. Waltman, "Judicial Activism in England," in *Judicial Activism in Comparative Perspective* 33–52 (Kenneth Holland, ed., 1991); Susan Sterett, *Creating Constitutionalism? The Politics of Legal Expertise and Administrative Law in England and Wales* (1997). For an older doctrinal exegesis of judicial review in UK courts, see C.T. Emery and B. Smythe, *Judicial Review* (1986).

Even if one believes that Parliament is still sovereign in the United Kingdom, the adaptability of the always-anomalous British unwritten constitution as a model is clearly declining. In Britain itself, academics widely agree that there is a crisis of constitutional legitimacy.[11] Furthermore, several countries that were historically recipients of the British model have recently departed from it. In the Caribbean, several former British colonies have joined together to establish a new supranational court of final appeal, the Caribbean Court of Justice, discontinuing the practice of appeal to the Privy Council in London. Other former colonies have adopted constitutional acts or amendments entrenching new rights in the constitution.[12] In some countries, such as New Zealand and Israel, these acts are amendable by ordinary majorities and not entrenched as in other polities. Nevertheless, they maintain great normative power as constitutional legislation and politically speaking are more difficult to amend than legislation concerning routine matters of governance, even if not institutionally protected. There has even been a step in this direction in Saudi Arabia, although the Saudi government continues to take the formal position that it has neither a constitution nor legislation other than the law of Islam.[13]

The major bastions resistant to judicial involvement in constitutional adjudication have lowered their resistance in recent years. The concept of expanded judicial power has even crept surreptitiously into the international system, where there has been recent consideration as to whether there is a sort of inherent power of judicial review in international law.[14] The issue under consideration concerns whether the United Nations Security Council's findings that it is acting to defend peace and security under Chapter VII of the United Nations Charter (UN Charter) are reviewable by the International Court of Justice. There is no explicit

---

[11] For cites, see Tony Prosser, "Understanding the British Constitution," in *Constitutionalism in Transformation: European and Theoretical Perspective* 61, 68 n.33 (Richard Bellamy and Dario Castiglione, eds., 1996).

[12] For example, the Israeli Basic Laws of 1992, the Canadian Bill of Rights Act (1960), the Canadian Charter of Rights and Freedoms (1982), and the New Zealand Bill of Rights Act (1992).

[13] In 1992, the government adopted a Basic System of Rules that defines the structure of government and establishes a new mechanism for succession. See Rashed Aba-Namay, "The Recent Constitutional Reforms in Saudi Arabia," 42 *Int'l & Comp. L.Q.* 295 (1993).

[14] Dapo Akande, "The International Court of Justice and the Security Council: Is There Room for Judicial Control of Decisions of the Political Organs of the United Nations?," 46 *Int'l & Comp. L.Q.* 309 (1997); see also Jose Alvarez, "Judging the Security Council," 90 *Am. J. Int'l L.* 1 (1996).

provision for judicial review in the UN Charter, and a Belgian proposal to establish it during the drafting of the UN Charter was rejected. The International Court of Justice has, however, considered the issue in *dicta*. The court has thus far carefully avoided making an express finding that the security council has acted outside of the scope of its powers, but it refused to explicitly deny that the court has the power to review the security council's actions.[15]

The United Nations, of course, is not a democratic system, nor one wherein majority rule has ever been unconstrained, by virtue of the institutional entrenchment of particular founding nations through the veto power on the Security Council. It is nevertheless interesting that some of the same questions that confront new democracies are being asked at the international level as well. Is there any action by supreme organs in a legal system that are *ultra vires*? If so, who has the power to decide whether an action crosses the line? And if the answer is a judicial body, who guards the guardians of legality?

As the "third wave" of democracy has proceeded around the globe, it has been accompanied by a general expansion in the power of judges in both established and new democracies. Virtually every post-Soviet constitution has at least a paper provision for a constitutional court with the power of judicial review.[16] New constitutional courts have been established in many new democracies. The following table (Table 1.1) demonstrates the spread in new democracies of constitutional courts, that is, bodies with the explicit power to overrule legislative acts as being in violation of the constitution. Countries listed in the table are those characterized by the Freedom House survey as democracies in 2000 that had not been so as of 1986, plus other well-known "third wave" democracies.

Table 1.1 shows that although there are institutional variations, providing for a system of constitutional review is now a norm among democratic constitution drafters. Indeed, that such a norm exists is also evidenced by the fact that new constitutions in countries that still fall fairly short

---

[15] See "Questions of Interpretation and Application of the 1971 Montreal Convention Arising from the Aerial Incident at Lockerbie (Libya v. US; Libya v. UK)," 3, 114 *I.C.J.* (1992) (Provisional Measures). The issue was also raised in "Application of the Convention on the Prevention and Punishment of the Crime of Genocide (Bosnia/Herzegovina v. Yugoslavia (Serbia and Montenegro))," 3 *I.C.J.* (1996) (Request for Provisional Measures).

[16] See, for example, Rett R. Ludwikowski, "Constitution Making in the Countries of Former Soviet Dominance: Current Developments," 23 *Ga. J. Int'l & Comp. L.* 155 (1993), and Rett R. Ludwikowski, *Constitution Making in the Countries of Former Soviet Dominance* (1996).

TABLE 1.1 *Constitutional Review in Third Wave Democracies*

Country	Year of Constitution/ Last Major Amendment (*= amendment only)	Freedom House Rating 2000–01 (average)	Form of Constitutional Review (Key: CR = review by special body; JR = review by courts; L = scope of review or access limited)
Albania	1991*	4.5	CR
Argentina	1853	1.5	JR
Armenia	1995	4	CR
Bangladesh	1972/1991	3.5	JR
Benin	1991	2	LCR
Bolivia	1994	2	JR
Bosnia-Herzegovina	1995	4.5	CR
Brazil	1988	2	JR/CR
Bulgaria	1991	2.5	JR/CR
Burkina-Faso	1991	4.5	LCR
Cape Verde	1992	1.5	JR
Central African Republic	1994	3.5	CR
Chile	1981	2.5	LCR/LJR
Colombia	1991	3.5	CR
Croatia	1990	2.5	CR
Czech Republic	1993	1.5	CR
Dominican Republic	1996	2	JR
Ecuador	1979	2.5	JR/CR
El Salvador	1983	2.5	JR
Estonia	1992	1.5	JR
Ethiopia	1995	4	LCR
Fiji	1990/1997	3.5	JR
Gabon	1991	4.5	LCR
Georgia	1995	3.5	CR
Ghana	1993	3	JR
Greece	1975	2	CR
Guatemala	1985	3.5	JR/CR
Guinea-Bissau	1984/1990	4.5	JR
Guyana	1992	2	JR
Honduras	1982	2.5	LJR
Hungary	1949/1990	1.5	CR
Indonesia	1949	3.5	CR[†]
Jordan	1952	4	LJR
Korea	1988	2	CR
Kyrgyz Republic	1993	5	CR
Latvia	1922/1991	1.5	LCR
Lesotho	1993	4	JR

(*continued*)

TABLE I.I *(continued)*

Country	Year of Constitution/ Last Major Amendment (*= amendment only)	Freedom House Rating 2000–01 (average)	Form of Constitutional Review (Key: CR = review by special body; JR = review by courts; L = scope of review or access limited)
Lithuania	1992	1.5	CR
Macedonia	1991	3	CR
Madagascar	1992	3	CR
Malawi	1994	2.5	JR
Mali	1992	2.5	CR
Moldova	1994	3	CR
Mongolia	1992	2.5	CR
Morocco	1972/1996	4.5	LCR
Mozambique	1990	3.5	JR/CR
Namibia	1990	2.5	JR
Nepal	1990	3.5	JR
Nicaragua	2000*	3	LJR
Panama	1972/1994	1.5	JR
Paraguay	1992	3.5	LJR
Peru	1993	3	JR/CR
Philippines	1987	2.5	JR
Poland	1997	1.5	CR
Portugal	1976	1	JR/CR
Rumania	1991	2	LCR
Russia	1993	4	LCR
Sao Tome & Principe	1990	1.5	JR
Senegal	1991*	3.5	LCR
Seychelles	1993	3	JR
Sierra Leone	1991	4.5	JR
Slovakia	1993	2	LCR
Slovenia	1991	1.5	CR
South Africa	1994	1.5	JR/CR
Spain	1978	1.5	LCR
Suriname	1987	1.5	JR
Taiwan	1947/1997	2	CR
Tanzania	1992*	4	JR
Thailand	1997	2.5	CR
Ukraine	1996	4	CR
Uruguay	1997	1	JR
Zambia	1991	4.5	LJR/LCR

† A Constitutional Court was proposed for Indonesia in 2001.

Source: Robert Maddex, *Constitutions of the World* (1995); United States Department of State, *Human Rights Reports* (1997); Freedom House, *Freedom in the World*. Dates of Constitutions were supplemented through the CIA Factbook at *http://www.theodora.com/wfb/*. Note that a lower Freedom House rating indicates a higher level of democracy.

of the conventional definition of democracy (such as Cambodia (1993), Mozambique (1990), Ethiopia (1995), and Eritrea (1996)) contain provisions for constitutional review that remained unimplemented for several years after their passage. Like democracy itself, constitutionalism commands such normative power as an aspiration that it is invoked by regimes that make no pretense of submitting to constitutional control.

The table shows that the centralized system of constitutional review, designed by Hans Kelsen for Austria and subsequently adopted in Italy and Germany, has been predominant in the recent wave of democratization.[17] In contrast, a 1978 study of constitutions found that only 26% of constitutions included provision for a designated constitutional court with the power of judicial review.[18] The centralized system reflected Kelsen's positivist jurisprudence, which incorporated a strict hierarchy of laws. Because constitutional rules are provided only to parliament and ordinary judges are subordinate to the parliament whose statutes they apply, only an extrajudicial organ could restrain the legislature.[19] This extra-judicial organ was solely responsible for constitutional review.

In new democracies, there may be particularly strong reasons to distrust a decentralized system.[20] After all, the judiciary was typically trained, selected, and promoted under the previous regime. While some judges may have been closet liberals, there is little ability to ensure that these judges will wield power in a decentralized system. Furthermore, there may be significant popular distrust of the judiciary. Giving the ordinary judiciary the power of constitutional review risks dragging the prestige of the

---

[17] Because designated constitutional courts in this tradition use adjudicative methods, we consider the term *judicial review* to apply to them as well as to systems of decentralized constitutional control. For a discussion of whether systems of abstract review are better characterized as engaging in a legislative or judicial process, see Stone, *supra* note 3, at 209–21.

[18] Henc van Maarseveen and Ger van der Tang, *Written Constitutions* (1978).

[19] Kelsen made his argument in Hans Kelsen, "La garantie jurisdictionnel de la constitution," 44 *Revue de Droit Public* 197 (1928). There, Kelsen characterized the Constitutional Court as a kind of negative legislature. For a discussion, see Elena Marino-Blanco, *The Spanish Legal System* 96–97 (1996) and Stone, *supra* note 3, at 228–30.

[20] One hybrid variation is to adopt a single hierarchy of courts, with a supreme court that is exclusively charged with constitutional control. See, for example, Constitution of Yemen (1991), Article 124; Constitution of Estonia (1992), Article 152 (ordinary courts can refuse to apply an unconstitutional act, but only the National Court can declare it null and void); Constitution of Eritrea (1997), Article 49(2)(a).

constitution down to the level of the adjudicators in the public eye. Setting up a specialized body, by contrast, designates constitutional adjudication as a distinct, important function. So one explanation for the shift toward centralized review may be that widespread democratization has occurred and that decentralized review is particularly unattractive in new democracies.

Accompanying the institutional spread of judicial review has been a normative turn in its favor in western scholarship on democratization. Conventional analysts of democracy are increasingly frustrated with the illiberal tendencies of democratically elected regimes and suggest that elections are not enough. Zakaria notes that "[t]he trouble with... winner-take-all systems is that, in most democratizing countries, the winner really does take all."[21] Huntington notes that thirty-nine "electoral democracies" are deficient in protecting civil and political liberties.[22] There is increasing concern for the constitutional elements of democracy, leading some analysts to distinguish between electoral democracy and liberal democracy, with the latter guaranteeing civil rights to a greater degree.[23]

Despite this fundamental shift in democratic practice and scholarship, there has been little inquiry into questions about the expansion of judicial review. We know very little about the conditions leading to the establishment of judicial review and about the successful exercise of judicial power. This is particularly acute with regard to non-European contexts, outside the core.[24] With development banks, scholars, and politicians insisting on the importance of the rule of law as a universal component of "good governance,"[25] the issue of judicial power merits more attention. We ought to know where judicial power comes from, how it develops in the crucial early stages of liberalization, and what political conditions support the expansion and development of judicial power. This study is an effort to examine these questions by focusing on the most visible and important

[21] Fareed Zakaria, "The Rise of Illiberal Democracy," *Foreign Aff.* 22, 42 (November/December 1997).
[22] Samuel Huntington, "After Twenty Years: The Future of the Third Wave," 8 *J. Democracy* 3, 10 (1997).
[23] See Larry Diamond, "Is the Third Wave Over?" 7 *J. Democracy* 20 (1996); Huntington, *supra* note 22, at 3–12 (1997); Guillermo O'Donnell, *Horizontal Accountability in New Democracies*, 9 *J. Democracy* 112, 117 (1998); Andreas Schedler, Larry Diamond, and Marc F. Plattner, eds., *The Self-Restraining State* (1999).
[24] C. Neal Tate, "Book Review of Paula Newberg's Judging the State: Courts and Constitutional Politics in Pakistan," 6 *L. & Pol. Book Rev.* 109–12 (1996).
[25] Thomas Carothers, "The Rule of Law Revival," 35 *Foreign Aff.* 23 (1997).

institutional manifestation of judicial power, constitutional constraint by courts.

One theory argues that the spread of judicial power is a reflection of a broader extension of rights consciousness around the globe.[26] This theory focuses on the *demand* for judicial protection of fundamental rights. The achievements of the human rights movement, the shift toward markets that rely on notions of private property, and the spread of democracy all reflect the importance of ideas of fundamental rights. As rights consciousness has spread, the argument goes, so, too, does the importance of courts as the primary political actors with the mission to protect rights.

I do not wish to contest the basic contours of this story. It would be difficult to deny that globalization and democratization have been accompanied by a dramatic spread in awareness of the importance of fundamental rights. What I wish to do is to supplement this story by examining specific contexts of judicial review, rather than simply accepting that a single uniform process is affecting the entire globe. In doing so, I will introduce considerations of power into the analysis, showing how politics shapes and is shaped by judicial review. If we were to accept the conventional argument that a shift in consciousness is the key factor behind the spread of judicial review, it would follow that differences in the way judicial review is structured and operates could be explained by variations in consciousness. My analysis shows that interests, as mobilized through institutions and politics, are at least as important in dictating outcomes in new democracies as rights ideology. In doing so, I shift attention from the demand for institutions of judicial review to the supply side, asking why it is that politicians would be interested in providing it.

CONSTITUTIONALISM IN EAST ASIA

I approach the problem of courts in new democracies by focusing on understudied constitutional contexts, particularly in East Asia. Asia has been called the home of illiberal democracy and represents perhaps the most difficult regional context for establishing the rule of law.[27] Although Asia has deeply rooted indigenous legal and political traditions, the assumptions and orientation of these traditions are often contrasted with

---

[26] See, for example, Heinz Klug, *Constituting Democracy: Law, Globalism and South Africa's Political Reconstruction* (2000); Charles Epp, *The Rights Revolution* (1998).

[27] Daniel Bell, David Brown, Kanishika Jayasuriya, and David Martin Jones, *Towards Illiberal Democracy in Pacific Asia* (1995); Huntington, *supra* note 22, at 10.

the western ideals associated with constitutionalism. Confucianism, in particular, would seem to present a difficult cultural environment for the development of judicial review. In contrast with western legal traditions organized around the notion of the autonomous rights-bearing individual, the Imperial Chinese legal tradition is usually depicted as emphasizing social order over individual autonomy and responsibilities over rights.[28] Law exists not to empower and protect individuals from the state, but as an instrument of governmental control. Any rights that do exist are granted by the state and may be retracted.

Furthermore, power is conceived as indivisible in the Confucian worldview, flowing solely from the emperor, who is the center of the cosmological and political order. No human force can check the emperor's power if he enjoys the mandate of heaven.[29] The notion of an intergovernmental check on the highest power is foreign to traditional Confucian thought. The emperor has "all-encompassing jurisdictional claims over the social-political life of the people."[30] The only human constraint on the emperor's power is the duty of scholar-officials to remonstrate the leader where he errs (a practice that varied in its practical impact in different periods of Chinese history).[31] This unified conception of power is a very different one from that of modern constitutionalism with its distrust of concentrated authority.[32]

---

[28] See the classic presentation of this position in Derk Bodde and Clarence Morris, *Law in Imperial China* (1967).

[29] See, generally, Tu Wei-ming, ed., *Confucian Traditions in East Asian Modernity: Moral Education and Economic Culture in Japan and the Four Mini-Dragons* (1996).

[30] Benjamin Schwartz, "The Primacy of Political Order in East Asian Societies: Some Preliminary Generalizations," in *Foundations and Limits of State Power in China* 1 (Stuart Schram ed., 1987), quoted in A. King, "State Confucianism and Its Transformation in Taiwan," in *Confucian Traditions in East Asian Modernity: Moral Education and Economic Culture in Japan and the Four Mini-Dragons* 228, 230 (Tu Wei-ming, ed.,1996).

[31] See Thomas Gold, "Factors in Taiwan's Democratic Transition," paper presented at Consolidating the Third Wave Democracies: Trends and Challenges, Institute for National Policy Research 12 (Taipei, Taiwan, August 27–30, 1995); Andrew Nathan, "China's Constitutionalist Option," 7 *J. Democracy* 43 (1996).

[32] See, for example, R. Fox, "Confucian and Communitarian Responses to Liberal Democracy," 59 *J. Pol.* 561, 572 (1997); Daniel Bell, *East Meets West: Human Rights and Democracy in East Asia* (2000). Of course, Confucianism offers a more general critique of law as a means of social ordering. For example, the Analects express disdain toward "guiding the people by edicts and keeping them in line with punishments." The classical opposition between *Fa* and *Li* is discussed in virtually every account of Chinese law. See, for example, Bodde and Morris, *supra* note 28; Janet E. Ainsworth, "Categories and Culture: On the 'Rectification of Names' in

To the extent that these traditional ideas about law and power continue to operate in East Asia (a highly contested question), they would seem to pose a challenge to the establishment of judicial power. Some authors have pointed to modern law as a reflection of a particularly western configuration of values and ideals.[33] A set of strong, secular, autonomous legal institutions capable of checking legislative and executive authority took centuries to develop in Western Europe.[34] With much less experience with the legal machinery of the modern nation state and with a legacy of strong and concentrated political authority, similar institutional development would seem to be a difficult proposition in Asia. Despite increasing public scrutiny and pressure from foreign donors and international financial organizations, reciprocity and personalism remain central to many descriptions of East and Southeast Asian politics and economies.[35] Many scholars and professionals remain skeptical about the possibility of the rule of law taking root, even after the economic crisis of 1997–98 led to political reforms in some countries in the region.[36]

This discussion echoes the now decade-old debates over the question of whether Asian values are incompatible with western notions of human rights and democracy.[37] Several leaders in the region have argued

Comparative Law," 82 *Cornell L. Rev.* 19 (1996); S. Lubman ed., *China's Legal Reforms* (1996); Ralph Folsom, John Minan, and Lee Ann Otto, *Law and Politics in the People's Republic of China* 13–18 (1992). *Li* refers to morality, custom, and propriety, while *Fa* is usually translated as criminal law, but refers more broadly to formal rules backed by sanctions.

[33] Roberto Unger, *Law in Modern Society: Toward a Criticism of Social Theory* (1976); see also Samuel Huntington, "After Twenty Years: The Future of the Third Wave," 8 *J. Democracy* 3 (1997).

[34] Harold Berman, *Law and Revolution* (1985).

[35] On donor efforts, see the *Bulletin on Law and Policy Reform* maintained by the Asian Development Bank at *http://www.adb.org/documents/periodicals/law_bulletin/*. On personalism, see, for example, David I. Steinberg, "The Republic of Korea: Pluralizing Politics," in *Politics in Developing Countries: Comparing Experiences with Democracy* 396 (Larry Diamond et al., eds., 1995).

[36] See Lester Thurow, "Asia: The Collapse and the Cure," *N.Y. Review of Books*, February 5, 1998, at 22. See also Enrique Carrasco, "Rhetoric, Race and the Asian Financial Crisis," *L.A. Times*, January 1, 1998; Enrique Carrasco, Tough Sanctions: The Asian Crisis and New Colonialism," *Chi. Trib.*, January 3, 1998; H. Patrick Glenn, *Legal Traditions of the World* 297 (2000).

[37] For contributions to the debate on "Asian Values," see William Theodore de Bary, *Asian Values and Human Rights: A Confucian Communitarian Perspective* (2000); Kishore Mahbubani, *Can Asians Think* (1998); Joanne R. Bauer and Daniel Bell, eds., *The East Asian Challenge for Human Rights* (1999); and Michael C. Davis, "Constitutionalism and Political Culture: The Debate over Human Rights and Asian Values," 11 *Harv. Hum. Rts. L. J.* 109 (1998).

that Asian political traditions, especially the Confucian legacy, are fundamentally incompatible with, and offer an alternative to, western-style liberal democracy. The western emphasis on civil and political rights, it is asserted, does not take into account an alleged Asian preference for economic well-being and communal goods. Asians prefer order over freedom, hierarchy over equality, and harmony over conflict. Hence, authoritarian governments in Asia actually reflect different cultural values that constrain democratic and constitutional development in the Chinese and more broadly Asian tradition.[38]

Others have challenged these views as simplistic and have called into question the cultural determinism that underlies the Asian values position.[39] The notion that Asian values are distinct presupposes an orientalist dualism between a monolithic Asian tradition of hierarchy and a western tradition of individualism. This dualism does justice to neither tradition, ignoring individualistic and liberal elements in the Confucian tradition as well as collective, hierarchical, and conflict-avoiding elements in the western tradition.[40]

In terms of thinking about the development of particular institutions, one problem with using culture as an explanatory category is that a tradition such as Confucianism is so broad it contains elements that might either support or hinder any institution under consideration. For example, Confucianism, once thought to be a hindrance to modernization, has in recent years been used to *explain* economic success in Asia.[41] Similarly, one might argue that certain aspects of the Imperial Chinese tradition, such as government by elite generalists, are compatible with judicial review.[42]

---

[38] Samuel Huntington, *The Clash of Civilizations and the Remaking of World Order* (1996). Lee Teng-hui's reflection on the contribution of Chinese culture to Taiwan's democratization is found in Lee Teng-hui, "Chinese Culture and Political Renewal," 6 *J. Democ.* 3 (1995).

[39] See Davis, *supra* note 37, and Randall Peerenboom, "Answering the Bell: Round Two of the Asian Values Debate," 42 *Korea Journal* 194 (2002).

[40] William Theodore de Bary, *The Liberal Tradition in China* (1983); Tatsuo Inoue, "Critical Perspectives on the 'Asian Values' Debate," in *The East Asian Challenge for Human Rights* 27, 37–45 (Joanne Bauer and Daniel Bell eds., 1999).

[41] See, for example, Gary Hamilton and Kao Cheng-shu, "Max Weber and the Analysis of the Asian Industrialization," Working Paper No. 2, University of California, Davis Research Program in East Asian Culture and Development (1986); Benjamin A. Elman, "Confucianism and Modernization: A Reevaluation," in *Confucianism and Modernization: A Symposium* 1 (Joseph P. L. Jiang, ed., 1987); Cal Clark and K. C. Roy, *Comparing Development Patterns in Asia* 61–93 (1997).

[42] See Tom Ginsburg, "Confucian Constitutionalism? The Emergence of Judicial Review in Korea and Taiwan," 27 *Law and Social Inquiry* 763 (2002).

The point is that, because of their very breadth, cultural and legal traditions do not dictate outcomes in predictable ways. The Confucian legacy as conventionally interpreted poses barriers to the emergence of constitutionalism and judicial review of legislation in Chinese society. But cultural and legal traditions are flexible and dynamic and can provide rationales for a wide range of political institutions.[43] This suggests the difficulty of building a workable theory of the adoption and function of judicial review on cultural factors.

This study will explain the emergence of judicial review as a result of institutions and politics, rather than culture. By focusing on the spread and transfer of a central practice of constitutional democracy, judicial review, outside of its core areas in the United States and later Western Europe, this study is an effort to broaden the empirical and theoretical base of comparative constitutional law. The core areas have been at the center of comparative projects documenting the vast expansion of judicial review in recent decades.[44] Studies of nonwestern countries have been far less frequent. By demonstrating that judicial review can function outside the core, this study will challenge culturally deterministic accounts of the rule of law and judicial power.

AMERICAN EXCEPTIONALISM?

How ought one approach the study of judicial review in countries beyond the core? There may be several dangers in treating the American experience as the benchmark against which other countries' practices are measured. One way that American constitutionalism is distinctive is the fact that there is no explicit constitutional provision for judicial review in the American constitution. This has consequences that may not apply to other systems, including the embedding of the constitution into ordinary law.[45] (Technically, there is a distinction between judicial review, in which ordinary judges play the role of constitutional check, and constitutional review, in which the function is given to specialized judges or political actors. This study uses the terms interchangeably.) The primary role of the

---

[43] *Cf.* Huntington, *supra* note 38. See de Bary, *supra* note 40; William Theodore de Bary, "The 'Constitutional Tradition' in China," 9 *J. Asian L.* (1995); Davis, *supra* note 37; Michael C. Davis, "The Price of Rights: Constitutionalism and East Asian Economic Development," 20 *Hum. Rts. Q.* 303–37 (1998). See also Michael C. Davis, ed., *Human Rights and Chinese Values: Legal, Philosophical and Political Perspectives* (1995).

[44] *The Global Expansion of Judicial Power, supra* note 7.

[45] Stephen Griffin, *American Constitutionalism: From Theory to Politics* (1996).

United States federal judiciary is resolving disputes among private parties, and it need not exercise judicial review to do so. Because judicial review is incidental to the basic functions of the courts, the legitimacy of judicial review is always in doubt. Scholars of American constitutionalism have responded by focusing almost exclusively on normative issues of judicial legitimacy rather than positive issues of judicial power. But these issues may be less important in contexts where there is a clear constitutional moment and a designated court whose only role is to safeguard the constitution.

Another risk of focusing exclusively on the American origins of judicial review is that one might overcharacterize the insular, purely national character of the practice. American courts are notoriously reluctant to acknowledge the normative or legal importance of other countries' case-law or international instruments.[46] Yet, in the international context, domestic practices of judicial review draw extensively on international treaties, other countries' case-law, and normative rhetoric from other national experiences. The danger of beginning with the American experience is missing the significant international dimension of contemporary judicial review. The rule of law ideal has strongly universalist overtones, and courts may invoke their fraternal duty to defend it in specific cases. This often involves an examination of how other judiciaries have dealt with a particular problem. This practice of borrowing has long been a feature of the common law tradition, but also occurs in civil law jurisdictions.[47] Citing cases from other contexts is a strategy of legitimation for courts.[48]

---

[46] See, for example, *Sei Fujii v. California*, 38 Cal. 2d 718, 242 P. 2d 617 (1952). But see *United States v. Then*, 56 F. 3d 464, 469 (2d Cir. 1995) (Calabresi, J., concurring).

[47] See, for example, T. Koopmans, "Comparative Law and the Courts," 45 *Am. J. Comp. L.* 545, 550–55 (1996); Anne-Marie Slaughter, "The Real New World Order," 76 *Foreign Aff.* 183 (1997) (arguing that such "transgovernmentalism" by both judges and bureaucrats is the primary response to globalization, and represents the future of governance in an era when the traditional territorial state seems less able to cope with growing regulatory demands). Another form of judicial use of comparative law involves looking to practices consistent with notions of a "free and democratic society," an approach reflected in Israeli Supreme Court practice as well as in the case-law of the European Court of Human Rights. The European Court of Justice itself engages in comparative law exercises under Article 287 (formerly Article 215) related to noncontractual liability of the community, where it must compensate based on principles common to the laws of the member states. See T. Koopmans, *supra*.

[48] See, for example, Herman Schwartz, "The New Courts: An Overview," 2 *E. Eur. Const. Rev.* 28 (1993).

Finally, the origin of the practice in the United States may lead us to look for *Marbury*-type "grand cases" wherein the court asserts its power to overrule political authorities.[49] The danger is that a grand case is not the only way judicial review can be established. Beginning with an American orientation may lead us in the wrong direction by focusing our attention on the search for nonexistent "grand cases" in new democracies. This approach may misread *Marbury*, which after all did not include any command to a political branch.[50] More accurately, observers looking for "grand cases" that establish institutions of judicial review have in mind *Brown v. Board of Education*, where the Supreme Court overturned the American caste system with a single blow.[51] But *Brown* is another highly atypical case. First, it explicitly overrules a precedent in contrast with the usual characterization of common law courts. Second, *Brown*'s rhetoric is primarily moral rather than legal.

Only in the sense that the Warren Court was highly conscious of the political ramifications of its decision was *Brown* a "normal" constitutional case. And it is precisely here that the U.S. experience *is* helpful. For studies of courts in new democracies will have to consider the delicate political contexts in which they operate. Just as the American courts are concerned about securing compliance with their decisions, so courts in new democracies face the same fundamental political problem: how to convince the losing party to abide with their decisions.[52]

APPROACH AND PLAN OF THE BOOK

This book addresses three questions concerning judicial review. First, why is it that countries adopt judicial review during periods of democratization and constitutional design? After all, if judicial review is undemocratic as scores of scholars have argued, it should be unattractive to newly empowered democrats. Second, what explains variation in the design and powers of new constitutional courts? One might think that there would be little variation in the design of new courts across different countries, but in fact there is variation, as Table 1.1

---

[49] *Marbury v. Madison*, 5 U.S. (1 Cranch) 137 (1803).
[50] See Michael J. Klarman, "How Great Were the 'Great' Marshall Court Decisions?" 87 *Va. L. Rev.* 1111 (2001).
[51] *Brown v. Board of Education*, 347 U.S. 483 (1954) (overruling *Plessy v. Ferguson*, 163 U.S. 537 (1896)).
[52] Martin Shapiro makes a similar argument for courts in all times and places. See Martin Shapiro, *Courts: A Comparative and Political Analysis* (1981).

suggests. Third, why is it that some constitutional courts exercise the power of judicial review more aggressively than others? Variation in institutional design plays a role, but there may be other more important factors.

The answer I offer to all three questions is that politics matters. I begin by treating the first two questions together: Why is it that judicial review is adopted in the democratic constitution, and why does it take the form it does? I consider why judicial review makes sense from the point of view of those who write the constitution. The answer has to do with the time horizons of those politicians drafting the constitution. If they foresee themselves in power after the constitution is passed, they are likely to design institutions that will allow them to govern without encumbrance. On the other hand, if they foresee themselves losing in postconstitutional elections, they may seek to entrench judicial review as a form of political insurance. Even if they lose the election, they will be able to have some access to a forum in which to challenge the legislature. I argue that the particular institutional design of the constitutional court will tend to reflect the interests of powerful politicians at the time of drafting, with optimistic politicians preferring less vigorous and powerful courts so they can govern without constraint.

The third question concerns the operation of the system of judicial review after it has been established. Here I focus on the decisions by judges, but also on the political constraints in which they operate. I show that the more diffused politics are, the more space courts have in which to operate. In contrast, where a dominant disciplined political party holds power, judicial review is more constrained. Drawing a distinction between systems with active judicial review and those where it appears relatively dormant, we can see a clear correlation between active review and diffused politics.

The second half of the book consists of historical analysis of the emergence of judicial review in three transitional political systems. The objective here is both descriptive and theoretical. Descriptively, I present data on the development of judicial review in unlikely and understudied contexts. Theoretically, my goal is to use the studies to test some of the propositions developed in the first part of the book and to demonstrate the utility of the theoretical framework for understanding the exercise of judicial power in new democracies.

The three cases selected for full study are Korea, Taiwan, and Mongolia. These cases are particularly useful given the influence of

Imperial Chinese legal institutions on all of them.[53] Judicial review has grown in all three environments in recent years as democratization has proceeded, a significant result given the supposed aversion of Asian societies to legal ordering. Although this selection of cases may be termed *intraregional* because all three countries are in Northeast Asia, the three represent very different environments with regard to a number of other important independent variables that might plausibly affect the development of judicial review. Of special importance are political and institutional variations.

The book concludes with a comparative analysis of the three cases and argues that political and institutional structure, rather than cultural factors, are the keys to understanding the development of judicial review in new democracies. The evidence in the case studies is consistent with the political theory of constitutional court design and performance offered in the first part of the book. Political uncertainty leads to the adoption of judicial review as a form of insurance to protect the constitutional bargain. Political diffusion after the bargain is concluded allows courts to exercise greater power. By increasing uncertainty, democratization leads to greater demand for judicial review; the extent of political diffusion determines how successful courts can be in asserting the power.

[53] Two of the case studies, Taiwan and Korea, are conventionally viewed as Confucian societies (with Confucian influence even stronger in Korea than in the Chinese society on Taiwan). Although it was a part of the imperial Chinese system that promoted Confucianism as official ideology, Confucian influence on Taiwan was probably less pervasive than on the mainland. After 1895, Chinese Confucian influence was subordinated under Japanese rule to State Shinto ideology and growing militarism. Some scholars therefore argue that Confucian influence was minimal on Taiwan. See, for example, Lucien Pye, *Asian Power and Politics: The Cultural Dimensions of Authority* (1985). Others, including a prominent former grand justice, assert that Taiwan is a Confucian society. See Herbert Han-pao Ma, *The Rule of Law in a Contemporary Confucian Society: A Reinterpretation*, presentation to Harvard Law School's East Asian Legal Studies Program (spring 1998). It is difficult to reconcile these two views. As the issue of Chinese and Confucian influences touches on the question of national identity, it is subject to intense contestation within Taiwan. In any case, the precise level of Confucian influence on Taiwan is not empirically verifiable. Nevertheless, as Taiwan is universally acknowledged to be a part of the "greater Chinese cultural system," it seems reasonable to consider the possible effects of the dominant Chinese legal and political philosophy on developments there. Mongolia, by contrast, has a strong historical aversion to Chinese culture and is not conventionally included in the Confucian world. Mongolia was, however, a former part of the Manchu Empire, which ruled China and has a long history of interaction with Chinese culture. All three cases, then, were historically influenced by Imperial Chinese legal institutions to varying degrees.

Ultimately, an examination of the development of judicial power in Asia can help us understand one of the most important questions of sociolegal studies, namely how a political system can transform itself from one governed by personalistic forms of authority toward one in which the rule of law prevails. In a region where prevailing traditions have emphasized an instrumental approach to law, the emergence of law as a *constraint* on political authority is a remarkable development with potentially broader implications. Cultural and legal traditions are not insurmountable barriers to institutions of liberal democracy. While this is good news for advocates of liberal democracy, the account offered here also suggests limits on the ability of outside intervention to facilitate institutional change. How does judicial power emerge? The answer suggested by this book is that domestic political diffusion is a necessary condition for the development of judicial power.

I

Why Judicial Review?

Modern scholarship on judicial review begins with the countermajoritarian difficulty.[1] This famous problem focuses on the propriety of unelected judges, who lack democratic legitimacy, overturning duly enacted decisions of democratic assemblies. This normative challenge has been bolstered by theorists of democracy who argue that judicial power comes at the expense of representative institutions.[2] Judicial review, from these perspectives, is not only unnecessary for democracy, but in fact suspect. In the face of these critiques, most legal scholars discussing judicial review have self-consciously adopted a defensive tone at the outset, trying to justify the role of courts in terms of democratic theory.

The conventional move to solve the problem of courts in democratic theory is to celebrate the role of judicial review in democracy as a check on majority power. Judicial review in this view can facilitate the democratic process by clearing out obstacles to its advancement.[3] Such obstacles can emerge, for example, through majority impositions on the electoral process: It may be in the narrow self-interest of permanent majorities to disenfranchise political minorities, who then have no recourse through ordinary legislative processes. In such instances of systemic failure, the

---

[1] Originally identified in Alexander Bickel, *The Least Dangerous Branch: The Supreme Court at the Bar of American Politics* (2d ed., 1986). See Barry Friedman, "A History of the Countermajoritarian Difficulty, Part One: The Road to Judicial Supremacy," 73 *N.Y.U. L. Rev.* 333 (1998) for a history of the problem.

[2] Most prominently, Robert Dahl, *Democracy and Its Critics* 188 (1989).

[3] Ely is the most well-known proponent of this view, elaborating on footnote 4 of *United States v. Carolene Products Co.*, 304 U.S. 144, 152–53 n.4 (1938). See John Hart Ely, *Democracy and Distrust* (1980).

courts can clear the channels of the political process by striking statutes. By serving as a countermajoritarian institution, judicial review can ensure that minorities remain part of the system, bolster legitimacy, and save democracy from itself.

Several scholars have recently articulated a more majoritarian view of constitutionalism that emphasizes the need to empower rather than restrict majoritarian processes.[4] Democracy is at bottom about deliberation and debate, they argue, and the function of a constitution is both to set boundaries for and facilitate this debate. The function of judicial review in these accounts is to provide another perspective on questionable policies. Courts are not the ultimate determiner of constitutionality but merely another governmental institution that helps deliberation take place through institutional dialogues with other branches of government. Judges, because of their special training and selection, can ruminate on fundamental principles of the democratic system.

Although normatively attractive, both of these accounts raise a fundamental difficulty, namely how it is that judicial review is adopted in the constitution in the first place. After all, why would a political majority adopt an institution that constrains itself in policy making? And why would it rely on judges to undertake the task of constraint? The recent wave of constitution drafting around the globe invites inquiry into the political logic of judicial review, beginning with the fundamental question of why it is adopted.

JUDICIAL REVIEW AS INSURANCE

Why would constitutional drafters choose to include provisions for judicial review in the constitutional text? To answer this question, we must begin with foundational questions about the constitution and whose interests it reflects. Since Locke, constitutional theorists have thought of the constitution as a contract between citizens and government. We imagine that citizens empower a state and develop a system of constitutional democracy as a mechanism to satisfy individual preferences through

---

[4] See Cass Sunstein, *Designing Democracy: What Constitutions Do* (2001); Jed Rubenfeld, *Freedom and Time: A Theory of Constitutional Self-Government* (2001); Bruce Ackerman, *We the People: Transformations* (1998); see also Amy Gutmann and Dennis Thompson, *Democracy and Disagreement* (1966); Jurgen Habermas, *Between Facts and Norms: Contributions to a Discourse Theory of Law and Democracy* (1996); Carlos Santiago Nino, *The Constitution of Deliberative Democracy* (1995).

collective action. This device enables us to ask normative questions about what institutions most approximate the good society, what citizens might have chosen behind a veil of ignorance, or what institutions best help the citizenry resolve collective-action dilemmas.[5]

The contractarian perspective analogizes the democratic constitutional scheme to a series of principal–agent relationships wherein the people rely on politicians as agents to satisfy their collective demands. If the people are the principal on whose behalf the constitution is created, constitutional adjudication should reflect the need to monitor their political agents. Judicial review of legislation exists to prevent politicians from reneging on the founding bargain with citizens.

This contractarian perspective is normative rather than positive, and it is open to criticism on empirical grounds. There are numerous reasons to be suspicious that actual constitutional design reflects the interests of citizens. Most obviously, constitutional design would only reflect citizen interest if the designer-politicians who actually draft and agree on the constitutional text were themselves pure agents of those citizens. But that can hardly be the case because citizens are subject to collective-action problems that prevent them from organizing to monitor constitutional debates. Under such circumstances, politicians who draft the constitution can seek to design institutions that benefit themselves, their institutions, or their interests narrowly rather than those of citizens more broadly. Much empirical evidence supports the assertion that constitution making is dominated by short-term interests of the designers rather than the long-term interests of the citizenry.[6]

In light of the agency problem of constitutional design, we must ask why self-interested politicians would design a system of judicial review. It is not sufficient to describe constitutional review as a device to protect citizens from future politicians without explaining why it serves the interests of present politicians who serve as a veto gate for the constitution. Although constitutional designers are subject to the same constraints of bounded rationality as everyone else, there are reasons for assuming that they consider their institutional choices carefully. Constitutional choices typically have a great impact on subsequent political outcomes, so there

---

[5] James Buchanan, *The Limits of Liberty* (1975); Robert Cooter, *The Strategic Constitution* 243 (2000); Dennis Mueller, *Constitutional Democracy* 61–67 (1996); John Rawls, *A Theory of Justice* (1973).

[6] Stefan Voigt, "Positive Constitutional Economics: A Survey," 90 *Public Choice* 11, 26 (1997); Mueller, *Constitutional Democracy, supra* note 5, at 316–18; Jon Elster, "Forces and Mechanisms in the Constitution-Making Process," 45 *Duke L. J.* 364 (1995).

are strong pressures on designers to choose institutions that will benefit their constituencies in the future.

I argue that the answer to the question of why self-interested politicians would design a system of judicial review depends on the prospective power positions of constitutional designers in postconstitutional government. Assume that constitutional drafters are themselves politicians, who are interested in governing after the adoption of a new constitution. It follows that they will seek to design institutions that maximize their ability to govern under the new constitutional order. The key factor from the drafters' perspective is the uncertainty of the future political configuration at the time of constitutional drafting.[7]

Consider two extreme constitutional scenarios. Where a single party believes it is likely to hold on to political power, it has little incentive to set up a neutral arbiter to resolve disputes about constitutional meaning. It would rather retain the flexibility to dictate outcomes without constitutional constraint. Flexibility allows policy change and maximum exercise of power. The absence of independent judicial review institutions under authoritarian constitutions reflects this desire to maintain the exclusive role of constitutional interpretation.

By contrast, where many political forces are vying for power, no party can have confidence that it is likely to continue to win future elections. A constitutional design allowing unlimited flexibility for electoral

---

[7] This theory is related to J. Mark Ramseyer's work on judicial independence. See J. Mark Ramseyer, "The Puzzling (In)Dependence of Courts: A Comparative Approach," 23 *J. Leg. Stud.* 721 (1994). Drawing on evidence from Japan and the United States, Ramseyer suggests that independent courts will be supported by politicians where they believe two conditions exist: (1) Continuing elections are likely, and (2) the ruling politicians are likely to lose a future election. In such an instance, it is in the interest of the ruling party to create independent courts to protect its policy preferences that are enacted as laws. The courts serve as the agents of politicians who are now out of office. Ramseyer's first condition is constitutional; the second is related to the character of the democracy. Where either one of the conditions does not hold, a ruling party will not choose independent courts that can only hinder that party's ability to act decisively. See also William Landes and Richard Posner, "The Independent Judiciary in an Interest-Group Perspective," 18 *J. L. & Econ.* 875 (1975). In Ramseyer's presentation, this decision's impact on the survival of the constitutional regime is exogenous to the model. The party making the choice to institutionalize independent courts makes a judgment about continuing elections and based on that judgment chooses to make courts independent or not. It is possible, even likely in the context of fragile new democracies, that such a decision will itself affect the probabilities of continued elections and maintenance of the constitutional order. Active systems of judicial review are not often associated with democratic failure.

winners, as in the model of parliamentary sovereignty, is much less attractive in a politically diffused setting than in a setting wherein a single party holds sway. While prospective governing parties would like flexibility, prospective opposition parties value limited government. Opposition parties want to minimize their maximum losses. They also value an alternative forum in which to challenge the policies of the majority, because they do not expect to win in the legislature. When the designers' party cannot count on reelection and may end up an opposition party, it will prefer a judicial forum in which to challenge its newly empowered political adversaries.

These considerations lead to a general prediction about judicial power and constitutional rights: *Explicit constitutional power of and access to judicial review will be greater where political forces are diffused than where a single dominant party exists at the time of constitutional design.* This is because dominant parties are likely to anticipate continued success in postconstitutional elections and therefore to prefer majoritarian institutions. Where political forces are deadlocked, or scattered, no party can confidently predict that it will be able to win postconstitutional elections. Because there are no parties that will be confident in their ability to win, all parties will prefer to limit the majority and therefore will value minoritarian institutions such as judicial review. The key factor in explaining variation in the extent of judicial power in constitutional design is the structure of the party system and the configuration of political forces at the time of constitutional drafting.

I call this the *insurance model of judicial review.* By serving as an alternative forum in which to challenge government action, judicial review provides a form of insurance to prospective electoral losers during the constitutional bargain. Just as the presence of insurance markets lowers the risks of contracting, and therefore allows contracts to be concluded that otherwise would be too risky, so the possibility of judicial review lowers the risks of constitution making to those drafters who believe they may not win power. Judicial review thus helps to conclude constitutional bargains that might otherwise fail.

Let us consider three objections to the insurance theory. One might argue that other minoritarian devices exist that can substitute for judicial review, such as difficult procedures for constitutional amendment, bicameralism, and proportional representation.[8] Because provisions about

---

[8] For some evidence of these propositions, see Elster, *supra* note 6, at 377–82; Jon Elster, "Limiting Majority Rule: Alternatives to Judicial Review in the Revolutionary Epoch," in *Constitutional Justice under Old Constitutions* (Eivind Smith, ed., 1995).

judicial review are embedded in the larger constitutional bargaining process, we cannot predict a perfect correlation between strong parties and weak judicial review. Judicial review can be traded off against other minoritarian institutions in the larger constitutional bargain. The precise configuration of the constitutional bargain will reflect tradeoffs across a number of different substantive and institutional issues. Nevertheless, in the proverbial state of other things being equal, more-optimistic parties will prefer less judicial constraint.

Why might judicial review be an attractive minoritarian institution for designers? As a form of insurance, judicial review is relatively inexpensive because it can be exercised by a court staffed with a few members. While a court, like other branches of government, may seek to expand its budget, it is certainly cheaper to run than, say, a second house of a legislature that could serve to protect the constitutional bargain because of a different representational system. Thus, judicial review, to the extent it serves the interests of the founders in constraining majorities, is cheap minoritarianism. This might explain why it is that judicial review may have been adopted more universally than other minoritarian institutions that could serve the interests of prospective losers.

Another reason judicial review may be a particularly desirable form of insurance is the international context of constitutional drafting. Constitutional designers do not operate in a vacuum, and there is a growing international norm that constitutions include some sort of institution to exercise constitutional oversight. The success of the institution elsewhere enhances its reputation. The formal submission of political power to the dictates of the rule of law is one of a package of institutions designed to express the break with the past. To a certain extent, like legislatures and presidencies, judicial review forms part of the "script" of modernity and is adopted for reasons of both external legitimacy and internal political logic.[9] Although other institutions might provide equally good protection for minorities, judicial review has a reputation for effective minoritarianism that makes designers particularly likely to adopt it. When designers must choose among alternative institutions that address a particular problem, one solution can stand out and become focal, even if other solutions would be effective substitutes.[10] The international context helps make

[9] John W. Meyer, John Boli, George M. Thomas, and Francisco O. Ramirez, "World Society and the Nation State," 103 *Am J. Soc.* 144 (1997).
[10] On focal points, see Thomas C. Schelling, *The Strategy of Conflict* (1960). See also Richard McAdams, "A Focal Point Theory of Expressive Law," 86 *Vir. L. Rev.* 1649 (2000).

judicial review a particularly focal solution to the problem of constitutional protection of political minorities.

Besides providing positive examples, foreign countries also play a more direct role in the spread of judicial review. By providing technical assistance to constitution-drafting exercises, foreign assistance programs subsidize the cost of evaluating different institutions. In some cases, international actors can also play an indirect or even direct role in the constitutional bargaining process. The extreme case is that of the Japanese constitution, which included provisions for American-style judicial review because it was imposed by the occupation authorities.

All these factors help to make judicial review an attractive form of insurance, but they do not dictate institutional choices. If we hold these international factors constant, weak judicial review is unlikely where political forces are evenly balanced; conversely, dominant parties are less likely to desire strong judicial review. Furthermore, foreign observers of constitutional drafting processes may pay scarce attention to the details of institutional design. The inclusion of a constitutional court may satisfy foreign interests concerned with rights protection and controlling legislative power, but the institutional details of standing law may be off the screen of foreign observers and hence susceptible to manipulation by local political actors.[11] Thus, the insurance theory still has a large explanatory role to play.

A second objection to the insurance theory concerns the use of the insurance analogy, which strictly speaking implies risk aversion. A risk-averse party is one that would prefer, for example, a sure chance to govern for one year over a one-in-four chance to governing for four years. While such risk-averse parties are sure to value judicial review, because they know they will be out of power, the assumption that parties are risk averse is not necessary for the theory as I have articulated it. All that is necessary is that there is intertemporal uncertainty between the time institutions are chosen and the time they will actually begin to operate. I use the term *insurance* in this looser sense. Certain other technical elements of insurance may in fact fit the analogy to judicial review, but they are not necessary for the theory.[12]

---

[11] Jodi S. Finkel, "The Implementation of Judicial Reform in Peru in the 1990s," paper presented at the American Political Science Association Meeting, San Francisco, August 2001.

[12] For example, one might argue that the effective insurance of judicial review can create a kind of moral hazard for political party members, who may work less hard to win the next election because they do not fear the consequences of loss as severely

A third potential objection concerns signaling. Even a dominant party controlling constitutional design may wish to provide for a system of judicial review as a way of signaling its serious intention to abide by the constitution. This illustrates a competing rationale for judicial review that I call the "commitment theory." Whatever the problems they seek to solve, constitutional drafters face the challenge of making their commitments credible.[13] Judicial review is an answer to problems of constitutional commitment. By setting up an independent institution to adjudicate disputes arising under the constitution, the drafters signal that they are serious about upholding their promises. Judicial review is thus a form of self-binding on the part of constitutional designers.[14] Of course, this signal of self-binding is only effective to the extent that the threat of independent judicial review is itself credible: The court must have both power and insulation from political control.

Although they are similar in many respects, this "commitment" rationale can be contrasted with the insurance theory in terms of its empirical implications. Whereas the insurance theory predicts *less* powerful institutions of judicial review with a dominant party, the commitment theory might predict *more* powerful institutions of judicial review with a dominant party. This is because demand by smaller parties for commitment during constitutional design will increase with party strength of the dominant party. On the other hand, if a dominant party is strong enough, it will be able to dictate the constitution without concern for the smaller parties' desires.

To illustrate, imagine a constitutional bargain among two parties where a two-thirds majority is needed to pass a constitution. The first column in Figure 1.1 represents the relative strengths of the two parties. Under the commitment theory, the level of predicted judicial review rises as one party becomes stronger, so long as it needs the cooperation of the weaker party to pass a constitution. This is reflected in the move from Low to Medium along the first two rows. Once the dominant party has a secure enough majority to dictate a constitution, there is no more need to accede to the minority by including judicial review in the constitution. Under the

as a party without the protections of judicial review. Thanks to Eric Rasmusen for this point.

13 Stephen Holmes, "Precommitment and the Paradox of Democracy," in *Constitutionalism and Democracy* (Jon Elster and Rune Slagstad, eds., 1988); Landes and Posner, *supra* note 7.

14 See, generally, Jon Elster, *Ulysses Unbound* 88–174 (2000).

Party Configuration of Seats in Constitutional Assembly	Predicted Level of Judicial Review Power under Commitment Theory	Predicted Level of Judicial Review Power under Insurance Theory
50–50	Low	High
60–40	Medium	Medium
70–30	Low	Low

FIGURE 1.1. Competing Theories of Institutional Design

insurance theory, the predicted level of judicial review declines consistently as one party becomes stronger.

The commitment theory focuses on the stronger party in constitutional negotiations, while the insurance theory focuses on the weaker, prospectively losing parties. Other than the different empirical implications for situations of evenly divided parties, the commitment theory is not really very different from the insurance theory. Both theories have elements of commitment, in that a truly dominant party that can dictate a constitution has little need for any form of judicial review. Only when cooperation is required does judicial review enter the picture.

In short, some of the objections to the insurance rationale really provide supplementary theories that complement rather than replace the insurance framework. Other minoritarian institutions may indeed render judicial review less attractive from the perspective of constitutional drafters; but judicial review is a relatively cheap form of minoritarianism so we should see it included in many constitutional bargains. The international context is also an important consideration and actually helps make judicial review a kind of focal point for drafters concerned about minoritarian interests. Ultimately, domestic politicians form a veto gate, so we should also expect their interests to be reflected in the details of institutional design. The commitment rationale is in part an alternative theory in that it predicts greater constitutional constraint where designers are stronger, up to a point. It remains to be seen whether this is a superior account of the design of judicial review.

Although the insurance theory is clearly minoritarian in character, it need not rely on a view that courts will *always* serve minority interests or that courts will always be effective when they do so. Recent work on deliberative democracy ties in with literature emphasizing that judicial decisions are not in fact final, but rather involve a kind of dialogue with political branches of government. The court is one actor among several that participate in the governmental conversation. The crucial point that all these theories share is that the court provides an alternative forum to the legislature and can thus allow the articulation of views that would otherwise not be heard. Whether or not this increases the quality of democracy, as the deliberative theorists argue, is not our concern here. What is important for present purposes is that, as a positive matter, judicial review potentially expands the range of voices to include political losers. Two fora are always better than one for the party that loses in the legislature. Thus, the insurance rationale is compatible with a variety of normative theories.

INSURANCE IN NEW DEMOCRACIES

Now let us consider more carefully judicial review in the context of new democracies and political transitions. There are two features of such contexts that contrast with more established democratic regimes. First, future political outcomes are more uncertain relative to autocracy. The presence of electoral competition means that even the most dominant and popular party faces a relatively higher chance of losing power than it would under a one-party system. Information on future outcomes is more difficult to assess. There is ample empirical evidence that constitutional designers sometimes misjudge the probabilities of their electoral success.[15]

Second, by definition the institutional structure of the political system is in a period of transition, of movement from one equilibrium toward another. I do not mean to suggest in teleological fashion that all democratic transitions lead to the same place. There is a wide range of institutional configurations that are possible even within the category of democracies. Indeed, this range itself is a source of uncertainty. As institutional structure changes, parties are even less certain that their power will remain intact. In sum, changes in the party system and institutional structure characterize transitional environments, so that outcomes are more uncertain.

Other things being equal, uncertainty increases demand for the political insurance that judicial review provides. Under conditions of high uncertainty, it may be especially useful for politicians to adopt a system

[15] See, for example, Jon Elster, "Introduction," in *The Roundtable Talks and the Breakdown of Communism* 1, 17 (Jon Elster, ed., 1996).

of judicial review to entrench the constitutional bargain and protect it from the possibility of reversal after future electoral change. Because rational politicians believe they may not remain in power under the terms of the constitution, they choose to set up independent courts to protect their bargain from repeal.[16] Judicial review in such circumstances provides insurance for the past against the future. In short, the presence of elections – the sine qua non of democracy – increases uncertainty and thus the demand for judicial review. The expansion of judicial power around the globe reflects democratization and is not antidemocratic as suggested by some analysts.[17] Judicial review may be countermajoritarian but is not counterdemocratic.

By relating judicial review to political uncertainty, this account provides a new perspective on the spread of judicial review around the globe in the latest "wave" of democratic constitution writing. The spread of judicial review does not merely reflect a norm among constitution drafters, but a response to the particular problems of electoral uncertainty that they face. This is not to argue that the international context is irrelevant. Given that no insurance contract is perfect or infallible, constitution writers must consider various institutions that might achieve their goal of reducing risk. Demand for any particular institution will rise with the perception that the insurance it provides is likely to be effective. As judicial review spreads to new environments and appears to function successfully, it becomes easier for new democracies to adopt it as they engage in constitutional reform and drafting. The spread of judicial review is self-reinforcing as its institutional reputation grows. But the account offered here supplements the international story with an account of the domestic political logic of review.

Note that the "insurance" rationale for judicial review is not an originalist theory. Politicians need not anticipate that judges *always* interpret the constitution in accordance with the founders' wishes. There are agency costs associated with judicial review as in any situation where one body (constitution drafters) appoints another (court) to monitor a third (government). Judges may impose their own constitutional preferences on the polity, even where they are appointed by politicians. Certain aspects of the institutional design of judicial review, such as political control over appointments or the budget, are designed to minimize agency costs from the point of view of current politicians. If judges act too

---

[16] Ramseyer, *supra* note 7.
[17] See Robert Dahl, *Democracy and Its Critics* (1989).

outrageously, politicians can punish them through constitutional and extraconstitutional means.

These mechanisms to reduce agency costs create a new puzzle. If the tools of political control over judges are available to political majorities after the constitution enters into force, why should a prospective political loser set up judicial review to constrain those majorities?

Notions of legality and fidelity to text are crucial to reducing perceptions of judicial agency costs. Judicial agency costs are relatively low compared to those of other kinds of political functionaries because of the typical (though not universal) requirement of legal training to serve on a constitutional court. If judges were unconstrained in asserting their own policy preferences, as suggested by proponents of the attitudinal model in political science studies of courts, constitutional law becomes politics by other means, and there would be no inherent reason that constitutional interpretation should be limited to lawyers and judges. Legal training is a form of ideology that can help to reduce agency costs. From the perspective of politicians, it is an inexpensive mechanism because legal academia subsidizes the costs of training judges and developing jurisprudential solutions to particular problems and also subsidizes the cost of monitoring the court by rewarding commentators who analyze the work of the court.

Judicial review may also be attractive to minorities even in the face of majority dominance because political pressures on judges are costly. Authoritarians from Zimbabwe to Malaysia have been criticized for improper interference with the judiciary, and though the threat of such criticism does not always protect courts, it is effective much of the time. The presence of a third-party adjudicative body whose explicit mission is to safeguard the constitution raises the costs of violating the constitution, even if it does not provide perfectly complete protection against all contingencies. Judicial review, like insurance, is a risk-reduction device. No risk-reduction device is foolproof: Insurers can go bankrupt just as courts can be ineffectual. But if the expected gains from a relatively inexpensive insurance contract outweigh the potentially catastrophic risk of a failed constitutional scheme, judicial review should be adopted.

The discussion so far can be understood in terms of a simple inequality. Constitutional designers will choose judicial review if and only if the expected costs of electoral loss (the probability of electoral loss times the average expected cost) exceed the net agency costs of judicial review. As the risk of electoral loss increases, the incentive to adopt judicial review increases as well. Similarly, any increase in perceived loyalty of the judiciary to the constitutional designer, either for ideological or political reasons, will increase the incentive to adopt judicial review, holding electoral risks constant. Judicial review will be adopted where comparative institutional analysis suggests that courts' agency problems are likely to be less than the costs of having no third-party monitor at all.

Simply because I focus here on the self-interested motives of politicians does not mean that I believe that all constitutional design can be explained as the product of self-interest. Other forces clearly play a role. Constitutional designers may sometimes be motivated by passions about certain ideas and institutions; they may even on occasion try to choose the best possible institutions for their polity.[18] Accidents and miscalculations are no doubt more frequent than social scientists like to recognize. My argument is one of probability: Those who need political insurance will tend to prefer to adopt judicial review, but this theory does not purport to explain every case.

We have now sketched the outlines of a theory regarding why judicial review is adopted in a democratic constitution. Although judicial review is associated with the global ideal of the rule of law, the adoption of a constitutional court may reflect in large part the insurance needs of the founders. This hypothesis suggests a corollary, that the particular design of judicial review institutions reflects local political realities. In particular, we predict that where dominant parties control the constitutional drafting process, we should expect a weak, low-access form of judicial review. Where constitutions are designed in conditions of political deadlock or diffused parties, we should expect strong, accessible judicial review. The next chapter will consider this hypothesis in greater depth.

CONCLUSION

Judicial review reflects the incentives of constitutional designers to adopt a form of political insurance. By ensuring that losers in the legislative arena will be able to bring claims to court, judicial review lowers the cost of constitution making and allows drafters to conclude constitutional bargains that would otherwise be unobtainable. As democratization increases electoral uncertainty, demand for insurance rises. Although other institutions can also serve to protect minorities, judicial review has become particularly focal. This theory goes a long way toward explaining the rapid spread of judicial review in recently adopted constitutions.

---

[18] Jon Elster, "Forces and Mechanisms in the Constitution-Making Process," 45 *Duke L. J.* 364 (1995).

2

Constituting Judicial Power

What determines the character of judicial review as it operates in new democracies? One important factor is the institutional design of the court and access to it, which is the subject of this chapter. The institutional design of the judicial review mechanism is generally, though not always, a product of the written constitution itself. As such, it reflects, in large part, the choices of the constitutional designers. The political bargain struck at the outset of the democratic regime and embodied in the constitutional text will frequently include some provisions for judicial review. Some important features of the judicial review body, such as its jurisdiction, composition, and selection method of its members, may be detailed in the constitutional text.

Text is not the only source of judicial power, however. This qualification is necessary both because some systems of judicial review are not derived from constitutional text (the systems in Israel and the United States are two well-known examples), but also because nonconstitutional norms may be important in shaping the environment of judicial review. Frequently, matters such as terms and procedures are listed in ordinary organic statutes of the judicial review body. Furthermore, judicial decisions themselves will fill in many of the gaps in these frameworks. Particularly important are decisions related to jurisdiction and standing that play a major role in a court's self-articulation of its political role.

This chapter is primarily concerned with the institutional choices embodied in written constitutions and their importance in setting the stage for judicial review. It focuses on explicit design of judicial institutions from the perspective of politicians seeking insurance. By tying judicial review to the politics of constitutional drafting, this chapter offers a theory with more specific implications than the general argument that the spread of judicial review reflects a global rights consciousness.

Chapter 1 argued that the decision to include judicial review in the constitution reflects the political needs of constitutional drafters. We still need to consider why politicians choose a particular institutional design for the judicial review that they do. This choice can be analogized to tailoring the insurance contract to fit specific local conditions. Why, for example, do some constitutional designers choose to adopt a system with open access so that any individual citizen may invoke the machinery of constitutional control, while other designers limit access? This question, and others of institutional design, can only be addressed after an exploration of the dimensions along which systems of judicial review differ.

This chapter addresses five major dimensions on which systems of judicial review vary: access to the court; effect and timing of judicial decision; the institutional mechanisms for accountability to the political environment; the term length of constitutional justices; and the size of the court. Access refers to how cases are brought to the court, effect refers to the consequences of a finding of unconstitutionality, and accountability concerns how the court as an institution is composed and the mechanisms for political control and influence over the court. Term length concerns the length of time judges can serve and whether they may be reappointed. The size of the court refers to the number of judges.

We do not devote much explicit consideration here to what is perhaps the highest-order choice constitutional designers face with regard to court design – namely, whether to grant the power of judicial review to the ordinary judiciary (as in the United States) or to limit it to a designated body (as in the Kelsenian model). Rather, we consider this decision as being essentially related to access to judicial review. A word of explanation is in order here.

Countries that allow ordinary courts to conduct judicial review are almost exclusively those that for historical reasons were subject to Anglo-American legal influence. We see this decision as being driven in part by considerations of history or legal tradition, though it is important to note that many of these countries have opted for hybrid solutions to the question of centralization. For example, the South African Constitutional Court is really a court of constitutional appeals from ordinary courts, and the Indian Supreme Court has a designated constitutional bench.

The common law courts, with their myriad roles and long tradition of autonomy, are a resource in the Anglo-American world that is simply unavailable to countries with other legal traditions. Ordinary courts in most new democracies seldom have such institutional credibility. For this reason, the default choice for many countries is to adopt a German-style designated constitutional court, but to tailor the design along the various dimensions discussed as follows. Therefore, we do not spend much time considering the *political* incentives to adopt centralized or decentralized review: In many constitutional design situations, there is no real choice to be made here. The particular relationship between the ordinary courts and constitutional review does have significant effects on the *operation* of the system of judicial review, and this is a theme that will be apparent in the case studies.

Access

Constitutional review systems differ widely on the question of who has standing to bring a claim. One can array access to the court on a spectrum from very limited access, as in the original design of the Austrian model in 1920, in which only state and federal governments could bring cases, to the present design of the German Constitutional Court, where not only political bodies but individuals may enjoy direct access through constitutional petitions and ordinary judges may refer questions as well. The Indian Constitution guarantees direct access to the supreme court on questions of fundamental rights and also allows the court to hear advisory questions so that its jurisdiction is much broader than its American counterpart, whose jurisdiction is limited to concrete cases. The present Hungarian Constitutional Court has perhaps the widest access of any such body in the world today, as the right of abstract constitutional petition is not even limited to citizens.[1]

Like other elements of institutional design, access can change over time. For example, 1974 constitutional amendments in France extended the right of petition to any group of sixty parliamentary deputies, allowing

---

[1] However, the court does not engage in concrete review in the classical sense of intervening in the context of ordinary court decisions. As for other courts with wide access, the Slovak court allows petition by "anyone" whose rights are the subject of inquiry, but this right is probably limited to citizens. Slovak Constitution (1991), Articles 130(f), 127.

	Centralized	Decentralized
Open Access	Germany, Italy	United States, Canada, Japan, Scandinavian Countries
Limited Access	France 5th Republic, Austria 1920–29	

FIGURE 2.1. Type of Judicial Review Body and Access

minority parties to challenge governmental action on constitutional grounds. Judicial decisions can also expand or contract standing.[2] Standing doctrine in the United States Supreme Court has changed over time, reflecting different judicial agendas.[3]

Figure 2.1 describes these features for some of the major systems of judicial review, again keeping in mind that hybrids are possible between these ideal types.

Access to the court is perhaps the most important ingredient in judicial power, because a party seeking to utilize judicial review as political insurance will only be able to do so if it can bring a case to court.[4] Setting up a designated constitutional court, accessible only to a narrow set of organs, has the effect of limiting the insurance function of the constitutional court. But some designated courts, such as that of Hungary, have wide access. Figure 2.2 arrays access to constitutional courts on a spectrum, from very limited access to very open. Open access decentralizes the monitoring function widely and makes it more likely that politicians will be challenged in court should they fail to abide by constitutional limitations.

The design choice on access has much to do with the prospective position of political forces in the constitutional system. Other things being

[2] See, for example, *Flast v. Cohen* 392 U.S. 83, 88 S. Ct. 1942, 20 L. Ed. 947 (1968) (taxpayer standing in the United States).
[3] Maxwell Stearns, *Constitutional Process: A Social Choice Analysis of Supreme Court Decision Making* (2000), especially Chapter 6.
[4] Note, however, that some of the new courts also have limited power to initiate proceedings on their own prerogative, without a formal petition from outside.

Access Mechanism	Examples
Special bodies only	Austria 1920–29, France before 1974
Special bodies + legislative minorities	France after 1974, Bulgaria, Rumania
Special bodies + any court	Taiwan, Poland before 1997
Any litigant	United States
Special bodies + any court + citizen petition	Germany, Mongolia
Special bodies + any court + open petition	Hungary

FIGURE 2.2. Accessibility of Constitutional Adjudication (Lower on Figure = More Accessible)

equal, a dominant party will seek to limit access to judicial review, perhaps by restricting it to major political institutions. Political forces in rough balance will seek to maximize access to legislative minorities and ordinary citizens to provide insurance in the event of an electoral loss. Because they expect to lose in the legislatures, the availability of constitutional review provides the prospective minority with another forum in which to contest policies of the majority. This may be achieved by extending access to the court to minority groups in the legislature or to ordinary citizens. Open access also allows watchdog groups that might share the policy preferences of the politicians to make claims and assist in monitoring the government. We should thus expect a correlation between political uncertainty and open access.

Another distinction is whether the court can hear constitutional questions only in the context of concrete legal cases (as in the U.S. Supreme Court), or whether it can consider constitutional issues in the abstract. Concrete review requires litigation of constitutionality in the context of a particular case. Abstract review determines the constitutionality of a statute without a specific case. The French *Conseil Constitutionnel* may only hear issues in the abstract. The German and Spanish Constitutional Courts practice both abstract and concrete review.[5] In practice, the distinction between abstract and concrete review is not as important as it may appear, but it is a widely used theoretical construct.

A related issue concerns the *timing* of review: In the French system, review can only take place *ex ante* promulgation of legislation. This means that the law can be modified by the legislature to conform with the decision of the *Conseil Constitutionnel*; this form of review makes the

[5] For a discussion, see Alec Stone, *The Birth of Judicial Politics in France* 231–35 (1992).

conseil more akin to a third house of the legislature than a court. *Ex post* review allows for more types of claims: A claimant can argue not only that a statute is unconstitutional on its face and its purpose, but also in its effects. *Ex ante* constitutional review may increase the average quality of legislation – patently unconstitutional bills cannot be passed. But *ex post* constitutional review may also have a similar effect. By demonstrating that unconstitutional legislation cannot be effectively implemented, *ex post* review may reduce the incentives to pass such legislation.[6] To the extent that review after promulgation allows more information to be considered, there may be an advantage for *ex post* monitoring.

Although it does not occupy a central place in this study, we should also mention the ancillary powers of constitutional courts beyond judicial review of legislation and administrative action. Constitutional courts also have other functions, including such duties as reviewing referenda and international agreements for conformity with the constitution;[7] determining whether political parties are unconstitutional;[8] adjudicating election violations;[9] and impeaching senior governmental officials.[10] Recently, constitutional courts have been given a wide range of other powers that move even more far afield from their traditional role. The Azerbaijani draft constitution gave the constitutional court power to "dissolve parliament if it repeatedly passes laws that violate the Constitution."[11] Similarly, the Constitutional Court of the Russian Federation has the right to initiate

---

[6] Of course, politicians could pass the unconstitutional legislation to claim credit from their supporters and shift blame to the court for striking it. For example, members of Congress often proposed antiabortion legislation of dubious constitutionality in the aftermath of *Roe v. Wade*, 410 U.S. 113 (1973). See Neal Devins, *Shaping Constitutional Values: Elected Government, the Supreme Court, and the Abortion Debate* (1996).

[7] See, for example, Constitution of Bulgaria (1991), Article 149(4) (international agreements).

[8] See, for example, Constitution of the Republic of China, as amended (1997); Basic Law of Germany (1949), Article 21(2); Constitution of Bulgaria (1991), Article 149(5).

[9] See, for example, Constitution of France (1958), Articles 58–60; Basic Law of Germany (1949), Article 41(2); Constitution of Lithuania (1992), Article 105(3)(1).

[10] See, for example, Constitution of Bulgaria (1991), Article 149(8); Constitution of Hungary (1949), Article 31(a); Constitution of Mongolia (1992), Article 35(1); Basic Law of Germany (1949), Article 61.

[11] Rett R. Ludwikowski, "Constitution Making in the Countries of Former Soviet Dominance: Current Developments," 23 *Ga. J. Int'l & Comp. L.* 155, 190 (1993). The constitution was passed in 1995 without these provisions.

legislation.[12] The Thai Constitutional Court has the power to approve recommendations of the Counter-Corruption Commission to ban politicians from office for failing to accurately report income and assets, a power that it has already used several times in the short period of time since the adoption of the 1997 constitution. Indeed, in one notable case the constitutional court was asked to ban the incoming candidate for prime minister. All of these powers can be very important for understanding the political role of constitutional courts in a particular system.

Effect

Systems of judicial review also vary in the effect of their pronouncement on legislation in concrete cases. American courts, bound by the rule of *stare decisis*, do not actually void laws that they find to be unconstitutional. Rather, because subsequent similar cases must follow the rule in previous cases, the voided law remains on the books, if dormant for all practical purposes.

In centralized systems, by contrast, the court has the power to declare the laws unconstitutional and immediately void. This feature of direct annulment of laws in centralized systems is often said to follow from the lack of a *stare decisis* doctrine.[13] Without a clear principle that precedents must be followed, ordinary courts could vary in their application of the constitution, hampering predictability and consistency in the legal system. To avoid such a result, the declarations of some constitutional courts are given *erga omnes* effect, meaning they are binding for all future cases.

A variation found in the German tradition is that the constitutional court has two choices in rendering a finding of unconstitutionality.[14] It can either find legislation null and void (*nichtig*) or incompatible (*unvereinbar*) with the basic law. In the latter case, the court declares the law unconstitutional but not void and usually sets a deadline for the legislature to modify the legislation. Sometimes these decisions admonish the legislature to modify the legislation within particular guidelines.[15] The court becomes deeply involved in "suggesting" to the legislature language that ultimately finds its way into the statute. For example, in its 1975 decision voiding

[12] Herman Schwartz, "The New Courts: An Overview," 2 *E. Eur. Const. Rev.* 28, 30 (1993), quoting Constitutional Court Act of the Russian Federation (1993), Article 9.

[13] Mauro Cappelletti, *Judicial Review in the Contemporary World* (1971).

[14] Donald Kommers, *The Constitutional Jurisprudence of the Federal Republic of Germany* (1989).

[15] *Ibid.* at 53.

a permissive statute allowing abortion, the German Constitutional Court engaged in extensive suggestions for rewriting of the statute.[16] In other cases, the court will sustain a challenged statute, but warn the legislature that it is likely to void it in the future, or suggest conditions for the constitutional application of the statute.

These types of decisions are typically understood as pragmatic, designed to give the legislature time to adjust the content of major legislation for which a judicial declaration of unconstitutionality would cause too much social disruption.[17] Partial findings of unconstitutionality are indeed less politically dramatic, and courts in new democracies that have adopted this technique have been more willing to send legislation back to the legislature than to void it completely.[18] There is no doubt that the availability of "lesser" options to voiding a law allows courts to take a more nuanced view of the political process in which they are engaged and therefore facilitates a more subtle range of interactions with the political bodies.

Their pragmatism notwithstanding, such decisions are problematic from a rule of law perspective. After all, the court finds a law unconstitutional, but allows its continued application. Although the delay in voiding the legislation may provide some advantages in terms of predictability, it appears odd to allow an unconstitutional act to stand. In my view, these techniques can best be understood by viewing the court as a quasi-legislative actor engaged in democratic dialogue with political branches of government. This typically is a *negative* form of legislating, guarding the limits of the process rather than promoting policy initiatives. Nevertheless, through suggestions for revision the court may have significant impact on the *shape* of legislation.

In some systems with a legacy of parliamentary control of constitutionality, the decision of the constitutional court as to unconstitutionality is not binding, but rather is advisory to the legislature. The legislature retains some power to reject or accept the court's finding, either by majority or supermajority vote. A version of this model was extant in Poland during the life of its first Constitutional Tribunal, 1988–97, and remains intact in Mongolia, as will be discussed in Chapter 6. Similarly, the Brazilian Senate

---

[16] *Ibid.* See also Mary Ann Glendon, *Abortion and Divorce in Western Law* (1987).

[17] Kommers, *supra* note 14, at 54.

[18] For example, the Korean Constitutional Court has begun to use this technique as a matter of course, preferring it to outright striking of legislation. See *Constitutional Court of Korea, the Constitutional Court* 17 (1997); and discussion in Chapter 7, *infra*.

can choose to accept as binding *erga omnes* a decision rendered *inter partes* in a specific case, allowing it to convert a finding of unconstitutionality.[19]

Courts in Latin America make use of a device called *amparo*, wherein a successful constitutional complainant will be free from the application of the offending law or government act, but the act will continue to apply to others. This device is desirable from the perspective of politicians who do not want much judicial constraint, a fair characterization of many governments in Latin America during the twentieth century. The *amparo* channels constitutional protest into the courts, perhaps relieving a source of broader political pressure on the regime, but at the same time does not really limit the government's freedom of action. An unconstitutional act that affects 1,000 people might require up to 1,000 suits, with all the expense they entail, before it no longer has effect. The *amparo* may work well to provide redress against government actions that provide substantial burdens on small numbers of citizens, such as measures affecting property rights. But actions that provide only minor burdens, or those that affect populations less able to mobilize for legal action, are likely to remain effective tools.

Mechanisms of Appointment and Accountability

Appointments are among the most crucial of design issues. Constitutional designers are unlikely to adopt constitutional review unless they believe it will be carried out by impartial appointees. If designers believe they are likely to lose postconstitutional elections, they will not be in a position to appoint judges. So overly partisan mechanisms are especially unattractive. The normative task is to select an appointment mechanism that will maximize the chances that the judge will interpret the text in accordance with the intentions of the constitution writers. This, in turn, requires considering judges' utility functions, an issue concerning which there is no consensus in the literature.[20]

Appointment mechanisms are designed to insulate judges from short-term political pressures, yet ensure some accountability. The United States

---

[19] Constitution of Brazil, Article 52(X).

[20] Jeffrey A. Segal and Harold J. Spaeth, *The Supreme Court and the Attitudinal Model* (1993) (judges vote their political preferences); Lee Epstein and Jack Knight, *The Choices Justices Make* (1998) (judges are strategic maximizers); Lawrence Baum, *The Puzzle of Judicial Behavior* (1997) (reviewing evidence and discussing poor state of knowledge on this question); Richard Posner, *Overcoming Law* (1995).

federal judicial system has lifetime appointments for insulation, but puts tremendous effort into screening potential candidates in the appointment process. Other systems set up mechanisms for ensuring accountability for judicial performance *ex post* by providing for renewable terms. Many American states use a system of elections that allows a judge to be appointed by a governor upon recommendation by a committee of mixed composition.[21] Judges are then subjected to recall elections where they "run on the record," that is, without opposition. Judges in these systems are very rarely recalled, so the threat may not be much of a constraint in reality.

Mueller persuasively argues that a supermajority requirement for judicial selection will tend to protect the minority from losing in both the courts and the legislature and by extension will tend to produce more-moderate, acceptable judicial candidates.[22] Mueller also considers the merits of having the judiciary and the chief executive serve as appointing authorities for the judiciary. He favors such professional appointments by existing judges, noting that the judiciary has internal incentives for competent selection.[23] A judiciary that appears incompetent invites modification of the appointment system. Indeed, one design suggested by Mueller would allow judiciary-nominated judges to take office barring legislative intervention by supermajority.[24] This proposal combines accountability and independence, because most appointments would be routine, but there is a mechanism for political intervention should judges nominate candidates who are far out of step with political opinion.

I divide appointment mechanisms into three broad types: professional appointments, as in Mueller's proposal; cooperative appointing mechanisms; and representative appointing mechanisms. Theoretically, one can also have single-body appointment mechanisms where, for example, an executive can appoint all members of the constitutional court without legislative oversight. An example that is close to this is the Council of Grand Justices in Taiwan, whose members are appointed by the president from a list of nominees prepared by a committee he picks. Approval is required by the legislature, but because the president was historically the

---

[21] This is the so-called "Missouri plan." Mary Volcansek and Jacqueline Lucienne Lafon, *Judicial Selection* (1987).

[22] Dennis C. Mueller, *Constitutional Democracy* 281 (1996).

[23] Dennis C. Mueller, "Fundamental Issues in Constitutional Reform: With Special References to Latin America and the United States," 10:2 *Const. Pol. Econ.* 119, 125 (1999).

[24] *Ibid.*

head of the largest political party, this was not an effective check, and the mechanism was a de facto single-body appointment mechanism. Single-body mechanisms of this type are unusual in democracies because they can lead to all-or-nothing composition of the court. If the president can appoint all the judges, the presumption of effective constitutional constraint disappears. Therefore, the insurance rationale for judicial review loses its appeal.

Cooperative appointment mechanisms require the cooperation of two bodies to appoint constitutional justices; the American, Russian, and Hungarian procedure of presidential nomination followed by legislative confirmation is one example. These systems seem consistent with the objective of supermajoritarian requirements to ensuring broad support (institutional or political) for those who are to interpret the constitution. They risk deadlock, however, because they require the agreement of different institutions to go forward. Although there are no institutional barriers to such bargains being concluded, it is possible that in circumstances of political conflict, appointments would not be made.

Finally, *representative* mechanisms utilize multiple appointing authorities: For example, in Italy a third of the nine-member court is nominated by the president, a third by the parliament, and a third by the supreme court.[25] This system has been copied in such diverse places as Bulgaria, Korea, and Mongolia. Alternative versions provide for one-third of appointments by each house of a bicameral legislature and one-third by the chief executive. Representative systems can be distinguished from cooperative systems in that, theoretically, appointees can be much closer to pure agents of the appointers. Because no other institution must agree to the appointment, there is no need for compromise. There may also be, however, a dynamic that prevents politicized appointments where there are three appointing bodies. Each appointing body may seek to appoint persons sympathetic with its institutional interests. However, if it is too blatant in doing so, the other appointing bodies will respond by appointing their loyal partisans. Because only one-third of the membership is appointed by any one body, each can be assured that it will be *unable* to dictate outcomes if each judge acts as a pure agent. I characterize this institutional design as "mutually assured politicization." Each body that appoints a person who appears to be a pure agent signals that it may plan to engage in extraconstitutional action

[25] Volcansek and Lafon, *supra* note 21.

and needs to influence the court to uphold its action. By appointing someone who appears "neutral" and nonpartisan, the appointing authority signals that it does not anticipate needing or using the court to uphold its own controversial actions. Thus, representative mechanisms may provide, like cooperative mechanisms, an incentive for moderate appointments.

Despite their popularity, representative systems have a disadvantage compared with cooperative systems. Although a dynamic of moderation as described above may come into play, there is some possibility that politicians will simply nominate pure agents. Opinions issued by a court of pure agents are likely to be internally fragmented and of lower quality than those issued by a more centrist, consensual deliberative body as appointed through cooperative mechanisms. Cooperative mechanisms more closely approximate the supermajority principle of constitutional economics but risk deadlock in the appointing process. Representative systems ensure a smooth appointment process but risk deadlock on the court.

In the German system, wherein each house of the legislature can appoint an equal number of members to the Constitutional Court, supermajority requirements are used in selecting judges.[26] This has led to a norm of reciprocity that has established de facto party seats held by the three major parties. The norm produces a stable court that reflects broad political preferences without overrepresenting either of the two main factions. This version of the legislative-centered system turns parties, not institutions, into the important players. The system is stable because the party system is stable.

The dynamics of party systems are a crucial variable in evaluating selection systems. A system of self-appointments by the professional judiciary may be the most likely to produce accurate review if we assume judicial neutrality, but it can lead to a court that dominates the legislature if the party system is too fragmented and unstable to provide a constraint on judicial decision making. In stable party systems, supermajority requirements will produce moderate judges, but appointments may not be made if there is deadlock. Representative systems ensure appointments will be made but create other risks on the court. For example, if the chief executive is the head of the majority party in one or both houses of Parliament,

---

[26] The Bundestag appoints its members through a two-thirds vote of the Judicial Selection Committee with party representation proportional to that of the body as a whole and the Bundesrat through a two-thirds vote of the body as a whole. Kommers, *supra* note 14.

this system will lead to a court that is allied with the chief executive. Where there is little party discipline or where the chief executive is independently elected, however, institutional rivalries can lead to a more divided court.[27]

Term Length

Term length is typically seen as being a key component of judicial independence.[28] Other things being equal, it is argued, the longer the term of appointment, the freer a judge will be in exercising discretion. U.S. federal court judges serve for life, and this is considered an important guarantee of their independence. The longer the appointment, the more independent a judge can be of prevailing political sentiments. Like central bank governors, judges are at risk from undue pressure to advance short-term political interests rather than the long-term collective good. We should thus expect longer terms to correlate with politicians who value judicial accuracy and independence, namely pessimistic politicians with insurance needs.

Although one might think that lifetime appointments are always longer than designated terms, this is not the case because virtually all other systems with "lifetime" appointments provide for a mandatory retirement age of sixty-five to seventy years of age. Even if this were not the case, appointments could come late in life as a reward for political loyalty rather than an incentive for independent adjudication. Thus, actual time served on such courts may in fact be lower than judges on courts with specific and limited terms. For example, Japanese judges on the supreme court serve until mandatory retirement at age seventy, but this in fact produces very short terms, averaging around six years.[29] Politicians in these systems exercise preappointment scrutiny over prospective judges.[30]

Other constitutional judges have limited terms. French members of the *Conseil Constitutionnel* serve a single nine-year term, and judges on the

---

[27] Bailey proposes that constitutional issues be decided by a legislature, possibly the previous sitting legislature that appointed judges if the issue is legislation passed by the current legislature. Martin Bailey, "Toward a New Constitution for a Future Country," 90 *Pub. Choice* 73, 99 (1997).

[28] See, for example, William Landes and Richard Posner, "The Independent Judiciary in an Interest-Group Perspective," 18 *J. L. & Econ.* 875 (1975).

[29] J. Mark Ramseyer and Eric B. Rasmusen, "Judicial Independence in a Civil Law Regime: The Evidence from Japan," 13 *J. L., Econ. & Org.* 259 (1997).

[30] Masaki Abe, "Internal Control of a Bureaucratic Judiciary: The Case of Japan," 23 *Int'l. J. Soc. L.* 303 (1995); Ramseyer and Rasmusen, *ibid.*

German Constitutional Court serve a single twelve-year term. Judges of other constitutional courts, including that of Spain, are allowed to be reappointed. Other things being equal, the possibility of reappointment has the potential to reduce judicial independence, as judges late in their term who seek to remain in office must be sensitive to the political interests of those bodies that will reappoint them. Of course, judges serving a single limited term also have an incentive to act with an eye toward future employment possibilities, so to the extent political authorities have control over entry into the professorate or other postjudicial positions, judges may be subject to political discipline in such systems as well.

Court Size

The constitutional designer may specify in the constitution the number of judges on the court. The major tradeoff here is between speed and accuracy. The greater the number of judges, the higher the costs of deliberation. At the other extreme, a single judge deciding all cases would be a relatively inexpensive method of judicial decision making. The problem with a single judge is that the potential error costs of such a system are high.[31] Hence, it is common for judicial panels to grow larger as an issue rises through a system of appeal. For example, United States federal courts of appeals frequently decide cases in panels of three judges with appeal to the court *en banc.*

One might think that larger courts would always be more accurate and hence better able to fulfill the insurance function for constitutional designers. After all, it seems plausible to assume that error costs are reduced by deliberations, and there is ample empirical evidence that group decision making is of higher quality than individual decision making.[32] However, others have argued that once a group expands beyond a certain size it tends to make poorer decisions. For example, Richard Posner has recently argued that an expansion in court size may be associated with a decline in quality of decisions, in part because norms of work are less sustainable with larger groups. However, his evidence is not dispositive

---

[31] At an extreme, in the United States, we let the trial judge decide the initial matter himself or herself even though his or her preferences may not reflect those of the court as a whole or of the median judge. Warren F. Schwartz and C. Frederick Beckner III, "Toward a Theory of the 'Meritorious Case': Legal Uncertainty as a Social Choice Problem," 6 *Geo. Mason L. Rev.* 801 (1998).

[32] At least in certain contexts. See Stephen Bainbridge, "Why a Board? Group Decision-making in Corporate Governance," 55 *Vand. L. Rev.* 1 (2002).

on the question.[33] Furthermore, Posner considers overall court size on an appeals court that initially hears cases in panels, so his argument is not directly relevant to constitutional designers that are creating courts that hear matters *en banc.*

In the context of new democracies, we believe smaller courts should be associated with more dominant political parties. This is because there are less factions concerned with representation on the court, and hence less of a need for ensuring balance among the membership. Furthermore, each additional judge increases the budget of the court, and there is little reason a dominant party would want to incur these extra costs, other things being equal.

One might argue that the salient variable to examine is panel size rather than court size. But the size of panels is typically a matter left to ordinary law or the organic statutes of a constitutional court, rather than being specified in the constitutional text. Furthermore, because important cases will often be heard *en banc,* the overall size of the court is a relevant variable subject to influence by constitutional designers.

There is some empirical support for the proposition that designated constitutional courts are larger than their counterparts that are the courts of final appeal for all issues. For new constitutional courts set up after 1989 ($n = 25$), the mean number of justices was 11.25. For supreme courts given the power of constitutional review in the same period ($n = 8$), the mean size is 8.25. The fact that supreme courts are smaller even though they have nonconstitutional cases to consider might indicate that first-instance consideration of the issues by lower-level courts saves time later on.

Summary

To summarize the argument so far, each dimension of design choice has certain effects on the capacity of the court to render accurate review. Table 2.1 summarizes three prototype constitutional courts along these dimensions. Because there are numerous dimensions upon which the institutional design of a system of judicial review may vary, there is an almost infinite array of configurations, and no two courts share exactly the same design and institutional environment. The diversity of systems

---

[33] Richard Posner, "Is the Ninth Circuit Too Large? A Statistical Study of Judicial Quality," 29 *J. Leg. Stud.* 711 (2000). See also Kaushik Mukhopadhaya, "Jury Size and the Free Rider Problem," forthcoming, *J. L., Econ., & Org.* (2003).

TABLE 2.1 *Dimensions of Design Choice*

	Germany – Constitutional Court	United States – Supreme Court	France – Conseil Constitutionnel
Access/Standing	Petition, courts, requests from government	Access through courts only	Restricted standing
Justiciable Questions	Concrete and abstract review	Concrete review only	Abstract review only
Appointments	Representative – 2 houses parliament (supermajority)	Cooperative – president, parliament	Representative – president, 2 houses parliament
Term Length	12	Life – no age limit	9
Size	16	9	9

of judicial review can be seen in Table 2.2, which presents the structural features of selected new constitutional courts established after 1980.

EXPLAINING VARIATION IN JUDICIAL REVIEW

Judicial Review as Insurance: Anecdotal Evidence

Does actual design of judicial review reflect the insurance model? There is strong anecdotal evidence to support the hypothesis that judicial review will be more accessible and powerful where political forces are diffused at the time of the constitutional bargain and more limited when a single party controls the process.[34]

Take as an initial example the French system, sometimes referred to as limited constitutional review. Constitutional review is restricted to abstract, *ex ante* review by a centralized body. At the time of the establishment of the Fifth Republic, standing was restricted to certain designated governmental bodies, a fact perfectly consistent with the insurance theory. The *conseil* was adopted at the instigation of General De Gaulle, who wanted a strong executive to prevent the deadlock that had characterized the Fourth Republic. The constitutional scheme features a dual system of

---

[34] There is similar evidence that central bank independence is strongly correlated with politicians' time horizons. As politicians' time horizons shorten, independence increases. John B. Goodman, *Monetary Sovereignty: The Politics of Central Banking in Western Europe* (1992).

TABLE 2.2 *Constitutional and Supreme Courts in Selected New Democracies*

Country	Term in Years	Term Renewable?	Total # Judges	Appointing Authorities	Access
Albania	9	no	9	president with assembly approval	certain bodies, citizens
Argentina	life+		5	president with senate approval	courts
Armenia	life+		9	5 assembly, 4 president	certain bodies, 33% of deputies
Bangladesh	life+		N/A	president	courts, limited original jurisdiction
Benin	5	once	7	4 assembly, 3 president	certain bodies, citizens
Bolivia	10	no	12	parliament	courts, limited original jurisdiction
Bosnia-Herzegovina	life@	yes, initially	9	4 house, 2 by Serb assembly, 3 by European Court of Human Rights in consultation with president	certain bodies, 25% of deputies of either chamber, ordinary courts
Brazil	life		11	president with senate approval	special bodies, political parties, labor unions, and any citizen
Bulgaria	9	no	12	1/3 president, 1/3 parliament, 1/3 top courts	certain bodies, 20% of deputies
Burkina-Faso	9	no	9	1/3 president, 1/3 assembly, 1/3 judges nominated by justice minister	certain bodies, 20% of deputies
Cambodia	9	yes	9	1/3 king, 1/3 assembly 1/3 sup judicial council	certain bodies, courts
Cape Verde	life		5	1 president, 1 assembly, 3 judges	courts, limited original jurisdiction
Chile	8	N/A	7	3 supreme court, 1 president, 1 senate, 2 national security council	certain bodies, 25% of members of either chamber
Colombia	8	no	9	senate from lists given by president, supreme court, council of state	certain bodies, citizens

Croatia	8	yes	13	parliament	certain bodies, 33% of deputies of either chamber, any person
Czech Republic	10	once	15	president selects from parliament list with senate consent	certain bodies, open to citizens
Djibouti	8	no	6	1/3 president, 1/3 assembly, 1/3 judges	certain bodies, 10 deputies
Dominican Republic	life+		16	senate	courts
Ecuador	life		9	national judicial council	courts
El Salvador	9	yes	5	national judicial council	certain bodies, citizens
Estonia	life+		17	court president nominated by president; others by court president	any court
Ethiopia	life+		11	6 president, 3 house members and supreme court president and VP	certain bodies
Fiji	life+		N/A	president	certain bodies
Gabon	7	once	9	1/3 president, 1/3 senate, 1/3 assembly	certain bodies, 10% of deputies
Georgia	10	yes	9	1/3 president, 1/3 parliament, 1/3 supreme court	certain bodies, open to citizens
Ghana	life+		at least 10	judicial council	courts
Greece	2	yes	11	courts, state councils, and professors	citizens
Guatemala	5	yes	13	congress selects from list of 26	courts
Guinea-Bissau	life		17	assembly on presidential nomination	courts
Honduras	4	yes	9	congress	certain bodies, open to citizens
Hungary	9	once	15	parliament	certain bodies, open to anyone
Korea	6	yes	9	1/3 president, 1/3 parliament, 1/3 supreme court	certain bodies, open to citizens
Kyrgyz Republic	15	yes	9	assembly	certain bodies, courts

(continued)

TABLE 2.2 (continued)

Country	Term in Years	Term Renewable?	Total # Judges	Appointing Authorities	Access
Latvia	10	no, but later reelection OK	7	3 assembly, 2 cabinet, 2 supreme court	certain bodies
Lithuania	9	no	9	1/3 president, 1/3 parliament, 1/3 supreme court	certain bodies, 20% of deputies
Macedonia	9	no	9	assembly	certain bodies, open to citizens
Madagascar	6	no	9	3 president, 2 assembly, 1 senate, 3 by supreme judicial council	president any court
Malawi	life+		at least 3	president	courts
Mali	7	once	9	1/3 president, 1/3 president of assembly, 1/3 judges	certain bodies, 10% of deputies
Mauritania	9	no	6	3 president, 2 assembly, 1 senate	certain bodies, 33% of deputies of either chamber
Moldova	6	yes	6	1/3 president, 1/3 assembly, 1/3 supreme council	certain bodies
Mongolia	6	yes	9	1/3 president, 1/3 parliament, 1/3 supreme court	certain bodies, open to citizens
Morocco	6	yes	9	4 + president by king, 4 by assembly king on judicial council nomination	certain bodies, 25% of deputies
Nepal	life+	N/A	15	assembly on presidential nomination	courts
Nicaragua	6		at least 7	1 president, 1 assembly, 2 judges, 1 professor, 1 bar association, 1 human rights organization	courts
Niger	6	no	7		certain bodies
Panama	10	no	9	president with cabinet and legislative approval	solicitor general

Country					
Paraguay	life+		9	president with senate approval	courts
Peru	5	no	7	assembly	certain bodies, groups of citizens
Philippines	life+		15	president	courts
Poland	8	no	12	parliament	certain bodies, open to citizens
Rumania	9	no	9	1/3 president, 1/3 each house of parliament	limited to certain bodies or legislative minority
Russia	life+		19	appointed by federal council on presidential nomination	open to citizens
Senegal	6	no	5	president	certain bodies
Sierra Leone	life+		at least 5	president	courts
Slovakia	7	once	10	president appoints from candidates	open to citizens
Slovenia	9	no	9	national assembly on presidential nomination	open to citizens
South Africa	12	no	11	president after consultation with judicial commission; 4 must be judges	any court
Taiwan	9	no after 2003	15	president from list prepared by committee	certain bodies, ordinary courts
Tanzania	life+		5	judicial council	
Thailand	9+	no	15	5 supreme court judges, 2 supreme administrative court judges, 8 by committee	special bodies, 10% of deputies, or any court
Ukraine	9	no	18	1/3 president, 1/3 parliament, 1/3 assembly	certain bodies
Uruguay	10+	no, but later reelection OK	5	assembly	courts

53

Key: + = includes some age limitation; @ = after a five-year transitional set of appointments.
Source: Adapted from constitutional texts at http://www.oefre.unibe.ch/law/icl/index.html with country-specific supplementary sources.

law making, with certain subjects to be the province of executive decrees rather than parliamentary legislation. De Gaulle's confidence was such that he drafted the entire constitution around his personal popularity and did not trust parties or parliamentarians. By allowing the *conseil* to consider only statutes *before* promulgation, he placed a check on the Parliament's ability to dictate policy. Restricted standing allowed De Gaulle and government agencies to bring cases, but not ordinary citizens, who might challenge legislation that the government wanted. Furthermore, eliminating concrete review meant that the government would be able to act without constitutional scrutiny once policies were adopted.

This scheme changed radically when standing was broadened in 1974 to include any minority group from the Parliament. This change was initiated by President Giscard d'Estaing, who headed the small Republican Party that governed briefly. As a minority party heading a coalition government, the Republicans valued expanded standing that would provide a guarantee of access once they were out of power. These changes have had a profound effect on French constitutional law.[35] Predictably, expanded standing led minority groups in Parliament to complain to the *conseil* with greater frequency and to judicialize the very issues they had lost in the legislature. The Gaullists themselves were able to take advantage of this in the early 1980s, after the election of François Mitterand and the Socialist Party: The Socialists' extensive program of nationalization was challenged in and ultimately modified by the *conseil*.[36]

The German system features a centralized body that can engage in both abstract and concrete review. Standing is broad and includes constitutional petitions, as well as the so-called concrete norm control that allows ordinary courts to refer questions to the constitutional court in the context of ongoing legal cases. The design of the German system reflected a strong ideological desire to maintain an open and effective system in the wake of the Nazi experience and in this sense reflects the importance of the rights theory.[37] The strong emphasis on basic rights and the distrust of the ordinary judiciary meant that the centralized constitutional court was an attractive option. However, the insurance theory also has a role to play in explaining institutional design. The German Basic Law was in

---

[35] Stone, *supra* note 5.
[36] *Ibid.* at 140–72.
[37] Mauro Cappelletti, *The Judicial Process in Comparative Perspective* (1989).

many respects a compromise between those who emphasized "positive" economic and social rights and those who emphasized "negative" rights, such as the right to property. An easily accessible constitutional court served the interests of both groups in circumstances where neither felt that it could be assured of a victory in the political arena. Compared with France, a more divided political configuration led to a more powerful constitutional court.

The adoption of judicial review in South Africa in the early 1990s provides a textbook illustration of the insurance theory.[38] One might think that the African National Congress (ANC), as the dominant political force among the black majority, was the paradigm case of a dominant party that would prefer an unconstrained legislature after democratization. The ANC, however, needed to provide assurance to the white and Zulu minorities that it would respect their views or else risk the very stability of the transition process. These minorities, in turn, sought to ensure that the ANC would not ride roughshod over their interests after the inevitable transition to majority rule. The National Party, in particular, sought to ensure a system of rights protected by constitutional review, as well as other minoritarian devices such as group rights and decentralization.[39] These competing interests led to numerous deadlocks in realizing the transfer of power to the black majority.

The configuration of the South African transition, with one dominant party that was unable to dictate a constitution, is such that either the insurance or commitment theory provides an intelligible explanation for the emergence of constitutional review. Where the insurance analogy is perhaps more helpful is in explaining how the presence of judicial review enabled the transition to go forward, when it otherwise might not have been able to.

The key point in South Africa's negotiated transition occurred with the decision to use a two-stage constitution-making process.[40] The parties would establish an interim constitution based on certain agreed principles, during which period a final constitution would be drafted. Not only would the interim stage include a bill of rights and a constitutional court,

---

[38] This section draws on data presented in Richard Spitz with Matthew Chaskalon, *The Politics of Transition: A Hidden History of South Africa's Negotiated Settlement* 192–209 (2000).

[39] Spitz, ibid. at 24.

[40] Heinz Klug, *Constituting Democracy: Law, Globalism and South Africa's Political Reconstruction* 140 (2000).

but this constitutional court had the power to certify the proposed final constitutional text before it would take effect.[41] The presence of judicial review in the menu of constitutional design resolved a deadlock in the negotiation of South Africa's transition, just as the possibility of insurance allows the conclusion of private contracts that might otherwise not occur. Although the ANC might have preferred an unhindered majoritarian constitution, it was unable to dictate that result to distrustful minorities that were sure to lose. Because the National Party had an effective veto on the timing of the transition, the design of the constitutional order reflected its demand for insurance. The constitutional court became the alternative forum in which minorities could – and did – challenge the draft final constitution.

The particular design of judicial review, in the form of a special constitutional court, also reflected insurance dynamics. There were significant debates over whether constitutional review should be performed by the ordinary courts, dominated by appointees of the previous government or by a designated body. The chief advocate of decentralized review was the smaller Democratic Party, which had no hope of winning a major share of seats after the election and was unable to muster support for its position. The debates were resolved in favor of a designated body that would hear cases on appeal from the ordinary courts. Both sides sought to ensure some control over the composition of the proposed constitutional court in further debates on the qualification of potential appointees. The government argued for a ten-year period of service as an advocate or judge, which would have effectively barred many nonwhite candidates. Advocates of wider participation argued for the inclusion of academics and others in the pool of potential justices.

The final mechanism, agreed to by both the Nationalists and the ANC, was that justices would be appointed by the president of the country, sure to be Nelson Mandela. Some justices would come from the ranks of the supreme court, and others would be chosen by the president after consultation with the cabinet. The decision to give the president the dominant role in forming the court made sense to the ANC; it apparently also reflected the National Party's mistaken belief that it would have a significant role in the first posttransition cabinet and thus influence over

---

[41] Republic of South Africa Constitution Act (1993) §71(2) ("The new constitutional text passed by the Constitutional Assembly, or any provision thereof, shall not be of any force and effect unless the Constitutional Court has certified that all of the provisions of such text comply with the Constitutional Principles. . . .")

court composition.[42] If the National Party had some influence over the cabinet appointments and had a strong presence in the ordinary judiciary, it might have significant representation on the court.

These demands were based on overoptimism by the National Party. They understood that they were sure to be a minority in the midterm and hence desired constitutional review; but they hoped to be able to influence appointments. The Democratic Party, with no hope of influencing appointments, argued against this proposal and in favor of a role for the nonpartisan Judicial Service Commission. Apparently, this argument convinced the National Party that it had made a mistake in allowing the president such a prominent role in making appointments. Although a role for judges of the supreme court would provide some insurance against an executive-dominated constitutional court, the National Party and the Democrats made a last-minute, ultimately successful push to expand the role of the Judicial Service Commission in the court appointments. The need for the court in the first place and features of its institutional design reflect political insurance demanded by minorities certain to lose postconstitutional elections.

The Israeli system illustrates how judicial review can also be adopted in established democracies as political configurations change.[43] Demand for insurance should increase when established political forces believe that they will no longer be able to remain in power. In a deeply divided society at independence in 1947 (as today), Israel's founders chose not to adopt a constitution but rather to use a series of incrementally enacted nonentrenched Basic Laws to embody the nation's central political principles. For many years, a secular Ashkenazi elite dominated Israeli politics, and the Labor Party ruled uninterrupted for the first decades of the country's history.

The election of Menachem Begin in the late 1970s initiated an alternation of power between Likud and Labor Parties. As political outcomes became less predictable, the Israeli Supreme Court became more assertive as the expositor of the constitution. This move was tolerated, and in fact institutionalized, by secular politicians who passed two Basic Laws protecting civil rights and explicitly empowering the court to void any

---

[42] This belief was mistaken. See Spitz, 204–5.

[43] See Ran Hirschl, "The Political Origins of Judicial Empowerment through Constitutionalization: Lessons from Four Constitutional Revolutions," *L. Soc. Inquiry* 91 (2000). Israel's system of judicial review is structurally similar to the American system, with the exception that judges must retire at age 70.

legislation not in accordance with their provisions and the basic values of the State of Israel.[44] These politicians faced increased political uncertainty caused by the rise of religious parties in conjunction with a massive wave of immigration from Russia. Judicial review was an attractive way of ensuring that the values of the secular Ashkenazi elite remained protected from future attack.

What of the American founding? Any general theory of judicial review ought to be able to account for the premier case, namely that of the United States, though one must also recognize that the theory as I have articulated it assumes that judicial review is already on the menu of constitutional design. The conventional account suggests that judicial review in the United States flows not from constitutional text but rather from the early case of *Marbury v. Madison*.[45] This emphasis on the self-articulation of judicial review by judges is somewhat unfortunate because it draws attention away from the important question of how the founders thought about judicial review. This is a complex question; indeed, some consider it to be *the* central question of American constitutional scholarship.[46] Despite these complications, let us consider briefly whether there might be an insurance rationale behind the institution of judicial review.

It is important to remember that the United States Constitution was drawn up in an era before the existence of political parties. Therefore, framing the insurance issue as being one considered by formal political parties makes little sense. Nevertheless, there is plenty of evidence that judicial review was seen to be a minoritarian device, and those demanding judicial review were concerned with minimizing the maximum harm that could be imposed on them by a majority. Furthermore,

---

[44] *Basic Law: Human Dignity and Liberty* and *Basic Law: Freedom of Occupation* (1992).

[45] 5 U.S. (1 Cranch.) 137 (1803). For a discussion of *Marbury* as central, see, for example, Paul Kahn, *The Reign of Law: Marbury v. Madison and the Construction of America* (1997). It is safe to say that this is the orthodox position by examining the central position of *Marbury* at the outset of the standard American textbooks in constitutional law. See also Robert McCloskey and Sanford Levinson, *The American Supreme Court* (1994). But see Robert L. Clinton, "Game Theory, Legal History and the Origins of Judicial Review: A Revisionist Analysis of Marbury v. Madison," 38 *Am. J. Pol. Sci.* 285 (1994) (arguing against the conventional understanding of *Marbury*); and Robert L. Clinton, *Marbury v. Madison and Judicial Review* (1989) (stating that *Marbury* only stands for the proposition that judicial review is justified when Congress interferes with *judicial* power).

[46] Jack Rakove, "The Origins of Judicial Review: A Plea for New Contexts," 49 *Stan. L. Rev.* 1031 (1997).

the configuration during the constitutional bargaining process was one in which thirteen states of various sizes sought to negotiate a union. None of the thirteen was sufficiently large to be able to dominate the others. Rather, each state was concerned that its own welfare would be in jeopardy. In this sense, the key factor was political uncertainty among constituent political units, rather than a dominant party precommitting itself to constitutional constraint, as the "commitment" theory described.

The need for insurance is particularly acute in federal systems where a free trade regime is contemplated. Most federal systems provide for some kind of judicial review mechanism to police the law-making boundary between national and local levels of government. This not only reassures the component parts that the center will not trample their rights, but also solves a collective action problem among the components themselves. Free trade in federal systems is endangered by problems of securing credible commitments to the free flow of goods among the component parts.[47] Each state in federalist polities, the reasoning runs, would like to sell goods to all other states but, other things being equal, would like to protect its own market. Without a guarantor to ensure that states cannot enact protectionist legislation, this configuration will soon lead to a high-protection, low-trade outcome. It may be in the interests of each state to accept constraints imposed by independent courts as the price for keeping the other states in line as well.

Federalism provides an important rationale for active judicial review in comparative terms, evidenced by American history and also emphasized by "realist" protagonists in debates over the role of the European Court of Justice in European integration.[48] Federal polities illustrate how political diffusion promotes judicial power. The free trade rationale can be stated in terms of insurance needs or in terms of precommitment on the part of the constituent units of the federation, illustrating that the commitment and insurance theories need not always be inconsistent.

---

[47] See Martin Shapiro, "Federalism, the Race to the Bottom, and the Regulation-Averse Entrepreneur," in *North American Federalism in Comparative Perspective* (Harry Scheiber, ed., 1992).

[48] Geoffrey Garrett, "From the Luxembourg Compromise to Codecision: Decision Making in the European Union," 14 *Electoral Stud.* 289 (1995); Geoffrey Garrett, "The Politics of Legal Integration in the European Union," 49 *Int'l Org.* 175 (1995); Geoffrey Garrett and George Tsebelis, "An Institutional Critique of Intergovernmentalism," 50 *Int'l Org.* 269 (1996); *cf.* Anne-Marie Burley and Walter Mattli, "Europe Before the Court," 47 *Int'l Org.* 41 (1993).

The Design of Judicial Review: Empirical Evidence

The above examples illustrate that the insurance theory has explanatory power in several prominent cases of the establishment of judicial review. In this section, we develop a more systematic empirical test of the insurance model by examining the constitutional courts adopted in Latin America and the former Soviet bloc in recent years. Nearly every postcommunist country has adopted a constitutional court, usually following the German model of a centralized body. Latin American countries also began to move to this model, though some countries retain the decentralized model of review. The details of institutional design vary across countries. Table 2.3 presents some data on these countries and their constitutional courts. We consider some of the dimensions of institutional design mentioned above.

To examine whether demand for political insurance is a determinant of constitutional court design, we must evaluate the relationship between demand and those features of court design predicted to produce more-accurate constitutional review. To capture demand for insurance, we use a proxy variable "Party Strength," the difference in the first postconstitutional election between the seat shares of the strongest and second-strongest parties or blocs of parties in the legislature. This captures the extent to which there is a dominant party and should correlate with the degree of political uncertainty during constitutional drafting.[49] The lower the differential between seat shares, the less certain will be the leading party or bloc that it will end up in power. Note that in most cases we cannot use the political configuration *before* democratization, as the former configuration may have been a one-party system that did not reflect

[49] For our purposes, this indicator is superior to another one frequently used in comparative political studies, namely the effective number of parties. The effective number of parties is $N_s = 1/\Sigma p_i^2$ where p_i equals the percent share of seats in the legislature of the ith party. Markku Laakso and Rein Taagepera, "Effective Number of Parties: A Measure with Application to West Europe," 12 *Comp. Pol. Stud.* 3 (1979); Rein Taagepera and Matthew Soberg Shugart, *Seats and Votes: The Effects and Determinants of Electoral Systems* (1989); John Ishiyama and Matthew Velten, "Presidential Power and Democratic Development in Post-Communist Politics," 31 *Comm. Post-Comm. Stud.* 217, 222 (1998). Effective number of parties might correlate inversely with political uncertainty as the smaller number of parties indicates a greater chance of each to capture seats in government. However, it would not capture the situation of political deadlock between two equally large parties, which would create high uncertainty but a low number of parties. Thanks to Omri Yadlin for pointing out this problem in an earlier version of this chapter. See also Tom Ginsburg, "Economic Analysis and the Design of Constitutional Courts, 3 *Theoretical Inquiries L.* 49 (2002).

TABLE 2.3 *Constitutional and Supreme Courts in Postsocialist Countries and Latin America*

Country	Constitution Year	Court Size	Term in Years	Access (Dummy)	Party Strength
Postsocialist					
Albania	1991	9	9	1	0.37
Armenia	1995	9	life	0	0.58
Belarus	1994	11	11	0	0.03
Bulgaria	1991	12	9	0	0.17
Czech Republic	1993	15	10	0	0.04
Estonia	1992	17	life	1	0.21
Georgia	1995	9	10	1	0.31
Hungary	1949/1990	15	9	1	0.18
Lithuania	1992	9	9	0	0.39
Macedonia	1991	9	9	1	0.24
Moldova	1994	6	6	1	0.37
Mongolia	1992	9	6	1	0.2
Poland	1997	12	8	1	0.05
Rumania	1991	9	6	0	0.59
Russia	1993	15	life	1	0.06
Slovakia	1993	10	7	1	0.28
Slovenia	1991	9	9	1	0.09
Ukraine	1996	19	9	1	0.19
Latin America					
Argentina	1994	9	life	1	0.07
Bolivia	1967/1994	12	10	1	0.05
Brazil	1998	11	life	1	0.04
Chile	1997	7	8	0	0.05
Colombia	1991	9	8	1	0.47
Dominican Republic	1994	16	life	0	0.23
Ecuador	1998	9	life	1	0.07
El Salvador	1983	5	9	1	0.33
Guatemala	1993	13	5	0	0.28
Haiti	1987	10	10	1	0.12
Honduras	1982	9	4	1	0.12
Mexico	1917/2001	11	life	1	0.11
Panama	1994	9	10	0	0.03
Paraguay	1992	9	life	1	0.1
Peru	1993	7	5	0	0.44
Uruguay	1997	5	10	1	0.1
Venezuela	1999	15	9	1	0.28
Mean		10.57	8.97	0.68	0.22

Note: Constitution dates reflect major amendments for Albania, Bolivia, Hungary, and Mexico. Certain institutional features, such as the life terms for Russian justices and the size of the Hungarian court, may have been modified subsequent to the date given here. Because our argument concerns initial design, we do not reflect these changes in the table. For purposes of calculating mean term length, we assume life terms equal eleven years.

the true range of political views. The political configuration in the first election after the adoption of the court is a reflection, albeit an imperfect one, of the true extent of diffusion before adoption of the constitution. Therefore, we draw data from the first postconstitutional election.

The column "Term" provides the number of years in a nominal appointment to the constitutional court. The prediction is that as the level of party dominance rises, the term of judges will fall. This is because reappointments and short-term length give politicians the ability to influence judges, especially if a party anticipates staying in power through multiple reappointment cycles. In practice, judges may not actually serve as long as provided in nominal appointments, but the constitutional courts of Eastern Europe are too young to have reliable data on actual time served. There is the additional problem of assigning term length for purposes of statistical tests to judges with lifetime appointments. In the data analyses that follow, we therefore assume, somewhat arbitrarily, that "lifetime" appointments are eleven-years long, precisely the same length as the longest designated term in the dataset.

Figure 2.3 shows the relationship between term length and party strength in scatterplot form. In Figure 2.3, the countries tend to cluster in either the lower-right or upper-left quadrants. The lower right represents

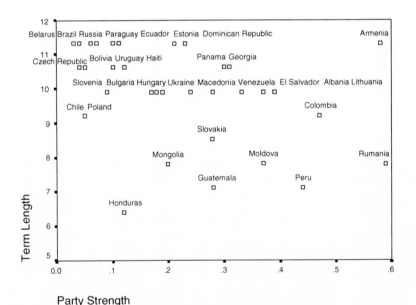

FIGURE 2.3. Term Length and Party Strength

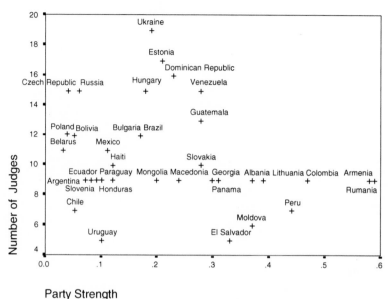

FIGURE 2.4. Court Size and Party Strength

a strong party with short terms, while the upper left represents a weaker party with longer terms for constitutional or supreme court justices. We note that Armenia is somewhat of an outlier, featuring a dominant party with lifetime appointments. Figure 2.4 presents a similar scatterplot diagram comparing the size of the court with the strength of the dominant party and shows similar results.

"Access" is a dummy variable that captures standing. The value is 1 if citizens have the right to petition the court or if ordinary courts can refer constitutional questions to the court. Thus, both a decentralized system such as that of Israel and a centralized system like that of Germany would carry an "Access" value of 1. Systems of limited access where only designated political institutions can bring questions to the court have an "Access" value of 0. This is a feature of the French model but also is found in some courts that otherwise look like the German model. The predicted relationship between extent of party dominance and access is negative. The stronger the dominant party in constitutional drafting, the less incentive there is to design an open system of access to the court.

To test whether the relationship is as predicted, Figure 2.5 presents the results of four separate least-squares regression operations with "Party Strength" as the sole independent variable. The dependent variables are

	Constant	Regression Coefficient (t-stat)	Regression Confidence Level
Regression one: y = court size	11.70	−5.26 (−1.46)	85%
Regression two: y = term length	9.94	−4.77 (−2.30)	97%
Regression three: y = access dummy	.87	−.89 (−1.78)	91%
Regression three: y = normalized index of court size, term length, and access	1.26	−5.85 (−3.08)	99%

N = 35

FIGURE 2.5. Regression Results: Insurance Model of Design

court size, term length, access, and an index variable, summing each of the other three variables after normalizing them.

The regressions demonstrate strong results for all three dependent variables. All coefficients have the predicted sign, and the results for term length and the index variable are statistically significant. Three features thought to enhance independence and accuracy of the court are those that are chosen in diffused party systems, where politicians should have an incentive to do so. This suggests that the insurance model has substantial explanatory power. If the precommitment model were superior, we would have expected to see that in many cases stronger parties led to *more* open access, longer terms, and larger courts because there would be greater need for precommitment.

To summarize the argument so far, judicial review provides an insurance policy for prospective losers in the electoral arena. The design of the system will reflect in part the configuration at the time of constitutional drafting, with the availability and power of judicial review increasing with political diffusion. In this sense, judicial review *reflects* democratization and is not antidemocratic, as asserted by theorists who focus on the countermajoritarian difficulty. While the precise institutional design has been less uniform than the spread of the practice itself, there are strong trends toward adopting a German-style designated constitutional court whose members have limited terms, open not only to particular political actors but also to courts or ordinary citizens as well. This open-access design not only ensures access to judicial review by prospective minorities but also provides courts with opportunities to become involved in a wide range of cases and to build up their power over time. It is to this process that we turn in the next chapter.

3

Building Judicial Power

Chapter 2 focused on the creation of constitutional courts and argued that the design of judicial review is to a large degree a function of politicians' insurance needs. However, courts that are created to do one thing can gradually adopt new roles for themselves. Courts are not passive players in the judicial review "game." Although politicians design judicial review with their own interests in mind as a way of reducing future political uncertainty, there is substantial evidence that courts behave strategically once they are established, both with respect to individual cases and with respect to their own position in the constitutional system.

Judicial activism leads to a potential problem with regard to the insurance theory. If courts are able to assume roles that differ from those anticipated by constitutional designers, would not constitutional designers discount the value of the insurance provided by constitutional courts? In other words, would not prospectively weak constitutional designers want to specify in some detail the norms to be used by courts in constraining political authorities? From the point of view of prospective minorities, however, this is not a problem as long as there is some positive probability that the court will use its powers to constrain political majorities. While the designers will try to channel judicial decision making into certain areas, for example, by specifying jurisdiction, enumerating rights to be protected, and listing sources of law to be considered – the intertemporal nature of the insurance contract means that they cannot do so with perfect confidence.[1] The question for designers is always whether they are

---

[1] See Stephen Holmes, "Precommitment and the Paradox of Democracy," in *Constitutionalism and Democracy* 195–240 (Jon Elster and Rune Slagstad, eds., 1988).

better off with or without judicial review. The fact that courts might take on new roles does not prevent the same courts from providing those protections that were envisioned at the outset of the constitutional bargain. Furthermore, to the extent that "mutations" in the court's role move in the direction of greater constitutional protection, prospective minorities will benefit from such changes. In this regard, the minoritarian focus of the insurance theory seems to fare better than the commitment theory, which emphasizes self-binding by prospective majorities.

Sometimes a shift in judicial role occurs because founding politicians have faded from the scene. During the presidency of De Gaulle, for example, the French *Conseil Constitutionnel* primarily played the role he had anticipated for it as a protector of executive law-making authority from legislative encroachment. It is only in the early 1970s after De Gaulle had faded from the scene that the *conseil* began to take a more active stance as a protector of individual rights. Once it had begun to assume this role, for example, by reading the 1789 Declaration of the Rights of Man into the constitution, the *conseil* was given an expanded role by politicians who sought to ensure access to constitutional review for legislative minorities. The story of the emergence of the *conseil* as a major constitutional and legislative actor in France involved the interaction of three factors: an initial design endowment, careful choices by judges to expand their power, and political acquiescence to the expanded scope of *conseil* decision making at a later time. To understand the emergence of judicial power in new democracies, we must pay attention to all three elements. Chapter 2 focused on initial design endowments. This chapter concerns the strategic choices of judges within their political environment.

This chapter develops the notion that constitutional courts wield *interdependent* law-making power, meaning that they are constrained by the preferences of politicians in interpreting the constitution. The central argument of this book, illustrated in the case studies that follow, is that within political constraints, courts can play an important role in constitutional development and democratic transition simply by asserting their own power in a careful fashion.

COURTS AS STRATEGIC ACTORS

This study draws on positive theories of courts and law that see the law as the product of interactions among various political institutions.[2] Courts

---

[2] See, for example, Lee Epstein and Jack Knight, *The Choices Justices Make* (1998); Rafael Gely and Pablo Spiller, "The Political Economy of Supreme Court

are assumed to maximize their substantive values and in doing so can be considered rational institutions in the broad sense of attempting to reach their goals. However, courts are not the only law-making institutions in a political system, so their ability to achieve particular outcomes is in part dependent on the preferences of other actors. For example, a legislature can overrule a judicial interpretation of a particular statute by passing a subsequent statute. In some systems, there exists a special procedure by which the court's constitutional decisions may be reviewed by other branches of government. Executive agencies can refuse to implement judicial decisions. Political branches can also affect judicial decisions through the appointment process. Through these various mechanisms of interaction with political actors, courts participate in constitutional "dialogues" with other forces, dialogues that create a shared understanding of what the constitution says over time.[3]

Several recent scholarly works on American constitutionalism emphasize the interactive character of the interpretive process.[4] They trace the interactions between the court and other actors in shaping the interpretation of laws and the constitution. In this analysis, the exercise of judicial power is directly affected by the preferences of other branches. Judges may wish to decide cases in certain ways, but they can be prevented from doing so by their awareness of the preferences of other branches. There is a growing body of evidence supporting this view of the dynamic nature of statutory interpretation, and the logic can easily be extended to constitutional adjudication as well. Because judicial review is the exercise of an interdependent law-making power, courts must behave strategically, that is, they must seek to achieve their goals taking into account the probable response of other actors to their choices. A rational court must be conscious of other actors in the political system.

Constitutional Decisions: The Case of Roosevelt's Court-Packing Plan," 12 *Int'l Rev. L. Econ.* 45 (1992); Keith E. Whittington, "Legislative Sanctions and the Strategic Environment of Judicial Review," *Int'l J. Con. L.* (forthcoming 2003).

[3] Louis Fisher, *Constitutional Dialogues* (1988); Sally J. Kenney, William M. Reisinger, and John C. Reitz, eds., *Constitutional Dialogues in Comparative Perspective* (1999).

[4] See, for example, Fisher, *ibid.*; Neal Devins, *Shaping Constitutional Values* (1996); Stephen Griffin, *American Constitutionalism: From Theory to Politics* (1996); Barry Friedman, "Dialogue and Judicial Review," 91 *Mich. L. Rev.* 577 (1993); Walter Murphy, "Constitutions, Constitutionalism and Democracy," in *Constitutionalism and Democracy: Transitions in the Contemporary World* (Douglas Greenberg et al., eds., 1993); William Eskridge, *Dynamic Statutory Interpretation* (1994); and William Eskridge, "The Judicial Review Game," 88 *NW. U. L. Rev.* 382 (1993).

To illustrate this intuition graphically, imagine a two-dimensional policy space with three political actors, a prime minister, a legislature, and a president. The space concerns some constitutional issue, such as the proper balance between free speech rights and national security. Each actor has a most preferred policy point in this two-dimensional space. The court is then called on to interpret the constitution. Actors will tolerate judicial decisions that are a certain distance from their most-preferred point. But if the policy is too far away from their most-preferred point, the actor will refuse to tolerate the policy.

We imagine that the function determining these tolerance zones reflects a variety of factors, including the particular policy preferences at stake, which vary from issue to issue; the institution's ability to ignore or avoid the court's decision; and the court's own store of political support, which increases the political cost of noncompliance.

If each institution is autonomous and can ignore the court outside its tolerance zone, the policy space in which the court can operate unconstrained consists only of the overlapping tolerance zones of all the political actors, that is the space denoted "A" in Figure 3.1. On the other hand, if all three institutions must cooperate – for example, to pass a constitutional amendment overruling the court – the court will have wide latitude to act. Any point the court chooses within *any* of the tolerance zones will be more favorable to one or the other actor than any alternative proposal, and the judicial decision will stand so long as it does not fall outside all the circles. The court has some discretion, but is not free to articulate *any* view it likes of the constitutional policy – rather, it must pay attention to the preferences of other actors.

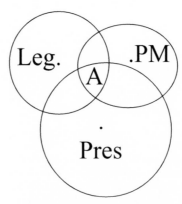

FIGURE 3.1. Judicial Policy Space

This view of judicial decision making as constrained is at odds with other potential approaches to judicial behavior. For example, a leading approach to the political study of courts in the United States, called *attitudinalism*, posits that judges seek to maximize their ideological preferences, without acting strategically.[5] Another view, sometimes called *formalism*, holds that judges simply apply the law and act apolitically. The law exists on a pure plane, and there are technically correct solutions to legal problems that are determinable through the application of legal science. Judges are trained in finding these answers and in determining what the law requires.[6] Formalism is the opposite of the attitudinal model. While the formal model asserts that judicial choices are "all law," attitudinalism claims it is "all ideology." The former stresses the quest for neutral principles of adjudication; the latter sees judges as politicians in robes.

We can begin by rejecting the attitudinal model as too extreme. Even casual observation of judges shows that they do not follow their personal motivations all of the time. Most judges follow the law most of the time. The question then becomes to what extent policy goals matter, if at all. The strategic approach provides an answer by highlighting the importance of institutional and political constraints in achieving policy preferences.[7] In this view, judges and politicians play a game of power using the law. Features of the law matter crucially in terms of framing what moves are possible and what strategies will be effective. But we must not lose sight of the players and their moves – constitutional law as developed by courts is not merely part of the immutable rules of the game.

Formalism is a particularly inappropriate theory for understanding how courts behave in new democracies. If courts simply apply "the law," there should be no difference in their willingness to do so across different political regimes. Courts with the power of judicial review under authoritarian regimes (for example, those in Taiwan until 1986, Poland from 1985–89, and Hungary from 1983–89) should be willing to exercise the power without regard to punishment. But judicial review is almost exclusively associated with democratic governance. Political liberalization

---

[5] Jeffrey Segal and Harold J. Spaeth, *The Supreme Court and the Attitudinal Model* (1993). For a defense of the strategic approach to the study of the U.S. Supreme Court, see Epstein and Knight, *supra* note 2.

[6] Larry Alexander and Frederick Schauer, "On Extrajudicial Constitutional Interpretation," 110 *Harv. L. Rev.* 1359 (1997); see also the rebuttal by Neal Devins and Louis Fisher, "Judicial Exclusivity and Political Instability," 84 *Va. L. Rev.* 83 (1998).

[7] Epstein and Knight, *supra* note 2.

is usually associated with an *increase* in judicial review, rather than a constant level.

To illustrate this point, let us suppose for a moment that for a particular country there is some "true" set of rules that the constitution requires, independent of any human agency. Suppose further that these are discoverable through expert textual interpretation of the type typically rendered by constitutional courts. In the early years of a democratic constitutional system, we should expect that there are more violations of the constitutional order than in a (hypothetical) equilibrium later on. This is true for two reasons. First, other things being equal, there is less information on what the "true" constitution actually requires. Ambiguous provisions have not been interpreted and alternative constructions not yet tested.

Second, to the extent that old political authorities remain in power and elites survive from the old system, norms of constitutional observance may be slow to emerge. Old patterns of behavior do not simply disappear at the moment of constitutional promulgation. Even after a new constitutional order is established in a political transition, ordinary statutes and administrative regulations are not automatically voided. The ministry of the interior does not change its handbook for police conduct simply because there is a new set of formal rules concerning the relationship between state and citizen. There are often hundreds of old laws and regulations remaining on the books that violate the text of the constitution, each awaiting revision by the legislative or administrative authority under the new regime. These interstitial violations of the constitution may in fact pose severe threats to individual liberties. And it is likely that the "old" agencies authorized by these statutes will continue to use them, whether or not they are aware of the conflict with the "true" meaning of the constitution.

Some transitional constitutional texts void with their passage all orders and laws that violate the constitution. However, this will often leave a gap in the law that must be filled in practice. Suppose in such a system old criminal procedure provisions violate the new constitution and were thus voided with constitutional promulgation. The morning after the adoption of the constitutional document, there will still be arrests that must be made, and those arrests will use *some* procedure. The officials carrying out the arrest are likely to use the techniques they know, the same techniques they used the day before the constitution was adopted. The culture of administration and government remains even where the formal legal framework has changed. If no constitutionally prescribed procedures have yet been formulated, the arrest under the old procedures may violate

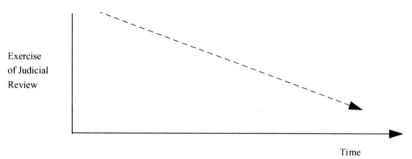

Exercise
of Judicial
Review

Time

FIGURE 3.2. Formalist Model of Judicial Review in New Democracies

any of dozens of new constitutional provisions. Such transitional contexts present ample room for exercises of administrative discretion that violate the constitution.

If judges can actually determine through interpretation the *true* meaning of the hypothetical constitution outlined previously and are unconstrained in their ability to articulate that meaning, then we should expect them to find many violations in the early years of constitutional democracy, with the number of violations decreasing gradually as consolidation deepens and the contours of the constitution become clearer. Figure 3.2 illustrates the implications of the formalist model.

In fact, the most common pattern of judicial review in new democracies is precisely the reverse of this. To anticipate the empirical results of this study, it is typical that the exercise of judicial review and the importance of judicial power *expands* with democratization. So the formalist story appears implausible. The pattern of increasing levels of judicial review suggests that in the real world courts must be *careful* to establish their power; they must consider the preferences of other political actors in the system and the possibility of reversal. Judicial power must be built gradually. The formalist contention that courts simply apply the law is empirically suspect.

It is my view that the function of judicial review in democracy has little to do with the neutral application of preexisting rules: Rather, judicial review is useful in developing the democratic constitution itself. Constitutions in this view are living, growing documents; they do not exist in some "pure" realm, ready for exposition by expert judges.[8] Judicial review is

---

[8] This view of the constitution as a living document originates with Holmes and became dominant during the New Deal. See G. Edward White, "The 'Constitutional Revolution' as a Crisis in Adaptivity," 48 *Hastings L.J.* 867, 872–79 (1997) for a history of the concept and its ultimate triumph over a more formalist notion of the

important in this view because it enables us to see more precisely what the constitutional boundaries of a system are. Judicial review invites a process of dialogue that will clarify the boundaries of political activity. This dialogue itself contributes to and enriches democratic self-articulation. The constitution is revealed, not through the pronouncements of a special class of wise people, but through continuous interaction among branches of government. Systems of effective judicial review, while not strictly necessary for constitutional systems, are useful for exposing the precise boundaries of the evolving normative framework that "constitutes" the community and structures political action.

Judicial review can play an important role in constitutional articulation by enunciating and refining what the constitution means. The ongoing process of interpretation means the constitution is continually being developed and subtly adjusting to new social conditions. Constitutionalism is deepened. The court plays a role in helping to grow the constitution, both in the sense of creating more and more law as well as ensuring a healthy relationship of mutual interchange between the constitution and its political environment.

This constitutive function can be particularly important in new democracies. New democracies are frequently fragile creatures without consensus on basic norms of governance. There is little time for gradually developing an unwritten constitution based on shared understandings, as in England. To the contrary, there are many pressures against nascent norms of constitutionalism. Democratic reversals and political crises are common. Uncertainty about the direction and pace of political change can hinder the development of constitutional norms, by preventing the formulation of common expectations of behavior among political actors. By contributing to constitutional dialogues, judicial review can play a key role in consolidating democracy and enhancing political stability. Judicial review can set in motion a virtuous cycle that encourages compliance with the constitutional order and respect for basic civil and political liberties. The very possibility of continuous articulation of the constitution itself contributes to the legitimacy of the democratic order by providing an alternative forum for losers in the legislative process. Those who become political minorities seek to constitutionalize policy disputes by taking them before the court. But the court is not unconstrained in its ability

---

constitution as static. Robert Post discusses several other "organic metaphors" for the constitution in "Theories of Constitutional Interpretation," in *Law and the Order of Culture* 13, 32 (Robert Post, ed., 1991).

to deepen constitutional legitimacy. There is also the risk of missteps and errors. A court that challenges a powerful political actor and provokes counterattack can set back the process of democratic consolidation.

A loose version of Albert Hirschman's classic framework of exit, voice, and loyalty is useful for illustrating this point.[9] A party unhappy with a government decision has three basic options. It can comply with the decision and remain loyal to the constitutional order. Compliance is unattractive where a party is unsure of the future survival of the regime or believes that it will indefinitely continue to be on the short end of governmental decisions. In such circumstances, a party may choose to "exit" the constitutional order entirely, either by ignoring the adverse decision, resisting enforcement, or, in extreme circumstances, taking steps to overthrow the regime. Finally, a party can seek to exercise "voice" and transform the constitutional order by challenging the legitimacy of the decision in another forum. Constitutional review is useful in this sense, not because constitutional politics are somehow of an entirely different order from ordinary politics, but simply because review provides another forum for appealing decisions one is unhappy with.[10] Another effective forum increases the probability that losers will exercise voice as opposed to exit. If the court develops a record of adjudicating fairly and finding at least some of the time for either side of a political cleavage, then the court gives the parties a stake in continuing to play by the constitutional rules. The democratic order is deepened, and its legitimacy is enhanced.

This view of the constitutional order as dynamic helps explain why judicial power often grows as democracy deepens. The court becomes an important site of political contestation and is frequently called on to resolve disputes. Losers in political arenas are likely to take their disputes, framed as constitutional issues, to court. Although from one perspective, this constitutionalization of politics may appear undesirable, in fact it enhances voice by providing another forum and another mode of political participation. Occasional victories before the court encourage further filings and enhance the court's role. I call this configuration, when a court is active, obeyed, and politically salient, the "high equilibrium" of judicial review.

There is another possible scenario, of course, namely that the court is not able to secure compliance from other political bodies. This can be

---

[9] Albert O. Hirschman, *Exit, Voice and Loyalty: Responses to Decline in Firms, Organizations and States* (1972).
[10] For a contrary view that constitutional politics are fundamentally different than ordinary politics, see Bruce Ackerman, *We the People: Foundations* (1993).

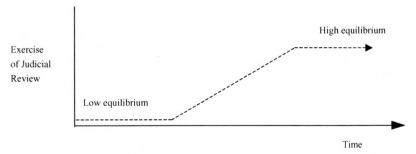

FIGURE 3.3. Strategic Model of Judicial Review in New Democracies

fatal for courts by leading to political counterattacks or marginalization. If a court is unable to convince parties that other parties will comply with its decisions, there is little incentive to bring disputes to court. Furthermore, there is little reason for a losing party to comply if it believes others will not comply. The perception of noncompliance becomes self-fulfilling. I call this the "low equilibrium" of judicial review. In the low equilibrium, courts do not often challenge politically powerful plaintiffs, with the result that they are rarely called upon to adjudicate truly important disputes. By failing to provide an alternative forum for voice, the court may subtly encourage exit. The constitution plays little role in social and political life, new issues are not constitutionalized, and the constitution is not renewed and becomes stagnant. A successful constitutional court in a new democracy will seek to shift from low-equilibrium judicial review to high equilibrium, through careful use of strategy. This is illustrated in Figure 3.3. A court effectively able to exercise the power of judicial review will not only enhance its own power, but will also benefit the constitutional order as a whole.

The equilibrium concept is useful for reminding us that systems of judicial review are not maintained by courts alone. The judicial process is typically conceived of as passive, usually requiring plaintiffs to bring cases to it. Plaintiffs bring cases to courts in anticipation of their future probabilities of success, based in part on past performance of courts. Another key political actor in determining how much judicial power can be exercised is the government, which must choose to comply or not with adverse decisions. Furthermore, even decisions not directed at government are usually not effectuated by courts themselves, but require implementation by the machinery of government. Government support is crucial for maintaining judicial power. The institutional weakness of courts has been a theme of judicial studies since Montesquieu noted that of the three powers of government, "the judiciary is in some measure next to nothing."[11] The interaction of courts with other political actors, not mere formal provisions in a constitutional text, creates a system of judicial review.

Might there be a tension between the strategic view of judicial decisions and the insurance theory of design articulated in Chapters 1 and 2? After all, if courts can be constrained by political authorities, would not constitutional designers be reluctant to trust that the insurance will be effective? The institutional weakness of courts appears to render them undesirable as a form of insurance "policy" purchased by politicians. But it remains true that attacking a court can be politically costly. The insurance theory does not stipulate that the court will *always* be able to protect prospective minorities. Rather, it asserts that the presence of constitutional review will raise the cost of attacking minorities. It therefore makes such attacks less probable, other things being equal, for it requires the abusive majority to undertake costly efforts to both attack the minority and intimidate the court. To the extent that the judicial review raises these costs, it can have a deterrent effect without being a perfect deterrent.

We speak of *the* court as a strategic actor, when of course there is no single court, but rather a set of many justices. We need a theory of how individual motivations are aggregated into the choice of the institution, and such theory is still in its early stages of development.[12] While a full-fledged theory is beyond the scope of this book, we will make the basic assumption that it is in the interest of each member of the court that the court as a whole behave strategically to maximize its own power over time. This assumption is valid regardless of whether one adopts an attitudinal, doctrinal, or strategic conception of judicial behavior. Even purely doctrinal judges will presumably wish to ensure that their interpretation of the law is authoritative and thus will be concerned with the legitimacy of the court and its power to make its decisions stick. Now let us assume the converse proposition, that judges are self-interested attitudinalists with policy preferences that they wish to maximize. Assume also that preferences are distributed across the court in some fashion.[13] Judges will compete to influence the outcomes of the court. One thing that all judges may agree on, however, is the need to expand the institutional

---

[11] Charles de Secondat Montesquieu, *The Spirit of the Laws*, Book XI, Chapter 6.

[12] See, generally, Lawrence Baum, *The Puzzle of Judicial Behavior* (1997).

[13] Selection criteria may mean that these preferences are heavily concentrated along the distribution curve rather than randomly distributed. The common requirement of legal training itself plays such a narrowing role.

power of the court. If judges believe they can advance their preferences through deliberation with other members of the court, then it serves the interests of all to expand the power of the court in terms of jurisdiction and influence. Thus, even when there is disagreement on substantive policy, there may be opportunities for agreement on efforts to expand judicial power. Even if I am in the minority today, I hope to be in the majority tomorrow and need the ability to exercise power when I am. Jurisdiction-expanding decisions serve this function. Each judge can rationally seek to advance the long-run institutional power of the court.

Another reason judges may wish to expand their institutional power has to do with prestige and professional identity. Professionals derive their status in part through their affiliation with organizations. The judge is a member of an important institution; therefore, she or he must be important. This is a slightly different argument from the assertion that judges are engaged in a common "professional project" with lawyers.[14] Although professional discourse has an important role to play in the development of corporate identities, I believe that institutional affiliation and organizational membership are prior to, and hence more significant than, the development of classlike professional motivations. In the first place, institutional affiliations are closer to the individual, in the sense of entailing more frequent and repeated social interactions. A second reason one's professional identity is probably somewhat subordinate to one's institutional identity is that material incentives flow directly from the employment relation and only indirectly from the broader membership in a profession.[15]

One problem with assuming that judges seek to maximize institutional power is that those judges who believe they will be in a permanent minority may wish to constrain their institution as a means of advancing their policy preferences. This is not a fatal problem for the theory presented here, because such judges, by virtue of being substantive losers on the court, are also less likely to be able to influence outcomes about "institutional" cases. Furthermore, the central role of deliberation and

---

[14] Martin Shapiro, "Lawyers, Corporations and Knowledge," 38 *Am. J. Comp. L.* 683 (1990) (reviewing Richard Abel and Philip Lewis, *Lawyers in Society* (1988)).

[15] This is the source of many problems involving the ethical regulation of lawyers. Ethical obligations are set at the level of the profession, but require monitoring at the level of the firm, where incentives for compliance are frequently less strong. Bruce Arnold and Fiona May, "Social Capital, Violations of Trust and the Vulnerability of Isolates: The Social Organization of Law Practice and Professional Self-Regulation," paper presented to Law and Society Association Annual Meetings (Toronto, 1995).

justification in the judicial process implies that judges may be somewhat optimistic about their ability to shape future pronouncements of the court. Again, it is reasonable to assume that judges are motivated to defend and expand the institutional power of the court even where they disagree on substantive law.

CONSTRAINTS ON THE COURT

If courts are strategic actors, as argued previously, what are the sources of constraint? A party unhappy with a court decision has, roughly speaking, four options. It can comply with the decision and accept the judgment. (All normative scholarship on judicial review proceeds on the assumption that this will be the case.) Alternatively, it can ignore the court decision and hope that whatever powers the court or other institutions have to enforce the decision will not be effective. Third, it can seek to overturn the court interpretation, through amending the constitution, or if such procedures are available, formally refusing to accept the decision. The final and most extreme option is for the party to attack the court as an institution, trying to reduce its jurisdiction or effective power in future cases. These options can be arranged in a simple figure (see Figure 3.4).

The first column of Figure 3.4 represents options that are formally consistent with the constitutional scheme. Complying with the decision or using legitimate procedures to seek a change in the law are constitutionally acceptable options. The second column, in contrast, represents formally unconstitutional options. Ignoring a binding decision or seeking to undermine the court are both outside the realm of procedures contemplated by formal constitutional documents. Nevertheless, they represent real-world options that must be considered in developing any positive account of judicial review. (A subset of methods of undermining the court,

	Formally Constitutional	Formally Unconstitutional
Accept	**Comply**	**Ignore**
Challenge	**Overrule/Punish**	**Attack**

FIGURE 3.4. Options after Decision

such as using the budget process to lower judicial resources, are perfectly constitutional and are called "punish" to distinguish them from unconstitutional "attacks." The distinction between these two is admittedly blurry.) It is important to remember that none of these weapons need actually be used to be effective. The threat of using them must simply be credible in order to constrain the judges' freedom of action. Let us describe each of these options in more detail.

Comply?

A rationalist approach to decision making suggests that a party will comply with an adverse court decision only when it expects a future benefit stream that is greater than the costs of complying with the decision. If the costs of exit are lower than the costs of compliance, a rational actor will choose to exit. This approach suggests two testable propositions. First, and rather obviously, if the court chooses to decide cases where the cost of compliance is high, it risks a decision on the part of the affected institution not to comply. This implies that the court ought to focus its early attention on matters that are not politically sensitive, where compliance is likely.

Second, it is important to realize that in the early years of a democratic system the probability of a favorable benefit stream from complying is itself in part a reflection of the probability of the continuation of the constitutional order. If the actor believes the court will not be operating at all in a few years, then the probability of a favorable future benefit stream is by definition lower. Thus, if parties *perceive* that the risk of any other actor "exiting" the constitutional arrangement, their own likelihood of compliance is lower. Courts must not only assure powerful players that it will not do anything to harm their interests, but also that it will not provoke other players to renege on the constitutional bargain. Such perceptions can create endgame norms and lead to the unraveling of the constitutional order. On the other hand, a cautious court that gradually builds up its power improves the track record of compliance and is likely to reduce institutional expectations of the fall of a regime in its calculation of compliance option.

Another observation to note is that it helps the court if various parties are optimistic in their assessments of future benefits. Assume for illustration that the constitutional order consists of legislature L, executive E, and the court. All disputes are bilateral between L and E. Assume further that costs and benefits are constant across decisions and all decisions are zero-sum. The court has in the past decided 45% of cases in favor of L and

55% in favor of E. If L sees past performance as a reliable signal of future patterns of judicial decision making, it may soon stop complying, unless L overestimates the probability of future victories. By framing its decisions in a manner that leads L to be overoptimistic, or to underestimate costs, the court can induce compliance. Decisions that are not zero-sum, or at least appear not to be zero-sum, are thus helpful in buffeting norms of compliance. Judges often look for ways to split the difference in controversial decisions as a strategy for ensuring compliance and optimism on the part of parties.

Ignore?

Compliance is one option for losing parties reacting to adverse decisions. What if an institution chooses not to comply? One alternative is to simply ignore the court. A classic example is the response to the 1984 *Chadha* decision of the U.S. Supreme Court.[16] At issue was the legislative veto, a device by which Congress wrote provisions in federal statutes that delegated power to administrative agencies, but allowed congressional intervention to override administrative decisions. The Court held the legislative veto device unconstitutional, invalidating over three hundred federal laws in a single decision. Congress has responded by passing several hundred statutes since 1984 that include various kinds of legislative veto schemes. The Court was unable to prevent Congress from continuing to pass such schemes.[17]

Overrule?

A third possibility is trying to overrule the court through normal channels – for instance, by passing constitutional amendments. To consider only one example, U.S. pro-life legislators frequently tried to overturn *Roe v. Wade*[18] by proposing amendments to the constitution to protect unborn life. Although not successful, the Supreme Court's subsequent decisions tolerating some state regulation of abortion illustrates the utility of threats to overrule. A more subtle version of this process occurs when legislators try to undermine the impact of constitutional decisions – for example, through attempts to restrict funding for abortions.

[16] *INS v. Chadha*, 462 U.S. 919 (1983).
[17] Louis Fisher, *Constitutional Dialogues* (1988).
[18] 410 U.S. 113 (1973).

The possibility of using the overrule option varies across constitutional systems with the difficulty of constitutional amendment. As amendment becomes easier, the court becomes more constrained by the threat of overruling. Donald Lutz has developed comparative data on constitutional amendment that shows that the structural ease of constitutional amendment varies across countries and that structural factors predict the level of actual amendment observed in various systems.[19] Other things being equal, ease of constitutional amendment should correlate with a low level of observed judicial review. The converse, however, is not necessarily true because overruling is not the only option available to political actors. As overruling becomes more difficult, the relative attraction of an unconstitutional response may grow.

Counterattack?

The unconstitutional response is for the political branch to attack the court. In Asia, a notable instance of this type of response occurred in Malaysia in the mid-1980s under Prime Minister Mahathir Mohamad. The courts ruled against the government in a number of cases in 1986–87, including one decision granting standing and an interim injunction to a prominent opposition politician challenging a major government-sponsored development project.[20] No doubt, the government saw in such decisions a threat to its power, for the opening of the courts as an alternative forum for challenging the state would potentially restrict the scope of action for the dominant UMNO Party. Accordingly, the politicians launched an attack on the supreme court, impeaching its president before a special tribunal. When five other judges of the high court, serving on the special impeachment tribunal, voted to issue a stay of the impeachment proceedings, they were impeached in turn.[21] In the aftermath of this attack, the Malaysian judiciary is a more cautious institution, which duly contributed to Mahathir's subsequent discrediting of his former deputy, Anwar Ibrahim.

Of course, some of the means of attacking a court are formally constitutional. Weapons include removing cases from the jurisdiction of the

---

[19] Donald Lutz, "Toward a Theory of Constitutional Amendment," 88 *Am. Pol. Sci. Rev.* 355 (1994).

[20] *Lim Kit Siang v. United Engineers (M) Sdn. Bhd. (No. 2)* [1988] 1 MLJ 182.

[21] See, generally, Khoo Boo Teik, "Between Law and Politics: The Malaysian Judiciary since Independence," in *Law, Capitalism and Power in East Asia* 205–32 (Kanishka Jayasuriya, ed., 1999).

court, impeaching justices, refusing to raise salaries in times of inflation, and underbudgeting for material factors related to the proper functioning of the judiciary, such as buildings and staff. For example, the U.S. Congress in the 1960s restricted salary increases for the Supreme Court but not for lower federal courts. The following case studies will present further examples of politicians seeking to constrain and restrain courts through various techniques.

Policy Space

Recall that Figure 3.1 presented the policy space within which a court can work as a function of institutional tolerance zones. It is clear that the amount of space available to a court will be dictated in large part by other political institutions' availability of mechanisms of noncompliance. Many of the noncompliance options, presented in Figure 3.4, require cooperation among institutions. The legislature, for example, can reduce judicial salaries and jurisdiction, but may need the cooperation of the government. The executive cannot overrule the court on its own without cooperation from other actors whose assent is required to amend the constitution. The more difficult it is for an actor to exercise such an option, the greater the tolerance zone and the greater discretion the court has in interpreting the constitution.[22] Suppose, for example, that legislation reducing judicial salaries requires drafting by the government, passage by the legislature, and signature by the president. No institution can overrule the court without agreement from the other two bodies, so the decision need only be tolerated by one institution to stand. The courts' policy space will be the entire set of tolerance zones, giving it wide discretion indeed.

Looking again at Figure 3.1 allows us to conceptualize why it is that dominant parties reduce the policy space for courts. Suppose that a single dominant party consolidates power and holds all three institutions. The most preferred policy points of the three institutions will converge to a single point. Even assuming that the size of each institution's tolerance zone is constant, the space the court has in which to work will shrink because the center points will converge. The policy space for the court is determined by a single actor, rather than three separate institutions,

---

[22] A related argument in one-dimensional space is made in Robert Cooter and Tom Ginsburg, "Comparative Judicial Discretion: An Empirical Test of Economic Models," 12 *Int'l Rev. L. & Econ.* 295 (1996).

even though three institutions formally still exist. Divided government, in contrast, means that the preferred policy points are further apart, giving the court more space to work in, at least with regard to forms of noncomplicance that require two institutions to effectuate.

The party system and substantive preferences will affect the locations of the different institutions' most preferred points. The size of the tolerance zone, and thus the space in which the court can work, will be determined in large part by the availability of mechanisms of noncompliance. For example, a legislature without a clear majority party is likely to have a larger tolerance zone than one with a single party, because securing legislative agreement to overrule or punish the court will require more negotiation. This will lead to more policy space for the court.

REGIME TYPE AND STRATEGIC CONSTRAINT

Each new democracy presents its own political context in terms of such variables as the strength of the old political forces, the constitutional environment of transition, and the party structure. This section briefly considers different features of the environment for their effect on judicial power. One useful way to draw a broad distinction among democratizing regimes is to consider the difference between dominant-party regimes and military authoritarian regimes.[23] Dominant party regimes are those in which the authoritarian institution is a dominant political party, archetypically a Leninist party. Dominant parties are often able to survive the democratic transition and exercise substantial power in the postauthoritarian era by virtue of their control of economic assets, their organizational structure, and their strong discipline. By contrast, military regimes are less able to effectively convert their power resources into a democratic era. For military rulers, there is no option but to return to the barracks and to withdraw from formal office, although attempts may be made to maintain behind-the-scenes influence over new civilian rulers or to create political parties to compete for power.

Dominant parties and military rulers have different capacities for exercising the options following an adverse judicial decision. By virtue of their legislative and electoral power, dominant political parties may be able to quite easily *overrule* adverse decisions or to *punish* the court through constitutional means, such as limiting jurisdiction. The party can influence

---

[23] Stephen Haggard and Robert Kaufmann, *The Political Economy of Democratic Transitions* (1995).

postjudicial job prospects and thereby induce passivity on the part of the court. In addition to these *ex post* mechanisms of showing displeasure, the dominant party may have at its disposal many tools for influencing the court *ex ante*. The party may train and maintain a cadre of judicial candidates loyal to party interests. It may control the appointment process through the legislature. Also, it may have a well-developed ideology with jurisprudential implications that carries weight among those appointed to the court.

Military authorities, in contrast, have few such formal tools for influencing the court. They may be less inclined to overrule the court through the legislative process or to attack it in a constitutional manner. But this lack of tools does not mean that courts are freer under military regimes than under dominant parties. The threats that military authoritarians have are those of exit and counterattack, whereby the rulers essentially shut down the court. The severity of this reaction may be sufficient to induce utter deference on the part of the court.

Ackerman notes that judicial review is associated with weak militaries, and our framework provides some support for this assertion.[24] Note, however, the important limiting case of Chile, where a certain similarity of interests between the judiciary and the military put the two institutions on the same side of the table when confronted with Allendean socialism.[25] Like the military, the judiciary was a technically trained bureaucracy and had a strong corporate identity. Both the military and judiciary were threatened by the politically charged and revolutionary rhetoric of the Allende period; particularly offensive to the courts was Allende's use of legal loopholes to advance his programs of land reform and expropriation. The Chilean judiciary also had a strong formalist tendency that prevented it from emerging as a strong defender of human rights or exerciser of judicial review. Even after the transition to democracy, the courts have been cautious and conservative, in part because the outgoing leadership entrenched key allies in the judiciary to preserve their policies. The Constitutional Tribunal established as part of the transition was an instrument of the old regime, not the new, and three of its seven members were appointed by the military-dominated National Security Council with one

---

[24] Bruce Ackerman, "The Rise of World Constitutionalism," 83 *Va. L. Rev.* 771, 791 (1997).

[25] Jorge Correa Sutil, "The Judiciary and the Political System in Chile: The Dilemmas of Judicial Independence during the Transition to Democracy," in *Transitions to Democracy in Latin America: The Role of the Judiciary* (Irwin P. Stotzky, ed., 1993).

more appointed by the conservative Senate. Thus, in Chile judicial review served the interests of a departing autocrat rather than new democrats.

The type of regime is not the only variable relevant to the analysis. Perhaps the major question of constitutional design in new democracies has been that of presidentialism versus parliamentarism.[26] How might presidentialism or parliamentarism influence the level of judicial review? Ackerman suggests that presidentialism is good for courts by providing them with a role as an arbitrator among law-making powers.[27] He notes that in France under the Fifth Republic the *Conseil Constitutionnel* was nominally created to guard the line between the law-making authorities of the president and the parliament, but in fact it was designed to protect presidential authority. Ackerman's implication is that relatively strong forms of semipresidentialism would be accompanied with higher levels of judicial power.

Our framework suggests that the party system, rather than the institutional structure alone, is the key factor accounting for the development of judicial power. The reason presidentialism supports judicial power is because of the potential for institutional divergences between president and parliament. But these divergent policy views can be ameliorated by the presence of a dominant party that controls both institutions. The structure matters, but only where the party system is sufficiently diffuse to allow judicial power to exist. Thus, the party system is a variable prior to the institutional structure, although the latter has received far more attention in the literature to date.

Assuming divergence of policy views among institutions, presidential systems may generate more demand for judicial review from the government. But depending on the particular constitutional scheme, presidents also have greater power to influence the court or to ignore its decisions. Of particular importance is the availability of the "exit" option for presidents. Where the executive has the power of commander-in-chief, the president may find that exit is less costly than otherwise. Whereas the legislature's power is tied to the continuing maintenance of the constitutional system, the executive can "exit" and overthrow the constitutional order. Admittedly, this is a highly costly power to exercise.

---

[26] See, for example, Robert Dahl, "Thinking About Democratic Constitutions," in *Political Order* (Ian Shapiro and Russell Hardin, eds., 1996); Haggard and Kaufmann, *supra* note 23; Giovanni Sartori, *Comparative Constitutional Engineering: An Inquiry into Structures, Incentives and Outcomes* (2d ed., 1996).

[27] Ackerman, *supra* note 24, at 789.

Nevertheless, it means that the president is more easily able to exercise what we are calling the "counterattack" response to adverse judicial decisions. Legislatures can attack the court – for example, through manipulating judicial salaries – but they cannot risk overthrowing the whole constitutional system. Without the constitutional system, the legislature has no power.

Presidential or semipresidential systems can also be conducive to the exercise of judicial power simply because they typically require the cooperation of two political bodies in order to pass legislation. The option of counterattacking the court through the legislative process, for example, through restrictions on jurisdiction or budget, may prove more difficult in systems where the cooperation of two law-making authorities is required to pass new legislation.

To see how the party system and political structure interact, consider the famous instance of the court-packing plan in U.S. history. President Roosevelt was frustrated at the Supreme Court's striking of New Deal legislation in 1934–35. Deferring to the preferences of the Court was not an attractive option, nor did he have the luxury of ignoring the Court's decision. The third option was to overrule the court by amending the Constitution, either to constitutionalize the New Deal reforms or to create a mechanism for overriding the judiciary. Roosevelt considered this option seriously, but was faced with two problems. First was the question of the scope of the amendment. The New Deal reforms were radical changes in American government and relied on massive delegation of power to administrative agencies. Broadly drafted provisions in a constitutional amendment were desirable for such a delegation, just as they were with ordinary legislation; but these provisions would have to be interpreted by conservative courts that could exploit ambiguities in the language to undermine Roosevelt's intent. Second, Roosevelt was afraid of the electoral consequences if any proposed constitutional amendment became a campaign issue.[28] Given these uncertainties and the difficulty of the constitutional amendment process, overruling the Court was an unattractive option.[29] In light of these circumstances, changing the personnel on the Court through dilution of the "four horsemen" seemed the most attractive option. After all, there was no constitutional language designating the number of Supreme Court justices, and the number had varied in

---

[28] Stephen Griffin, *American Constitutionalism* (1996).
[29] David Kyvig, "The Road Not Taken," 104 *Pol. Sci. Q.* 473 (1989) (arguing that amendment was more feasible than Roosevelt thought).

American history, most recently when radical Republicans after the Civil War had successfully "attacked" the Chase Court in this manner.

Roosevelt announced his plan and was met with tremendous uproar. The source of the resistance to Roosevelt was not the Court itself pronouncing his plan unconstitutional, but rather was rooted in the Congress controlled by Roosevelt's own Democratic Party. Members were ambivalent about the plan, in part because it invited reciprocal action under a Republican president. Both the formal separation of powers and the party system of regular alternation of two parties facilitated the preservation of judicial independence under adverse conditions.

One of the most common constitutional configurations in new democracies is the combination of a French-style mixed governmental system with a German-style constitutional court. This is perhaps the ideal constitutional configuration for the development of active judicial power because it sets up numerous separation-of-powers disputes along with an open-access court that can conduct abstract and concrete review. Holding the party system constant, we would predict greater judicial power in those new democracies with this configuration than in those adopting a pure Westminster-style system or a pure presidential system. This is because of the combination of a difficult environment for passing new legislation to attack the court, along with high demand from government bodies for dispute resolution to resolve jurisdictional boundary problems and, where available, easy access to the court for citizens and plaintiffs.

This analysis is again subject to the important caveat that it is the party system that gives life to the institutional design of a constitutional scheme. Other things being equal, a mixed system of government with a designated constitutional court will provide numerous opportunities for judicialization. In the real world of new democracies, parties matter and dictate the extent to which courts can take advantage of structural opportunities.

THE STRATEGY OF CASE SELECTION

Broadly speaking, courts can concentrate attention on three different kinds of cases. The first category includes what may be called vertical separation-of-powers cases: those concerning the division of power between local governments and the national government. In a federal system, this involves center-state relations, but such cases arise even in nonfederal systems. From the point of view of a strategic court, these cases are straightforward in the sense that the national government typically has greater power to compel the performance of the constituent government as well as to discipline the court. Furthermore, constitutional courts are national institutions with a policy-making role. This does not mean, however, the national constitutional courts are always centralizers.[30] Precisely because the power of national institutions to discipline the court is typically greater, it may be in the court's strategic interest to forge a relative balance between national and constituent unit power. By balancing the two levels, the court might gain more policy space to work in. Diffusion itself is a strategy as well as a supporting condition for judicial power.

The second category of case may be called horizontal separation of powers, and it concerns the relationship among bodies in the central government. Typically, democratic governments set up multiple political institutions, whose jurisdictions and responsibilities are distinct. Jurisdictional disputes will often arise wherein one body questions whether another co-ordinate branch of the central government has the power to undertake a certain type of action. The court is a natural third party to turn to with its functional expertise in dispute resolution and nonpartisan mode of composition.

In these kinds of disputes, the court is most clearly serving in its role as dispute resolver rather than policymaker. But these kinds of cases are fraught with danger for the court. The minute the court decides the case, the situation shifts from triadic dispute resolution to two-against-one, upsetting the losing party.[31] The trick of constitutionalism is to induce the losing party to comply. If the court sides with the more powerful body, then the decision may be self-enforcing. If the court sides with the weaker body, then its rhetorical strategy will be particularly addressed to the need to secure compliance from the stronger or to communicating the possibility of repeated play with a long-run distribution of benefits in favor of the more powerful constitutional actors.

A third category of cases is that concerning constitutional rights. Like horizontal dispute resolution, these cases may sometimes involve challenging the powerful center on behalf of relatively marginal actors, namely individuals. Such rights cases, however, often advance policy goals of the central regime. For example, a revenue-maximizing state will find it in its own interest to set aside a realm of private property that cannot be easily

---

[30] The Supreme Court of Canada, for example, has presided over a federal balance that has shifted in favor of provincial rather than central authorities. See J. Snell and F. Vaughan, *The Supreme Court of Canada: History of the Institution* (1985).

[31] Martin Shapiro, *Courts: A Comparative and Political Analysis* (1981).

expropriated as a way of encouraging investment and the production of tax revenues. Furthermore, rights cases offer great legitimacy benefits to the court. Although the court will be deciding against a hypothetical majority represented by the government, the court provides a victory to an interest group likely to have intensely held preferences. Populism can provide a bulwark against counterattack; a court can cultivate it by broadening standing and encouraging litigation by a range of rights-seeking interest groups.

Which kind of cases should courts concentrate on? The strategy will be based in large part on what allies the court seeks to protect it from the fundamental problem of institutional weakness. Courts face a tension between this weakness and the need to expand institutional power to advance whatever policy goals judges may have. Therefore, it will make sense for courts to seek allies to minimize the threat of collateral harm. There is no uniform strategy that makes sense for all courts in all times and places. Nevertheless, some generalizations are possible. A centralizing approach to local-national relations might make sense for a young court subject to threats of attack or noncompliance, such as those repeatedly experienced by the U.S. Supreme Court up to the time of the Civil War.[32] Such decisions are largely self-enforcing. Separation-of-powers decisions, by contrast, are high risk for the court, especially where there is an asymmetrical institutional balance among the powers being separated.

The politics of rights decisions are more ambiguous. Where a court sides with an individual against the government, the reason cannot be the greater possibility of compliance. The power of the government to resist court decisions is always greater than that of individuals subject to governmental coercion. Rather, there may be some substantive goal the court is trying to advance, such as institutional autonomy, property rights protection, or social equality. Alternatively, the court may be striving to appeal to the public as a strategy of legitimation and a way of raising the costs of political attack on the court.

Where constitutional adjudication is centralized, as in the European tradition and most new democracies, the institutional structure may provide judges with another dimension of strategic choice. Courts in the German tradition sometimes have explicit power to give the legislature time limitations within which to correct defective statutes. They can also hold a statute constitutional as long as it is interpreted in a particular way.

---

[32] Most prominently, the threats of noncompliance by Thomas Jefferson and Andrew Jackson.

The institutional factors that allow courts to do this are not available to all courts, but where they are, they greatly facilitate judicial strategy.

To conclude, courts exercise interdependent law-making power. Judicial review does not exist in a political vacuum, but rather courts are constrained by the positions of other political actors. In new democracies, one of the key variables for the performance of judicial review is the power configuration of political forces. Other things being equal, a strong military or dominant party will hinder judicial power. On the other hand, divided government, or equally balanced political forces, will expand the court's room for interpretation and will help make it a natural arbiter to resolve political conflicts that arise. Political diffusion, either in the structure of the constitutional order or in the party system, allows courts the freedom to expand judicial power, build up legitimacy over time, and deepen the constitutional order.

4

Courts in New Democracies

The remainder of this book will apply the concepts developed thus far to real-world cases of the establishment of judicial review. This chapter begins the inquiry by taking a wide perspective, briefly considering the history of a few well-known courts and their strategic interactions with other branches of government. The three subsequent chapters look deeply at three particular cases of the establishment and expansion of judicial review in Asia.

Judicial review has spread around the globe in three waves. The first wave was that of the United States and the constitutions of its various constituent states. Although judicial review was adopted in a couple of European polities thereafter, particularly after Kelsen's reconceptualization of constitutional review in the early twentieth century, it was not until a second wave of constitution writing after World War II that the practice spread broadly. The third wave of judicial review has been the recent adoption of judicial review in the postcommunist world and other new democracies. In discussing cases from these three waves, we will examine successful cases as well as an instance where judicial review failed to contribute to democratic development and consolidation, namely postcommunist Russia. For each, we will consider the extent of political diffusion as the environmental condition supporting judicial review.

My argument is that, other things being equal, the insurance theory of design and the diffusion theory of judicial power will explain the behavior of courts and politicians. In individual cases, there are other factors at play and there may be other rationales for the adoption and functioning of judicial review. In any event, it would be impossible to "prove" the theory articulated here on the basis of three detailed case studies and numerous more-anecdotal cases. My goal is not to offer a definitive theory that explains all cases, but rather to articulate an important set of factors that have received insufficient attention in the discussion of the spread of judicial review around the globe.

THE U.S. SUPREME COURT AND THE ESTABLISHMENT OF JUDICIAL REVIEW

In considering the establishment of judicial review in new democracies, it is worthwhile to begin with the legal case usually, but erroneously, considered to be the origin of judicial review, namely John Marshall's 1803 decision in *Marbury v. Madison*. Marshall's decision is extraordinarily sensitive to the political conditions of the time.[1] The decision came in the middle of a bitter political dispute about the federal judiciary, one in which Marshall himself was deeply implicated as a prominent Federalist and late appointment to the court in the waning days of the Adams administration. The Federalist effort to expand the judiciary after its loss in the election of 1800 is a textbook case of the insurance theory. A party that knew it had lost two branches of government expanded the third branch to guarantee a forum.

From the point of view of an inquiry into judicial strategy, the beauty of the *Marbury* decision is the logic of compliance.[2] Confronted with a request to issue a mandamus to the secretary of state, which Marshall knew would provoke resistance, Marshall sidestepped. The opinion analyzed at great length why Marbury had a right to his commission, why mandamus was the proper remedy, and why the secretary of state was the proper object of judicial action. In this sense, it was a scathing attack against Marshall's political opponents. Then, in the final portion of the

---

[1] See, generally, Paul W. Kahn, *The Reign of Law:* Marbury v. Madison *and the Constitution of America* (1997). See also Robert McCloskey and Sanford Levinson, *The American Supreme Court* (1994). But see Robert L. Clinton, "Game Theory, Legal History and the Origins of Judicial Review: A Revisionist Analysis of *Marbury v. Madison*," 38 *Am. J. Pol. Sci.* 285 (1994) (arguing against the conventional understanding of *Marbury*).

[2] Kahn disagrees with this reading of *Marbury* as a political case about power and instead develops a theory of the case as central to the American institution of the rule of law. See Kahn, *supra* note 1. Marshall's feat, in Kahn's view, is to transform a political dispute into a legal one. From my perspective, Kahn's view is not inconsistent with the analysis offered here. By changing the terrain of the dispute from politics to law, Marshall ensures that his institution will continually be involved and will play the game on its home court.

opinion Marshall managed to say that the judiciary had no power to issue a mandamus to the secretary, because the explicit assignment of original jurisdiction to the Supreme Court by Section 13 of the Judiciary Act of 1789 went beyond the enumerated assignment of that jurisdiction in Article III of the constitution. Marshall says to Congress that its attempt to give the courts the power is an unconstitutional legislative act that is void. Because the grant of jurisdiction could only be exercised by the judicial branch itself, there was limited risk that Congress or the Executive could ignore the decision. Marshall's order is to his own branch of government, and it is a negative order at that: Do not issue a mandamus. By the way, Marshall goes on to say to Congress, you should not have allowed us to issue writs of mandamus, and we refuse to abide by your attempt to do so. By issuing an order to the judiciary itself in a manner consistent with the desires of the "political" branches, Marshall ensured there would be zero risk of noncompliance with the decision. Jefferson thus found himself in the position of attacking the decision that supported his position or accepting the decision with its potentially momentous future consequences. Marshall traded mandamus for judicial review and no doubt received the more powerful tool.[3]

The fragility of the court's power in the early era of U.S. history and the threat posed by noncompliance are evidenced by the history of the Marshall Court. Contrary to our contemporary image of the Supreme Court as prominent, powerful, and countermajoritarian, the Marshall Court was progovernment and served as a key ally of the central government against the states. It showed its willingness to serve the interests of national institutions and became seen as a useful part of government by those in the position to inflict greatest punishment upon the court. The states had larger tolerance zones for adverse decisions by virtue of their limited ability to attack the court.

The court had to move cautiously at first. In *Cohens v. Virginia* (1821), the court was confronted with the question of whether it had the power to hear appeals from state courts in cases where the state was a party. The court again deftly asserted a general power in a way that upheld the disputed state action, ensuring compliance. The state of Virginia was free to punish the Cohens brothers as it wished, said the court, but in

---

[3] Robert Lowery Clinton argues that *Marbury* stands only for the proposition that the court can exercise judicial review over statutes that interfere with the judicial power and not other statutes. See *Marbury v. Madison and Judicial Review* (1989). Suffice it to say that the verdict of history is otherwise.

doing so the court established the power to review state court decisions involving the state for conformity with federal law. Another nail in the coffin of state sovereignty was hammered down, and there was again no threat of noncompliance because the court did not order the release of the plaintiffs.

As is well-known, after *Marbury*, the court did not again challenge an act of Congress until *Dred Scott v. Sandford* (1856).[4] In striking a balance between institutional expansion on the one hand and institutional protection through upholding regime interests on the other, the court leaned heavily toward the latter. This caution was due perhaps to early threats of noncompliance by Andrew Jackson. Judicial power was also subject to executive interference, such as when the Jeffersonians sought, unsuccessfully, to impeach Justice Chase. Far less risky was a strategy of upholding central authority vis-à-vis that of the states, as in the cases of *Fletcher v. Peck*,[5] where the court first held a law of a state unconstitutional; *McCulloch v. Maryland*,[6] where the court used the necessary-and-proper clause to find that Congress had implied constitutional powers, including the power to charter a national bank; and *Gibbons v. Ogden*,[7] which developed an expansive view of the commerce power.

The early political system of the American republic was by today's standards not a democracy, in that the franchise was restricted to white male property holders. Nevertheless, it provides important evidence for our theory. Judicial review served an important function for the national government in controlling regulation by the subsidiary units. Why was judicial power not exercised more actively against the central government? No doubt, the threat of collateral attacks on the court played an important role. And although the basic two-party structure of American politics, which is conducive to judicial power because it features evenly balanced opponents, developed quite early on, political diffusion in the early United States was not accompanied by a sense of constitutional boundary that would prevent exit. Indeed, the issue of secession dominated politics and

---

[4] 60 U.S. 393 (1856).

[5] 10 U.S. (6 Cranch) 87 (1810). Note that *Fletcher* involved the attempt by the Georgia legislature to overturn earlier land grants made by a corrupt predecessor. This decision was an explicit challenge to Georgia, but in terms of the logic of compliance demanded only nonaction from Georgia rather than demanding affirmative steps.

[6] 17 U.S. (4 Wheat.) 316 (1819).

[7] 22 U.S. (9 Wheat.) 1 (1824). *Gibbons* provides broad language about federal authority under the textually vague commerce power, but fails to rely on that power for the decision, which is instead made under the supremacy clause of Article VI of the Constitution.

required careful handling by the court in its program of extending national power. The fiasco of *Dred Scott* illustrates the impossibility of finding effective mediate solutions to this issue.

The early rounds of judicial review in the United States can be characterized as repeated iterations of a game. The initial decision establishing review was a game that the court and Jefferson both "won."[8] The court struck a law passed by the previous legislature, while producing the policy outcome desired by Jefferson. Because it was a self-enforcing order to the judiciary in line with the president's preferences, there was no question of noncompliance. In subsequent rounds of the game, the Marshall Court largely avoided compliance challenges by siding for the federal government. The court avoided the possibility of noncompliance by maintaining low-equilibrium judicial review.

The Chase Court was the first to routinely exercise the power of judicial review during a period that corresponded with a deepening of American democracy, as the franchise was expanded in the aftermath of the Civil War. Judicial review of federal statutes was not uncontroversial, however. The 1866 case of *Ex Parte Milligan* came in the midst of a battle of words with radical Republicans in Congress.[9] The issue concerned the Civil War practice of trying civilians before military courts. By holding that military tribunals could not try civilians while ordinary courts remained open, the court defended its own jurisdiction, even though it had waited until after the Civil War to interfere with military authorities in this way. *Milligan* can be characterized as a separation-of-powers decision disguised as a rights decision, in which the court protected its own turf against executive interference while appearing to vindicate the civil rights of an individual. This is consistent with a view of courts as concerned with their own institutional power.

The Chase Court continued striking Republican-backed laws requiring loyalty oaths for voting in Missouri and for the practice of law in federal courts.[10] Republicans responded with a number of proposals to amend the judicial process in the aftermath of these decisions, including one proposal to require a unanimous vote to strike a statute, which would have hindered the court from acting. Later, in *Ex Parte McCardle* (1868), the

---

[8] Clinton, *supra* note 1, at 285.
[9] 71 U.S. (4 Wall.) 2 (1866); Robert J. Steamer, *The Supreme Court in Crisis* 102 (1971).
[10] *Cummings v. Missouri*, 71 U.S. (4 Wall.) 277 (1867); *Ex Parte Garland*, 71 U.S. (4 Wall.) 333 (1866).

court was presented with a challenge testing *Milligan*.[11] McCardle was a Mississippi newspaper editor charged with seditious libel and inciting insurrection for anti-Republican rhetoric. Using the 1867 Habeas Corpus Act, intended by Congress to protect loyal unionists in the southern states, McCardle petitioned the Supreme Court. Congress was outraged and repealed the act, explicitly prohibiting the court from hearing cases under it even if already docketed.[12]

This early history illustrates the caution with which judges established the system of judicial review in the United States and their susceptibility at every stage to intervention from political authorities. Where the Supreme Court set out to "definitely set to rest a controversy that has so long plagued the country," as Justice Catron said about *Dred Scott*, it provoked backlash and controversy.[13] Where it acted sensitively and supported regime interests, it was more successful. Caution and care, it would seem, are crucial for establishing judicial power until the threat of exit by political forces is diminished.

There is a paradox here. To develop effective institutional power, justices must sometimes restrain themselves from exercising it. What determines how daring courts can be in exercising power? Keith Whittington has recently argued that judicial power in the United States is most limited during periods when new legislative majorities come into power.[14] The four periods of greatest pressure on courts from political branches are the 1800s, 1820s, 1860s, and 1930s. Each of these historical periods witnessed the rise of a new majority political party: the Jeffersonians, the Jacksonian Democratic Party, the radical Republican Party, and the New Deal Democratic Party. Each of these periods saw explicit threats to the court. The Chase Court, for example, may have been the first to regularly strike legislation, but it also provoked a serious backlash in the form of Grant's packing of the court to reverse *Hepburn v. Griswold*, the case that held that the federal government had no right to issue paper money.[15] Grant was successful in his effort, and it was not until much later, when Roosevelt tried his similar scheme to protect the New Deal from judicial interference, that norms of judicial independence had developed sufficiently so that the court was seen to be "off limits" to institutional

---

[11] 73 U.S. (6 Wall.) 318 (1868).
[12] Steamer, *supra* note 8, at 107.
[13] Neal Devins, *Shaping Constitutional Values* (1996).
[14] Keith E. Whittington, "Legislative Sanctions and the Strategic Environment of Judicial Review," *Int'l J. Con. L.* (forthcoming 2003).
[15] 75 U.S. (8 Wall.) 603 (1870).

attacks. Combined with the diffusion that has always been a feature of American politics, the New Deal defense of judicial autonomy prepared the way for the unparalleled judicial activism of the Warren and Burger Courts.[16] The Warren Court, in particular, presided over the improvement of American democracy through the effective extension of the franchise to blacks and other minorities. The court was thus able to draw on its stock of capital developed through decades of caution to withstand an institutional attack and entrench its position in national political life.

The institutional caution of the U.S. Supreme Court, its strategy of serving as an instrument of centralization for many years, and its widespread legitimacy illustrate how a court can successfully expand its power over time. We are so familiar with this story that we risk forgetting the great threats that the court was under at particular moments in U.S. history and the strategic caution that allowed the court to survive as an institution. It could easily have been otherwise, as judges in some circumstances have learned.

THE SECOND WAVE OF JUDICIAL REVIEW: POSTFASCISM AND
POSTCOLONIALISM

The years immediately following World War II saw the development of a new wave of judicial review. Powerful centralized constitutional courts were established in Germany and Italy in the wake of the fascist experience, as political forces sought to ensure that basic rights would be protected. Kelsen's model of a designated constitutional court, access to which originally was restricted to certain political bodies and state governments, was modified to include access by the citizenry. A new constitution in Japan explicitly gave the judiciary the power to strike legislation and administrative action for unconstitutionality. In some new nations formed through decolonization, such as India, the highest courts were granted the power of supervising the constitution.[17] In the case of these new nations, the supreme courts simply took over the former role of the colonial power's courts in supervising local rules.

---

[16] The Warren Court is typically portrayed as much more activist than the Burger Court, but in terms of numbers of state and federal statutes overturned per year, the latter court was more active.

[17] In the case of India, this power was apparently contemplated well before decolonization. See Adarsh Sein Anand, "Protection of Human Rights through Judicial Review in India," in *Judicial Review in International Perspective: Liber Amicorum Lord Slynn* 381–82 (Mats Andenas, ed., 2000).

India's experience illustrates the gradual approach the court has taken to building up its power. During the early years of the Indian Constitution, the Supreme Court took a relatively passive role in interpreting the constitution, despite the explicit list of fundamental rights and the extensive powers granted to the court as protector of those rights.[18] The court's early years saw it challenge a series of governments on the issue of nationalizing property. Because property was a fundamental right, the court insisted that full compensation was required, but government responded by amending the constitution to overrule judicial decisions.[19]

In 1971, after the Twenty-fifth Amendment sought to preclude judicial review of property rights claims, the Supreme Court struck down parts of the amendment as conflicting with the constitution's "basic structure."[20] Indira Gandhi's government attacked the court as an institution, announcing publicly that it intended to limit appointments to those sympathetic to it and bypassing the usual seniority norm concerning appointments to the chief justiceship. When Gandhi declared emergency rule in 1975, the Parliament passed a constitutional amendment preventing the court from scrutinizing future constitutional amendments for conformity with the constitution. In the face of these attacks on jurisdiction and threats to judicial independence, the court largely submitted to politicians' desires.

While this stance was criticized by many, it did mean that the court was able to maintain institutional integrity to fight another day. After emergency rule ended, the court became bolder and rejected the amendment that had purported to prevent review of constitutional amendments. It became much more active in criminal procedure, restraining the power of the state. Judicial review of administrative action in India has also developed rapidly in recent years.[21] The court also created, in effect, a right to legal aid.

The controversy over the power to review constitutional amendments is at bottom a controversy over jurisdiction. Even if the court was unable to "win" its confrontation with political authorities in the short term,

---

[18] Article 32 of the Indian Constitution guarantees the right to petition the court to protect the fundamental rights and gives the power to the court to issue orders or writs as necessary to enforce those rights.

[19] See, generally, Charles Epp, *The Rights Revolution* (1998); George Gadbois, "The Institutionalization of the Supreme Court of India," in *Comparative Judicial Systems: Challenging Frontiers in Conceptual and Empirical Analysis* 111–42 (John Schmidhauser, ed., 1987).

[20] *Kesavananda Bharati v. State of Kerala*, AIR 1973 SC 1461.

[21] See, for example, *Dwarka Dass Marfatia and Sons v. Board of Trustees, Port of Bombay*, AIR 1989 SC 1642.

its acquiescence allowed it to defend its jurisdiction in the long term. Regardless of how the court decided the substantive rights issues before it, then, we see a concern with institutional power that allowed the court to emerge as a central political institution in the 1980s and 1990s, when the Congress Party was less dominant and new political forces were on the rise.

One sign of a more activist court has been its willingness to broaden standing requirements since the 1980s. Broadening standing to encourage public-interest litigation helps ensure that the court will remain an important locus of consideration for many important issues of social policy. By creating its own demand, the court has been able to engineer high-equilibrium judicial review. According to Charles Epp, the court is upholding individual rights claims with much greater frequency, another sign of high-equilibrium judicial review.[22] This expanded judicial activism may also serve the interests of the Congress juggernaut that now finds itself in opposition.

Although India's experience demonstrates the ability of a court to challenge political authorities, even in difficult political circumstances, and also to spur a higher-equilibrium level of judicial review, the Supreme Court of Japan appears to follow a path of great restraint. A classic example of a party ignoring a constitutional decision is the response of the Japanese Liberal Democratic Party (LDP) to Supreme Court decisions on electoral malapportionment. The LDP was able to rule uninterrupted for thirty-eight years in large part because of an electoral system that severely underrepresented urban areas. The Supreme Court has twice held the electoral system unconstitutional and suggested the Diet correct its error.[23] The court, however, was concerned about its own ability to force compliance and refrained from voiding elections held under this unconstitutional system despite specifically finding them illegal. The unenthusiastic reaction of political forces to these cases is often seen to have contributed to Japanese judicial passivity on constitutional matters.

Because a single party has ruled uninterrupted for so long, it has been able to signal its constitutional preferences quite clearly. Indeed, its noncompliance with the adverse malapportionment decisions can be seen as

---

[22] See Epp, *supra* note 19, at 89.
[23] *Kurokawa v. Chiba Prefecture Election Commission*, 30 Minshu 223 (April 14, 1976); *Tokyo Election Comm'n v. Koshiyama*, 37 Minshu 1243 (November 7, 1983); William Somers Bailey, "Reducing Malapportionment in Japan's Electoral Districts," 6 *Pac. Rim L.J.* 169 (1997).

a signal to the court not to challenge it on core policy matters. The court appeared to heed its warning and did not rule a statute unconstitutional from the second apportionment case until 1997.[24]

The Japanese court has also been subject to political influence in the appointments process. The Supreme Court members are appointed by the Diet, and some have argued that the justices are more conservative than their fellows at other levels of the court system.[25] With the notable exceptions of the electoral cases, the supreme court has been able to obtain compliance with its decisions; but the number of decisions challenging core interests of the governing party have been few and far between. The court exercises what we have characterized as low-equilibrium judicial review.

THE THIRD WAVE OF JUDICIAL REVIEW

Hungary: Compliance

Hungary's Constitutional Court was created in the wake of communism and against the background of political deadlock among the Communists and the opposition. Indeed, in many respects the political forces were unable to agree on the fundamental rules of the game, as reflected by the fact that they reformed the Hungarian constitution through a process of amendments rather than drafting an entirely new document. The court itself had been proposed by the Communists, through the ministry of justice, at the roundtable talks ending one-party rule.[26] Indeed, the roundtable agreement called for the naming of five of the ten initial justices of the constitutional court, including two each by the major political forces and a fifth judge agreed to by both. Consistent with the insurance theory, a party that knew it would soon lose power sought to enshrine certain constitutional guarantees to prevent its emasculation at the hands of new democratic forces. Besides the constitutional court, the constitutional scheme required a supermajority of two thirds for the passage of certain important laws, another minoritarian device.

---

[24] The 1997 case concerned the constitutionality of public funds used for a Shinto shrine.

[25] J. Mark Ramseyer and Eric Rasmusen have compiled an extensive set of data demonstrating the political influence on the Japanese judiciary, in their forthcoming *Measuring Judicial Independence: The Political Economy of Judging in Japan* (2003).

[26] Gabor Halmai and Kim Lane Scheppele, "Living Well Is the Best Revenge: The Hungarian Approach to Judging the Past," in *Transitional Justice and the Rule of Law in New Democracies* 159 (James McAdams, ed., 1997).

For the former Communists, the insurance policy proved effective when the court took an absolutist stand against legislation designed to allow prosecution of members of the former regime. Hinging its decision on rule-of-law values, the court identified itself as an instrument of "Europeanizing" Hungary's constitutional culture through an absolute commitment to the development of a *rechtstaat*.

Politics in the years following the Revolution of 1989 remained convoluted, as numerous parties sought to control the Parliament. The first parliamentary election in 1989 brought to power a fragile coalition of three parties that was subsequently preoccupied with their internal conflicts. In such circumstances, it is perhaps no surprise that the Hungarian Constitutional Court emerged as a major political actor, taking an active role in shaping the new constitutional order under its first president, László Sólyom. Relying on a broad theory of constitutional interpretation, the court issued important decisions on the death penalty, on a right to data privacy, access to information, and many conventional rights, such as the right to property and freedom of expression and association.[27] Its activism led it into all sorts of other policy areas as well.

In all these areas, the court was able to secure compliance from political authorities whose actions were constrained by the court decisions. No doubt the strong pull of the European Union had much to do with the culture of compliance that developed around the first constitutional court, but another essential element was the political diffusion in the legislature that gave the court the space in which to work as it articulated its vision.

The court did not remain so active however. Upon the completion of the nine-year terms of the initial set of justices in 1998 (and the retirement of other justices), the court was filled with new appointments. This turnover in staffing reflected, in part, a decision by the Parliament not to renew the terms of Justice Sólyom and others from the original set of justices. The subsequent turn of the court to a more formalist mode of interpretation led to a reduced role for the court[28] and can be read as a reining in of an activist institution that played an important role in Hungary's reintegration in Europe.

---

[27] See cases presented in László Sólyom and Georg Brunner, *Constitutional Judiciary in a New Democracy: The Hungarian Constitutional Court* (2000); Ethan Kingsberg, "Judicial Review and Hungary's Transition from Communism to Democracy," 41 *B.Y.U. L. Rev.* 41 (1992).

[28] Kim Lane Scheppele, "The New Hungarian Constitutional Court," 8 *E. Eur. Const. Rev.* 81 (fall 1999).

Russia: Counterattack

Boris Yeltsin's 1993 attack on the first Russian Constitutional Court is one well-known example of political interference with a new court. The history of this institution illustrates the dangers to judicial bodies of acting precipitously in new democracies. The court had been created at the very end of the Gorbachev era through amendments to the 1978 Russian Constitution and came into life with passage of the Law on the Constitutional Court in 1991.[29] The court was composed of fifteen members, two of whose slots were never filled. Six of the new justices were academics, six were parliamentary deputies, and one was a prosecutor. During its two years of existence, the court played a central role in Russian politics. It received roughly 30,000 petitions from the public and heard twenty-seven cases.[30] Nineteen of these involved reviewing laws and administrative acts at the request of government agencies, with eight cases responding to citizen petitions. This limited pool of cases allows us to determine the court's implicit strategies of case selection and rhetoric. In particular, the experience of the Russian Court illustrates the dangers of deciding separation-of-powers disputes.

Although in its two years the court struck down an equal number of parliamentary laws as presidential decrees,[31] it developed a reputation for challenging presidential authority in particular. Its first major decision overturned President Yeltsin's decree merging the police and internal security forces into a single ministry. Yeltsin's use of the decree power, according to the court, violated the separation of powers by infringing on parliamentary authority. Yeltsin abided by this decision, and Russia appeared to be on its way to an effective constitutional regime for the first time in its history.

Soon, however, came the Communist Party case, which occupied the court for most of 1992. Yelstin, in a series of decrees after the 1991 coup attempt, had disbanded the Communist Party and seized its property and assets.[32] Early in 1992, the Communists challenged these decrees as exceeding presidential power, prompting a cross-petition by opponents of the Communist Party who asked for a decision on the party's legality

[29] Law of 12 July 1991.
[30] Robert Ahdieh, *Russia's Constitutional Revolution* 79 (1997).
[31] *Ibid.*
[32] Decree No. 79 of August 23, 1991; Decree No. 90 of August 24, 1991; and Decree No. 169 of November 6, 1991.

and constitutional status. The two petitions were joined by the chairman of the court, Valery Zorkin, bringing together genuinely legal issues with deeply political ones.[33]

The court was faced with a difficult situation. It could uphold the president's actions, even though they did not follow the relevant legal procedures for banning political associations; or it could strike them and side with the anticonstitutional Communists who had supported the coup. Neither option appeared particularly attractive. Thus caught, the court attempted to split the difference by finding a mediate solution. In a decision published on November 30, 1992, the court upheld Yeltsin's decrees against the organs of the national Communist Party of the Soviet Union, but not against its local bodies. The court relied on a federalist rationale to find that local political party offices could not be implicated in the national coup. As to the true character of the party, the court abdicated and declared the question moot. This decision provoked disappointment on all sides.

With legislative-executive relations reaching a crisis point, the next month the court's Chairman Zorkin negotiated a compromise document between Yelstin and the Parliament. This constitutional compromise marked the deep involvement of the court, and Zorkin in particular, in the realm of pure politics as opposed to law. The image of the court as a neutral, technical body devoted to the law was dashed. Internally, the court began to drift. Its decisions, which had been almost entirely unanimous in its first year of operation, frequently included dissents in 1993. When Yeltsin dispensed with the compromise and announced a decree granting himself emergency powers in March 1993, the court issued an opinion declaring the action unconstitutional, even before the decree was issued.[34] Zorkin appeared on television to denounce Yeltsin's actions. Within months, Yeltsin dissolved the Parliament and suspended the court's operation.[35] It was not reconvened until February 1995, with reduced powers.[36] In particular, it lost the powers to declare parties unconstitutional and issue

---

[33] The legal grounds of the case were complicated, and they are better elaborated elsewhere. Suffice it to say that the case featured some bizarre arguments, such as Yeltsin's position that the decree to ban a political association was legal under a 1932 Stalinist decree that permitted the executive to undertake such action. See, generally, Ahdieh, *supra* note 30.

[34] In fact, the decree never materialized. The court thus issued an advisory opinion.

[35] Decree No. 1400 of September 21, 1993, and No. 1612 of October 7, 1993.

[36] Ahdieh, *supra* note 30, at 149; Sergy Pashin, "A Second Edition of the Constitutional Court," 3:3–4 *E. Eur. Const. Rev.* 82 (1994).

an advisory opinion on the impeachment of the president. Terms were reduced from life to twelve years.

Other analysts have criticized the court, and particularly its chairman, for getting too involved in politics[37] and for focusing on separation-of-powers issues rather than individual-rights cases.[38] Some argue that the court could have utilized a form of political-questions doctrine to avoid such controversial, no-win cases and that its chair could have assumed a lower profile. Such criticisms are warranted, but they risk obscuring the problem. The court's mistake was not involvement in politics, per se, but the manner in which it became involved. In particular, the court was insufficiently sensitive to the problem of compliance. By consistently siding against the president in a fragile period of Russian political history, the court appeared to take the position of the Parliament and prompted the president's actions. It forced an endgame, which it could not win.

Of course, it would be unfair to place all the blame on the court. The particular structure of Russian politics encouraged extraconstitutional behavior. Norms of constitutional compliance were fragile at best after seventy years of communism. The outcome of the crisis was adoption of a new constitutional system by referendum in December 1993, which sets up what one observer has called a "superpresidential" system.[39]

Nevertheless, the first Russian court illustrates the problems that can result from poor strategy. The Communist Party decision hinged on a decentralizing approach to federalism, in contrast with the Marshall Court's centralizing approach at a comparable stage of U.S. history. It also led to continued conflict. In terms of our framework, Russia in 1992 had a great deal of political diffusion, but few effective boundaries on political action. The court through its eagerness to enter the fray did little to develop these boundaries by inducing compliance. It continuously challenged the constitutional actor, the president, whose only available option was to

---

[37] See, for example, Lawrence Lessig, "Introduction: Roundtable on Redesigning the Russian Court," 3:3–4 *E. Eur. Const. Rev.* 72–74 (1994); Ahdieh, *supra* note 30, at 84.

[38] Ahdieh, *supra* note 30, at 84–90.

[39] M. Steven Fish, "The Perils of Russian Superpresidentialism," 96 *Current Hist.* 326 (1997). With a relatively weak legislature to provide a voice option for political losers, there is a tremendous amount riding on presidential elections, such that actors may be willing to emasculate the constitution to keep the office. See also M. Steven Fish, *Democracy From Scratch: Opposition and Regime in the New Russian Revolution* (1995).

counterattack the court and destroy the constitutional order, leading to greater concentration of political power and less diffusion. The reduced powers of the second Constitutional Court resulted from the poor strategic choices of the first court. Had the court been willing to provide greater political benefit to the dominant authorities, it might have been able to safeguard its long-term interest by enhancing the zone of tolerance for its decisions.

CONCLUSION: CAUTIOUS COURTS

Judicial review is not only a function of institutional design. The choices of courts are crucial for determining how the system of judicial review operates and whether or not it will emerge as an important part of the political order. The contrasting strategies of the first Russian Constitutional Court and the United States Supreme Court illustrate how the choices of justices can affect the overall development of judicial review. Both countries had new courts exercising the power of judicial review for the first time early in their democratic history. In both countries, there were serious divergences among the political forces, with continuous threats of exit. The two courts, however, pursued different strategies. The United States Supreme Court spent decades building up its power by providing positive benefits to the regime through centralizing decisions on issues of federalism. In contrast, the Russian Constitutional Court plunged immediately into bitter separation-of-powers disputes. Not only did it choose cases poorly, but it sought allies in precisely the wrong places. Its Communist Party decision, for example, challenged Yeltsin directly, provoking him into disbanding the court. It also allowed the dissolution of the national-level Communist Party, leaving only local parties intact. It therefore weakened any support that it might have drawn on from the national-level legislature to protect it from the president.

It is important to remember in these discussions of judicial strategy that the institutional weakness of courts is likely to render them cautious as a general matter. The potential risk of counterattack, and the vulnerability of courts, requires great emphasis on the delicate normative balance that preserves judicial power. There is no small irony here. Constitutional courts are institutionally cautious; yet through careful decision making they can entrench the constitutional system by inducing actors to remain in the constitutional order and comply with seemingly adverse decisions. Judicial power expands through apparent deference and minor incremental decisions, performing the insurance function for which they are designed.[40] Where courts become bold, they may generate a backlash that actually reduces their freedom of action.[41]

As argued in Chapter 3, there is no contradiction between the observation that courts are constrained and the insurance theory of constitutional design. Minority parties that may desire insurance will certainly be no worse off having an alternative forum in which to challenge the majority. Although courts may be unable to constrain truly dominant majorities, they will be able to constrain lesser majorities and raise the costs of unconstitutional action.

Finally, it is important to recall a point raised in the Introduction – namely, the danger of drawing too much from perceptions of American experience in examining the operation of courts in new democracies. The search for "great cases" not only misreads *Marbury*, but risks obscuring the subtle interactions between courts and politicians in the early years of the establishment of new democracies. The real story of the establishment of judicial power may be in the shadows, in the detailed interactions between courts and other political actors. The remainder of this book demonstrates this through a detailed examination of the emergence of judicial review in three Northeast Asian countries: Taiwan, Mongolia, and Korea.

---

[40] Martin Shapiro's 1964 observation still holds true that it is "the day to day power over small decisions rather than the ability to change dramatically the whole course of government that often constitutes the key to judicial policymaking." Martin Shapiro, *Law and Politics in the Supreme Court* 41–42 (1964).

[41] Menachem Hofnung, "The Unintended Consequences of Unplanned Constitutional Reform: Constitutional Politics in Israel," 44 *Am. J. Comp. L.* 585 (1996).

5

Confucian Constitutionalism? The Grand Justices of the Republic of China

INTRODUCTION

Political constraints on judicial power can become most apparent as they disappear during transitions from authoritarian rule. Conceptually, the simplest kind of transition involves a replacement of one regime by another and the formation of a new constitutional structure as the basis for government power. The task for constitutional courts in such circumstances is to speak for the new democratic order. By contrast, courts in gradual political and constitutional transitions face a more ambiguous environment. They may be unclear on the shifting preferences of key political forces. Furthermore, where courts had formerly served as instruments of government suppression, they are likely to face problems of legitimacy. As guardians of the old order, they may be under pressure to slow reform. They are subject to residual political controls and more subtle pressures.

How can a constitutional court that served an authoritarian regime become an instrument for democracy and human rights? This chapter discusses the Council of Grand Justices in the Republic of China (ROC) and its careful use of doctrine to expand constitutional review power where it had previously been constrained. In contrast with a "grand case" model of judicial review, wherein Herculean judges force the governing powers to comply with the dictates of the rule of law, the Taiwan example illustrates the merits of careful expansion of judicial power through a gradual, step-by-step process. Individual cases illuminate the judges' careful process of testing how much judicial power political authorities would tolerate in an ambiguous, shifting, but continually liberalizing political environment.

Although formally constituted since the establishment of the ROC government on mainland China in the late 1940s, the Council of Grand Justices of the Judicial Yuan has historically been a quiet institution. After some early efforts to constrain the exercise of political power, the grand justices were disciplined by the legislature in the late 1950s. From that time until the recent liberalization, the justices were cautious. But as the Kuomintang (KMT) regime liberalized beginning in 1986, the council became more active and has slowly expanded both the scope of its power and the exercise of constraints on government. Taiwan's democratization culminated in the election of longtime oppositionist Chen Shui-bian as president in 2000, and a period of divided government ensued. As democracy has become consolidated, the council appears to have settled into a position as a central actor in Taiwan's vigorous constitutional democracy.

The development of a constitutional rule of law in modern Taiwan is the first historical instance of the entrenchment of modern constitutionalism in a Chinese context, a cultural environment perceived to present severe barriers for the development of independent judicial power.[1] The story may have implications for the future development of judicial review in other Chinese political systems, including the People's Republic of China (PRC) itself.[2] Of course, the democratic transition in Taiwan also had its own unique dynamics, in part related to the nature of the KMT regime that combined features of Leninism, personalism, and military rule. As a quasi-Leninist political party that ruled uninterrupted after its withdrawal from the mainland in 1949 until 2000, the KMT would seem to be a classic dominant-party regime. Unlike most other Leninist regimes, however, the KMT had strongly personalistic elements, as the Chiang family controlled the presidency for forty years. Personalism and Leninism both limited the development of legal authority as an independent check on

---

[1] This description of Taiwan as the first successful Chinese constitutional order is similar to that of Chao and Myers, who describe Taiwan as the first Chinese democracy. Linda Chao and Ramon Myers, *The First Chinese Democracy: Political Life in the Republic of China on Taiwan* (1998). After this chapter was completed, I read the excellent study by Chang Wen-chen, *Transition to Democracy, Constitutionalism and Judicial Activism: Taiwan in Comparative Constitutional Perspective*, Unpublished S.J.D. Thesis, Yale Law School, June 2001.

[2] This issue was confronted in early 1999 with a dispute over the power of the Court of Final Appeal in Hong Kong, which claimed the power to restrict application of decisions of the National People's Congress in Beijing when they conflict with the Basic Law of Hong Kong. Ultimately, the court reversed its position under pressure from Tung Chee-hwa, chief executive of Hong Kong.

political power. The KMT can also be understood as a regime of military occupation because of the monopoly of mainland-born Chinese in the military's upper ranks for many years. "Mainlanders" (those who emigrated after the loss of the mainland and their descendants) represent only around 15% of the population, but they controlled the government for its first four decades of existence.

Another distinctive feature of the Taiwan experience is its ambiguous international context. Having lost the mainland, the KMT insisted on maintaining the "one-China" paradigm as the key to its legitimacy and argued that it was the sole legitimate government for all of China. At the same time, Taiwan had many of the features of an independent country. Continuing pressure from the PRC regime constrained democratic discourse, as talk of "Taiwan independence" was anathema to both the KMT and PRC authorities. The need to preserve the rhetorical "face" of the one-China paradigm was a constraining condition on constitutional reform and judicial politics, as well as on the broader political terrain in which judicial decision making took place. Another international element to the story is American influence, enhanced by the regime's military dependence on the U.S. security umbrella to counter the continuing threat from the PRC. The need to distinguish the ROC regime from that of communist China and the ideological promise of an eventual return to the mainland operated as constraints on KMT choices and reinforced the constitutional limits on the exercise of political power, even in the authoritarian period.

The gradual and extended democratic transition is also a distinctive element of Taiwan's experience. Pressure for democratization in Taiwan in the 1970s and 1980s grew not because of the regime's failures, but at least in part was produced by the regime's economic success in generating the Taiwan miracle.[3] Furthermore, the particular ideological program of the KMT had from the beginning called for an eventual return of political power to the people, so democratization can be viewed from one perspective as the culmination of successful leadership, rather than the failure of the regime. This is different from the experience of formerly communist states in Eastern Europe.

This chapter begins with background to the 1947 Constitution and the role of Sun Yat-sen's thought in its construction. It then describes

---

[3] Thomas Gold, *State and Society in the Taiwan Miracle* (1986); Cheng Tun-jen and Stephen Haggard, eds., *Political Change in Taiwan* (1992); Chu Yun-han, "Taiwan's Unique Challenges," 7 J. Democ. 69 (1997); Tien Hung-mao, *Taiwan's Electoral Politics and Democratic Transition: Riding the Third Wave* (1999).

Taiwan's democratization process and proceeds to a detailed account of the evolving role of the Council of Grand Justices. Although the council was created to fulfill the insurance needs of the constitutional drafters, the need for such a role diminished over time as the KMT consolidated its rule. Only with the decline of the one-party state was there sufficient political space for the council to operate in. As the possibility of alternation in government increases, the council is likely to continue to play an important role.

THE DEVELOPMENT OF CONSTITUTIONAL THOUGHT IN CHINA

Modern Chinese constitutional thought began to develop in the late nineteenth century through increased contacts with the western world and Japan.[4] During the years of turmoil associated with the collapse of the Ching dynasty in 1911, several draft constitutions were presented. Consistent with conventional democratic and revolutionary theory of the time, all the republican drafts relied on notions of parliamentary sovereignty, without provision for constitutional control by courts. This was also consistent with the Imperial Chinese notion of undivided sovereignty, simply substituting "the people" for "the emperor." If the people are sovereign, in accordance with the first principle of democratic theory, then they must speak unchallenged through their representative institutions. There is neither need nor proper basis for a judicial check on the decisions of the sovereign.

In Sun Yat-sen's political thought, the judicial power was one of the governmental powers and not intended to constrain the sovereign itself.[5]

---

[4] The transformation of Japan after the Meiji restoration in 1868 into a modern industrial power by the early 1890s, accompanied by the passage of the Meiji Constitution in 1889, was an important influence on Chinese thought about how to modernize the country and led to a famous call by the intellectual Kang Yu-wei in 1895 for a form of modern constitutionalism with separation of powers. Chiu Hungdah, "Constitutional Development and Reform in the Republic of China on Taiwan," 29 *Issues and Studies* 1, 3 (1993); Chao and Myers, *supra* note 1, at 47.

[5] There is a tension in Sun's theory, however. Sun distinguished between the people's "right to rule" as sovereign and the government's "right to rule" as administrator. Paul Linebarger, *The Political Doctrines of Sun Yat-sen* 218 (1937). The people's power is exercised through their representatives in the National Assembly, while the governing powers are exercised through the five branches of government. As eventually manifested in the Five-Power Constitution of the Republic of China, ordinary legislation is passed by the Legislative Yuan and not by the National Assembly. Hence, there ought to be no objection to courts overturning legislation, because both branches are merely administrators of the people's will.

Sun's writings suggest that he saw the judiciary as a feature of western constitutionalism that, in combination with the other governmental powers, would serve to prevent abuses of power.[6] But his broader thinking on the role of law drew on traditional Chinese notions as well as his particular conception of the challenges facing China in the early part of the century. Sun viewed the radical social upheavals of China as resulting from the impact of western ideas on a stagnant imperial institution. The ideological balance of China had been disrupted. To restore ideological balance would require a government-led transformation, so that a new ideological consensus could be formed. Law, as an instrument of governmental power, was an essential component of this transformation. A greater role for the state required greater use of law, but Sun's conception of law was not fundamentally different from that of imperial China. It was not a limit on government per se, but rather a necessary component of the state power that would eventually restore balance in the society.

Although Sun did not contemplate judicial review of legislation, it was already present in the marketplace of concepts available to constitutional theorists, and it appeared in some early draft constitutions for China.[7] The American experience was well known, and scholars were no doubt familiar with the emerging Austrian model. Just as in the "third wave" of global judicial review in the late 1980s, international factors played a role in institutional design in that the experience of earlier constitutional orders presented a menu of choices for later drafters.

Following the establishment of the Nationalist Government, the quasi-Leninist KMT declared a period of "political tutelage" in 1928. This notion modified earlier republican notions of parliamentary sovereignty with the overlay of a Leninist "vanguard" party. Although the people were ultimately sovereign, they were understood as being incapable of

---

[6] Sun, "Address on Democracy," in Sun Yat-sen, *Six Lectures Delivered in Canton*, in *The Teachings of Sun Yat-sen: Selections from His Writings* 111 (N. Gangulee, ed., 1945).

[7] Fa Jyh-pin, "Constitutional Developments in Taiwan: The Role of the Council of Grand Justices," 40 *Int'l & Comp. L. Q.* 198, 199 (1991). The first provision for judicial review in China was found in the Draft Constitution of the Temple of Heaven in 1913, but the legislature retained the power of interpretation of the constitution. In the 1919 Draft Constitution, this power was shared with leaders of the judiciary as both branches joined together to interpret the constitution. The next constitutional document, the Constitution of 1923, continued to rely on notions of parliamentary sovereignty, but allowed the highest court to decide conflicts between national and provincial law, setting the basis for a kind of judicial federalism that was never to be developed.

exercising power, given China's level of education and the tumultuous political circumstances of the time. The prospective challenge of governing a large and uneducated populace in the context of an ongoing civil war led the KMT to deploy Sun's notion of political tutelage, whereby the party would serve as a leading force in society, gradually educating the people to the point where they could exercise their political rights. This notion of tutelage reflected the elitism of the Chinese political tradition and the old notion of rule by intellectuals.[8]

Leninist notions of tutelage are incompatible with judicial review, and no Leninist Party has ever successfully subordinated itself to a system of constitutional control.[9] But as China began the search for a "final" constitution, judicial review made a comeback. The 1936 Draft Constitution mandated that questions of whether laws were in conflict with the Constitution would be settled by the Judicial Yuan upon submission by the Control Yuan.[10] A 1940 attempt to revise the draft proposed a Constitutional Interpretation Commission with nine commissioners. However, China's continuing civil war and Japan's invasion in 1936 prevented the implementation of any of these provisions for constitutional control over the government, weak as they were.[11]

THE CONSTITUTION OF 1947

The current constitution of the ROC was drafted on the Chinese mainland by the KMT government and adopted by the National Assembly in 1946, entering into force on December 25, 1947. The constitutional structure reflects the particular political philosophy of Sun Yat-sen and his theory of

[8] But whereas elites in the old system were required to abide by and maintain old traditions, Sun's class of "geniuses" was supposed to serve as social engineers and initiators of change. Linebarger, *supra* note 5, at 113–14.

[9] This deserves some qualification. In the late communist period, a number of countries tried to set up constitutional courts and councils to provide a check on law making. In the USSR, for example, the Committee for Constitutional Supervision was created under Gorbachev in 1989. Robert Ahdieh, *Russia's Constitutional Revolution* 28 (1997). Yugoslavia established a system of judicial review in the 1970s to oversee the country's federalist balance. Such systems were part of efforts to reconcile one-party rule with wider political participation and remained "low-equilibrium" systems of judicial review, with few cases and little real power or authority.

[10] Lawrence Shao-liang Liu, "Judicial Review and the Constitution: A Tale of Two Institutions," 10, paper presented at the conference on The Evolving U.S. Constitution 1787–1987, Institute of American Culture (Taipei, Taiwan, June 2–4, 1988).

[11] Andrew Nathan, *Chinese Democracy* 112 (1985).

the three powers of the people (*sanminzhuyi*), as well as Chiang Kai-shek's preference for a strong presidency.[12]

Five-Power Scheme and Executive Dominance

The complex scheme of powers devised by Sun Yat-sen and put into force by the ROC Constitution of 1947 included five branches of government, as well as a National Assembly outside the five-power scheme, representing the sovereignty of the people. The five governmental powers are the Legislative, Executive, and Judicial Yuans corresponding to the typical Montesqueiuan scheme, along with the Control and Examination Yuans, inspired by institutions from Chinese history.[13]

Since 1991, several stages of constitutional reform accompanying political liberalization have modified the scheme from that intended by the drafters in 1946. Most importantly, the direct election of the president, implemented in 1996, marked the first time in Chinese history that the head of state had been directly elected. The National Assembly, formerly required to meet every year, has seen its role reduced to the point where it is an ad hoc body that meets only to consider constitutional amendments and impeachments. The result is a dual-executive system leaning heavily toward the presidency; judicial duties split among the Council of Grand Justices, the other elements of the Judicial Yuan, and the Control Yuan; and a unicameral Legislative Yuan. The overall coherence of the system has suffered from incremental reform.

The president remains at the center of government and has significant powers. He is commander-in-chief of the armed forces, convenes the National Assembly, and appoints the premier (head of the Executive Yuan) as well as the grand justices and all members of the Examination and Control Yuans. He can issue decrees in certain policy areas. After

---

[12] The three principles are nationalism, democracy, and people's livelihood. Zhao Suisheng, *Power by Design: Constitution-Making in Nationalist China* (1996), describes the struggle between advocates of presidentialism and parliamentarism in the years leading up to the passage of the constitution and argues that Chiang's military power and eventual emergence as top leader was crucial to the decision to adopt a presidential model.

[13] The Control Yuan was originally an elected body conceived as the successor to the imperial Censorate and responsible for controlling the behavior of officials. It has the power to investigate and impeach high officials and to audit the budget. The Examination Yuan is a separate body responsible for the recruitment and selection of government officials by administering the national civil service examinations that were another legacy of China's imperial system.

constitutional amendments in 1997, the Legislative Yuan no longer needs to approve the president's appointee for the premiership.[14] Among other powers, the president exercises the authority to resolve interbranch disputes where there is no relevant constitutional provision.[15] This provision to resolve interbranch disputes gives the president a power that is often allocated to the judiciary in other systems and likely reflects Chiang Kai-shek's desire to place the presidency at the center of the governmental system. It would also appear to set the stage for jurisdictional disputes between the president and the grand justices over who has the authority to resolve particular interbranch disputes.

Temporary Provisions

For forty years, formal constitutional structure on Taiwan was emasculated by the actual exercise of political power, heavily concentrated in the presidency during the period of the "Temporary Provisions Effective During the Period of Communist Rebellion." These were adopted in 1948 at the first meeting of the First National Assembly in Nanjing and came into effect on May 10 of that year.

The Temporary Provisions revised the constitution to eliminate the need for Legislative Yuan approval of presidential powers to declare martial law and to govern by decree power during a natural calamity, epidemic, or economic crisis.[16] The Temporary Provisions also suspended

---

[14] Additional Articles of the Constitution of the Republic of China (July 21, 1997), Article 2. The 1997 revisions limited the range of decrees of the president requiring countersignature of the premier, strengthening the president relative to the other executive. The president also gained the power to dissolve the Legislative Yuan in the event of a no-confidence vote in the government. To balance this power, the Legislative Yuan was given the power to pass a motion of impeachment against the president, a motion then requiring a two-thirds vote in the National Assembly to pass. This counterweight is less significant than it might otherwise appear. The National Assembly is now elected on a proportional-representation basis according to the percentage of votes captured in the presidential election, so the president is guaranteed that his party will enjoy a plurality there. As long as he maintains the support of his party, the president need not be threatened by divided government. It is probable that the French experience of *cohabitation* was an important negative example for this institutional design. See issues of *National Policy Dynamic Analysis* No. 73 (November 16, 1993) and No. 85 (May 3, 1994).

[15] Constitution of the Republic of China (1947), Article 44. This provision has not been frequently used in ROC constitutional history.

[16] Articles 39 and 43 of the ROC Constitution. The Temporary Provisions did allow the Legislative Yuan to criticize emergency measures through the use of Article 57(2) procedures. Temporary Provisions, Provision 2. This procedure allows

the two-term limit on the presidency, allowing Chiang Kai-shek to rule until his death in 1975.[17] Martial law and strong presidential rule became the core features of the regime from 1949 through 1987. For example, Article 8 of the martial law decree suspended civilian judicial proceedings for certain categories of offenses. Under these procedures, some 10,000 cases involving civilians were heard by military courts during the one-party period, despite an explicit constitutional provision prohibiting the practice.[18]

The adoption of the Temporary Provisions was considered unconstitutional by democratic activists and opponents of the regime.[19] Other analysts seem to indicate that the Temporary Provisions were themselves constitutional.[20] The provisions stipulate that they are adopted in accordance with amendment procedures detailed in the constitution that require passage of a resolution for amendment by three-quarters of National Assembly members present at a meeting with a quorum of two-thirds of all elected members. However, the constitution nowhere provides for a "temporary" amendment that can be abrogated by the National Assembly. One might argue that to interpret the temporary amendments as constitutional requires a reading of their adoption that includes a further, implicit amendment to the constitution: namely, to provide for temporary amendments in the first place. The Grand Justices never interpreted the constitutionality of the provisions, so their constitutionality is only a matter of speculation.

---

the Legislative Yuan to request policy changes of the premier. The text of the Temporary Provisions is available as an appendix to Chiu Hungdah, "Constitutional Development and Reform in the Republic of China on Taiwan," 29 *Issues and Studies* 1 (1993), as reprinted in University of Maryland, Occasional Reprints Series, No. 115.

[17] Temporary Provisions, Provision 3. In addition, the Temporary Provisions provided for the continuing exercise of power by legislators elected on the mainland until elections could again be held there. The president was empowered to promulgate election regulations for central government offices without regard to ordinary constitutional restrictions as laid out in Articles 26, 64, and 91. Temporary Provisions, Provision 6.

[18] Tien Hung-mao, *The Great Transition: Political and Social Change in the Republic of China* 111 (1989). The prohibition is contained in Article 9 of the Constitution of the Republic of China.

[19] Records of the National Assembly I (*Guomin dahui shilu diyibian*), 219–21, trans. Shih Chih-yu, "The Style of Chinese Constitutional Development: China and Taiwan," 23 *Int'l J. Soc. L.* 371, 382 (1995). The rationale for adopting the Temporary Provisions was, ironically, the need to protect the constitutional order.

[20] F. Fraser Mendel, "Judicial Power and Illusion: The Republic of China's Council of Grand Justices and Constitutional Interpretation," 2 *Pac. Rim. L. & Pol'y J.* 157, 162 (1993).

In short, the authoritarian regime was constrained by the 1947 Constitution only to the extent that it felt it necessary to secure legal blessing for extraconstitutional actions. It would be a mistake to say that the regime was completely unconstrained; at the same time, the serious encroachments on individual liberties pose problems for those who would characterize the regime as constitutional in the substantive sense that liberal democrats ascribe to the word.

Centralized Judicial Review: The Dynamics of Design

As discussed in Chapters 1 and 2, the adoption of judicial review involves two distinct questions. First, should judicial review be included in the constitution or not? Second, if it is to be included, in what form? Judicial review could have been omitted from the 1947 Constitution – after all, there had been no strong tradition of judicial constraint on the rulers in Chinese political thought.[21]

However, several features of the legal and political environment supported the adoption of some form of judicial review. First, there was a long tradition of review of administrative procedures and actions dating back to imperial China. Although not used to constrain the sovereign, the Chinese tradition celebrated the use of law by the sovereign as an instrument to ensure that its agents acted in accordance with their orders. Second, provisions for constitutional control were included in various forms in the draft constitutions from 1913 to 1940. Third, China had dealt with a variety of countries, including Germany and the United States, that had traditions of judicial review. So the idea of judicial review was present on the menu of choices under consideration by the drafters.

Chapters 1 and 2 argued that political insurance plays a crucial role in the design of judicial review. In the Taiwan case, it is likely that the inclusion of judicial review was also, in part, a product of the ideology of modernization that underpinned the desire to rule through a constitution in the first place. The modern, western nations with whom China aspired to be compared all had constitutions and increasingly provided for judicial review in their text. In particular, postwar constitutional drafting efforts underway in Europe contemplated judicial review as a reaction to the perceived errors of parliamentary sovereignty that had allowed for fascist takeovers through constitutional means.

---

[21] Zhao, *supra* note 12, does not even mention judicial review in his excellent study of constitutional politics up until 1947.

If international factors contributed to the decision to adopt judicial review, the particular choice of the form of review ultimately included in the 1947 Constitution was rooted in the political dynamics of the day and the uncertainties of insurance. The National Political Consultation Conference brought together the feuding Nationalists and Communists in early 1946. Their effort was to find a formula for national unity in the wake of Japanese aggression. Neither side trusted the other, and earlier national unity governments had fallen apart. Indeed, the two parties were engaged in continued fighting among themselves as negotiations proceeded. The Nationalists saw themselves as the dominant party in the negotiations, as the Communists had a smaller military force. Nevertheless, even at the conference, the legitimacy of the nationalist government was fragile and prospective electoral outcomes were uncertain. The conference decided on a unified judicial system along the lines of the American model, headed by a set of grand justices.[22] This would have involved a single hierarchy of courts hearing civil, criminal, administrative, and constitutional matters. In effect, judicial review would have been distributed or decentralized through various levels of the court system. Two parties, uncertain about their own positions in any future government, called for a decentralized mechanism for judicial review, ensuring open access.

In the end, however, that choice was never implemented. Negotiations between the two parties broke down with the outbreak of full-fledged civil war. The constitutional assembly revised the constitution and separated the task of constitutional adjudication from the ordinary courts, entrusting it exclusively to the Council of Grand Justices of the Judicial Yuan. The reasons behind this decision are still unclear to scholars, but a number of broad political factors can be discerned.[23]

First, once it was decided to include the power of judicial review, the decision to concentrate it in a distinct set of grand justices appointed by the president is consistent with the tendency toward centralization of authority under the KMT. Second, once civil war broke out and intensified, there was little reason for the KMT to consider the preferences of the Communists in formulating the constitution. During the initial period of

---

[22] Fa, *supra* note 7, at 198, 199–200 (1991); Lawrence Shao-Liang Liu, "Judicial Review and Emerging Constitutionalism: The Uneasy Case of the Republic of China on Taiwan," 39 *Am. J. Comp. L.* 509 (1991).

[23] For example, one prominent observer believes that the rationale was that the ordinary courts, then as today, were severely backlogged and that they neither wanted nor were believed to be able to handle the additional work. Interview with law scholar, National Chengchi University, April 1, 1998.

the civil war, the KMT considered itself to be the dominant player, so that when the Communists left the scene, the rather sudden decision to centralize judicial review limited the power of the prospective opposition to pursue politics by other means in the courts. One reason centralized judicial review may be attractive to authoritarian rulers is that the small number of justices makes political control easier. By contrast, decentralized judicial review assumes an autonomous legal hierarchy that usually is bureaucratically organized. While there is some room for political controls over ordinary courts through the appointments and appeals processes, the possibility of a wayward lower-court judge declaring a law unconstitutional is much greater. The early history of the council illustrates how the KMT was correct in its calculations.

THE AUTHORITARIAN REGIME, CONSTITUTIONAL CHANGE, AND DEMOCRATIZATION

As the KMT regime retreated to Taiwan following the defeat on the mainland, it faced local resistance and suppressed it brutally in the infamous massacre known as the 2/28 Incident in 1947.[24] The KMT subsequently decreed martial law, and the regime repressed dissidents through the Taiwan Garrison Command, the Security Bureau, the police, and the military courts. Thousands of dissidents were jailed, anticommunism was promoted, and the regime transformed itself from the corrupt loose party it had been on the mainland into a disciplined, organized Leninist political party.

At the same time, the regime continued to promote an ideology of democracy and constitutionalism, based on Sun's philosophy. Repression was justified on the grounds of anticommunism and the objectively delicate international situation. But as long as individuals and groups did not advocate Taiwan independence or communism, an authoritarian pluralism prevailed with some space for free discussion in cultural and social realms.

An important factor in Taiwan's ultimate liberalization was continuing international pressure on the regime from the United States, as well as increasingly sophisticated and broad-based movement around the so-called *dangwai* (non-KMT) politicians. The critical role of foreign support

---

[24] The incident began with an island-wide uprising against the Nationalist government and culminated in a series of massacres by government troops. Chao and Myers, *supra* note 4, at 22.

for the regime and the particular configuration of U.S. policy placed real constraints on the performance of the government and ensured a formal commitment to constitutionalism that remained intact throughout the authoritarian period. This commitment was brought to the fore as pressure for democratization grew steadily while the economy boomed. Urbanization, education, and a broad middle class developed. Dissidents suffered continual and brutal repression, but had an outlet among the overseas community in the United States, where many spent time during the most repressive years.

After Chiang Kai-shek's death, his son Chiang Ching-kuo became president of the ROC and chairman of the KMT. The younger Chiang brought more Taiwanese to the fore of the party as a way of building up legitimacy, picking Taiwan-born Lee Teng-hui as his vice-president. Chiang was interested in reforming the system to advance the paradigmatic goal of reunification with the mainland. He decided the answer to the problem of reunification lay in deepening Taiwan's democracy, then transferring the experience to the areas under PRC control.[25] Just as KMT was a vanguard party, Taiwan would serve as a vanguard province for democratization of the mainland. At the KMT's Third Plenum in March 1986, Chiang announced these ideas in a speech that proposed to "initiate democratic constitutional government . . . return political power to the people; and make them entirely equal before the law."[26] This speech signaled the beginning of a long and steady reform period.[27] The dynamic of the period was one of continual demands by opposition politicians, followed by cooptation and liberalization by the mainstream faction of the KMT.

A few months after Chiang's speech, in September 1986, opposition leaders tested the sincerity of his words when they formed the Democratic Progressive Party (DPP) in violation of existing law. Chiang decided to tolerate the new party. The next year, martial law was lifted and the gradual dismantling of the authoritarian rule began in earnest. Liberalization accelerated under Lee after the death of Chiang in 1988. Lee placed constitutional restoration at the center of his program.[28] The process was by no means smooth, and Lee's mainstream KMT faction weathered numerous crises. It maneuvered between the democratic opponents of the regime

[25] Chao and Myers, *supra* note 4, at 112.

[26] *Lienhebao*, March 30, 1986, at 3, quoted in Chao and Myers, *supra* note 4, at 126.

[27] Some have argued that Chiang sought to liberalize as a way of undercutting rivals within the National Assembly and government.

[28] See inaugural address for eighth-term presidency, as quoted in Lee Teng-hui, National Day Message, July 10, 1994, at 3.

and the old guard of the party, especially the National Assembly members who had been frozen into office since their election on the mainland some forty years before.

A crucial point in the transition process came in 1990 when Lee, facing pressure from both sides, called the National Affairs Conference to bring together social elites for a discussion of the future directions of the country, with an emphasis on constitutional reform. In doing so, he consciously echoed the Political Consultation Conference that had preceded the 1947 Constitution, which had initially included communist and nonpartisan leaders.[29] The National Affairs Conference marked a crucial point in Taiwan's liberalization and the acceptance of a common set of rules for competition. All the main political forces came together to negotiate the political reform process and agreed to proceed with reforms under the 1947 Constitution, rather than replace it with a new document. This sense of constitutional boundary, that no major player would exit the constitutional order, combined with increasing political diffusion, presented the Council of Grand Justices with new opportunities to exercise power.

Key reforms that followed included the 1991 subjection of the president's emergency powers to the approval of the Legislative Yuan, the termination of the Temporary Provisions that same year, and the amendment of the constitution to allow for election of a new National Assembly. Subsequently, in 1994, the constitution was amended to provide for the direct election of the president and vice-president, a long-standing DPP demand. This led to the direct election of Lee Teng-hui in 1996, the first popularly elected chief executive in Chinese history, and subsequently led to the victory of DPP leader Chen Shui-bian in 2000, the first peaceful democratic transfer of power in Chinese history.[30]

Amid all the reforms of electoral institutions, the Council of Grand Justices has received relatively little attention from scholars of democratic transition.[31] Even today, there is a perception that courts are subject

---

[29] Shih, *supra* note 19, at 384. For more on the 1946 National Political Consultation Conference, see Zhao, *supra* note 12, at 146.

[30] See, generally, Chao and Myers, *supra* note 4, and Steven J. Hood, *The Kuomintang and the Democratization of Taiwan* (1997).

[31] See, for example, Chao and Myers, *supra* note 4; Gold, *supra* note 4; Hood, *supra* note 30; Cheng Tun-jen, "Democratizing the Quasi-Leninist Regime in Taiwan," 41 *World Politics* 471 (1987); *Political Change in Taiwan* (Cheng Tun-jen and S. Haggard, eds., 1992); Tien, *supra* note 18.

to special political influence.[32] However, a careful consideration of the council's decisions shows that it has played a quiet but important role in contributing to the environment of political liberalization and advancing reform in the interstices of political institutions. It has done so by carefully expanding its own power.

THE COUNCIL OF GRAND JUSTICES: STRUCTURE AND OPERATIONS

Formation

Under the 1947 Constitution, the council is composed of seventeen members who are appointed by the president with approval of the Control Yuan for renewable nine-year terms. Constitutional amendments in 1997 lowered the number of grand justices to fifteen, shortened the terms to eight years and made them nonrenewable, and provided for staggered appointments that coincide with the four-year presidential election cycle.[33] This little-discussed set of reforms will ensure that each incoming president can appoint roughly half the council.

Selection of nominees is the responsibility of a nomination committee led by the vice-president. The president chooses candidates from the list approved by this committee. Prospective justices then appear before a confirmation hearing in the National Assembly. According to participants, matters of substance have played little role in the confirmation hearings.[34] Rather, the Assembly members view the hearings as an opportunity to cultivate a sense of personal obligation on the part of the potential justices.

There are five alternative sets of requirements one can meet to be eligible for appointment to the council. One must have:

1. served for ten years on the Supreme Court in distinguished fashion;
2. served as a member of the Legislative Yuan for nine years;

---

[32] *See* Julian Baum, "Under My Thumb," *Far E. Econ. Rev.* 26 (Feb. 26, 1998) and "Confidence in Judges has Declined: Survey on Dissatisfaction with Politics, Courts," FBIS CHI 95-015 (October 1, 1994) (summarizing article by Chia Chih-yun, "How People View Major Issues," *Hsin Hsin Wen*).

[33] Additional Articles of the Constitution of the Republic of China, Article 5. The article also provides that the Judicial Yuan's draft budget may not be eliminated or reduced by the Executive Yuan in its submission of the budget to the Legislative Yuan.

[34] Interview with a former member of the National Assembly, March 31, 1998; Interview with Grand Justice, April 1, 1998.

TABLE 5.1 *Council of Grand Justices, 2001*

Name	Year of Appointment	Previous Career	Foreign Education
Liu Tieh-cheng	1985	Academic	United States
Wu Geng	1985	Academic	Austria
Wang Ho-hsiung	1994	Prosecutor	
Wang Tze-chien	1994	Academic	Germany
Lin Yung-mou	1994	Judge	
Vincent Wen-sheng Sze	1994	Academic	United States
Sun Sen-yun	1994	Judge	
Chen Chi-nan	1994	Judge	
Tseng Hua-sung	1994	Judge	
Tun Hsiang-fei	1994	Academic/ Government	
Yang Huey-ying	1994	Judge	
Tai Tung-hsiung	1995	Academic	Germany
Su Jyun-hsiung	1994	Academic/ Government	Germany
Hwang Yueh-chin	1999	Academic/ Government	Austria
Lai In-jaw	1999	Government	United States
Hsieh Tsay-chuan	1999	Judge	United States

3. taught for ten years at the university level and written in the field of law;
4. been a justice of the International Court of Justice or author of books on public or comparative law; or
5. a legal education and experience and renown in politics.[35]

Justices meeting any one of the above categories may not compose more than one-third of the total membership, meaning that in practice the council must draw from at least four different categories of persons to fill seventeen seats.[36] The council is thus provided with multiple bases of legitimacy, mostly but not exclusively having to do with law. Although the trend is toward university and judicial appointments (see Table 5.1), political factors continue to play some role in the appointment process, as evidenced in 1994 by the National Assembly's rejection of a candidate for

---

[35] Organic Law of the Judicial Yuan, Article 4.
[36] This will decline in 2003 to three categories, when the total membership of the council declines to 15 per the recent amendments to the Constitution. See *supra* note 33.

the Sixth Council who had loose DPP ties.[37] Table 5.1 shows the current council membership as of 2001.

Another illustration of the hybrid status of the council between politics and law is that the grand justices, unlike judges, have no life tenure. Although the constitution grants "judges" life tenure, the grand justices are not considered to fall into that category.[38] But like judges, the grand justices are constitutionally required to maintain distance from partisan politics and enjoy protection from political interference.[39]

Despite this provision, the appointment mechanism allows for strong and centralized political control over the council. Unlike many other new democracies, particularly in the postsocialist world, nominations are concentrated in a single body, the presidency. There is no dynamic of "mutually assured politicization" that exists to prevent overly political appointments when multiple bodies must appoint constitutional justices.[40] Until 1994, the National Assembly confirmation had been a rubber-stamp process. Furthermore, until the 1997 constitutional amendments modified this provision, grand justices could be reappointed to multiple terms. This meant that they had an incentive to act in accordance with the president's policies so long as they wished to continue serving. Where reappointment is impossible, as in Germany, constitutional court members may be more insulated from short-term political pressures. The 1997 amendments in Taiwan eliminating reappointments may insulate the justices somewhat and enhance the policy space for independent decision making.[41]

Geographic balance was always a factor in appointments to the council, with distribution of seats among persons from certain provinces of China.[42] As the KMT regime gradually became more "Taiwanized" under Chiang Ching-kuo, the number of Taiwan-born justices gradually rose, but was still disproportionately low. Only three members of

---

[37] It is of interest to note that the DPP did not support her in the National Assembly hearings either.

[38] Article 81. The 1997 constitutional amendments, which explicitly provide for a set term of office for the grand justices, ended arguments about whether the term limitations in the council law were constitutional.

[39] Constitution of the Republic of China, Article 80.

[40] See *supra* Chapter 2.

[41] Concern with reappointment is not the only career-related factor affecting judicial independence, however. Where justices are appointed for only a single term, potential retirement positions become important. In the ROC, there are few positions for grand justices to retire to, because the professorate is a career position.

[42] Fa, *supra* note 7, at 198, 205.

the Fifth Council (1985–94) were from Taiwan. In 1994, with the appointment of the Sixth Council by Lee Teng-hui, the situation changed dramatically. Eleven out of fifteen grand justices were then from Taiwan, a complete reversal from the previous council. This has had significant impact on the jurisprudence of the council, as discussed as follows.

Functions and Operations

The Council of Grand Justices has two functions: to unify the interpretation of statutes and regulations and to interpret the constitution. Only government agencies may request a unified interpretation from the council while both government agencies and citizens may ask for a constitutional interpretation. This reflects the different political functions of the two: unified interpretations serve the interest of the sovereign in a uniform legal system, but the orientation is toward the administrative efficiency of the sovereign rather than the need to provide clear, consistent rules so that private actors may plan their affairs. Private parties may benefit from the coherence of the legal system, but these benefits are neither essential nor particularly desirable from the perspective of the sovereign except insofar as they advance the probability of compliance with positive law. Constitutional interpretations, on the other hand, may be requested by individual litigants, as long as constitutional rights have been infringed and legal remedies exhausted.[43] There is no requirement that the constitutional issue arise from a concrete case, and government agencies can ask the council to perform abstract review if a constitutional question is raised before the agency.

Both standing and jurisdiction have been expanded in the period of democratization. 1993 amendments to the Procedure Law extended standing to any group of one-third of the members of the Legislative Yuan who may submit a question to the council about pending legislation or the constitutional provisions on their duties. This is likely to result in a great expansion of the council's political role as pending legislation is brought before the council by minority parties in the legislature. Another procedural revision in 1993 grants the Supreme and Administrative Courts the explicit power to set aside ongoing proceedings when confronted with an issue of constitutional interpretation of a statute or regulation.

[43] Law of Procedure, Article 5, paragraph 2.

Constitutional amendments in 1992 provided for the grand justices to sit as the Constitutional Court in the event that there is a challenge against "unconstitutional" political parties, defined as those whose "goals or activities jeopardize the existence of the ROC or a free democratic constitutional order."[44] The Constitutional Court now has the power to dissolve unconstitutional parties. This power was thinly targeted at the Democratic Progressive Party (DPP), particularly its proindependence factions that would eliminate the ROC and declare a new state of Taiwan. The constitutional amendments were seen as progressive in that they took the determination of unconstitutional political parties away from an Executive Yuan "Political Party Screening Committee," which had the previous January agreed to punish the DPP for its proindependence plank.[45]

A STRATEGIC ACTOR IN A DYNAMIC ENVIRONMENT: A HISTORY OF INTERACTIONS WITH THE POLITICAL BRANCHES

Introduction

The history of the grand justices reflects the tension all courts face in their dual roles as both instruments of the regime and independent policy actors. Through the appointment mechanism, the council has been under the direct influence of the central actors in the ROC political system, namely the four presidents who have served since 1947. During the long period of tight authoritarian control, the scope of the council for independent decisions suffered accordingly. Although it was somewhat active in the early 1950s, the council suffered from interference by the political branches, and its role became marginal for the second and third terms. During the first three terms, only once did the council find a law unconstitutional, and it was ignored by the authorities on that occasion. As liberalization proceeded from 1986–96, the council gradually became more

---

[44] The addition of this power reflects continuing German influence in Taiwan's constitutional law. Under the Basic Law, the German Constitutional Court also has the power to disband political parties that "seek to impair or abolish the free democratic basis order." Basic Law, Article 21. See Donald Kommers, *The Constitutional Jurisprudence of the Federal Republic of Germany* 13, 223–29 (1989).

[45] "Party Screening Committee Puts Off DPP Independence Case," *Central News Agency* (February 20, 1992). Political parties are now ordinary "civic organizations." The council's substantive view on these provisions was revealed in a recent decision allowing public meetings that advocate independence. See *infra* text at note 100–2.

TABLE 5.2 *Council Interpretations by Term*

Term	First (1948–57)	Second (1958–67)	Third (1967–76)	Fourth (1976–85)	Fifth (1985–94)	Sixth (1994–01)
Number Petitions to Council	658	355	446	1145	2784	1623
Unified Interpretations	54	35	22	21	18	1*
Constitutional Interpretations	25	8	2	32	149	166*
Total Interpretations Rendered	79	43	24	53	167	167*

* *Note:* Sixth Council statistics only include seven years of nine-year term, through 2001.
Sources: The grand justices and Constitutional Court of the Republic of China (Taipei: Judicial Yuan, 1995), 40–41; Su Yong-chin, "Summary of Interpretations by Council of Grand Justices" in *Fifty Years of the ROC Constitution (Zhonghua minguo xing hsien wu shi nien)* (Taipei: National Assembly, 1997), 273–80; statistical report available at *http://www.judicial.gov.tw/juds/ eG-1.HTM*; author's calculations.

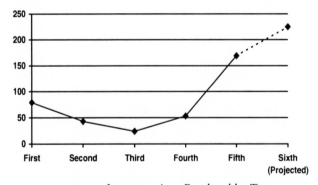

FIGURE 5.1. Interpretations Rendered by Term

active and daring. The council began to move toward high-equilibrium judicial review through a careful series of steps to expand its jurisdiction and enforcement capacity. This pattern of tentative initial steps, followed by a long dormant period and then a gradual rise in activism, is apparent from the statistical summaries in Table 5.2 of the number of petitions and interpretations rendered by the council by term. Figure 5.1 shows the drop in petitions after 1958 and the subsequent increase with the period of greater liberalization. The composition of the petitions by origin also reflects the transformation of the council from instrument of government rule to guardian of individual rights. During the first term, over 70% of petitions submitted for resolution came from government agencies as opposed to private individuals.[46] Many of these government petitions came from the Executive Yuan and asked the council to clarify the various responsibilities of government bodies or asked for unified interpretations of the law. They served the interest of the sovereign in coherent government, adjudicating boundary disputes between its components. By the fifth term, the council was playing a completely different function: Constitutional interpretations dominated its docket, and over 90% of petitions came from individuals. This reflected an expansion in public access engineered by the council itself, as well as the growing ability and willingness of the council to provide relief to citizens who challenge government action. Of those petitions still submitted by government agencies, the Legislative Yuan had replaced the Executive Yuan as the greater source of petitions.

The statistical record of the number of interpretations rendered, presented in Figure 5.1, has followed a similar pattern as that of petitions. The first term of the council rendered a relatively high number of interpretations, but following the "punishment" of the council by the authorities in the late 1950s, the number of petitions and interpretations decreased, only rising gradually after the death of Chiang Kai-shek in the fourth term. The pattern is also continuing with the sixth council, which released 167 interpretations in the first seven years of its nine-year term, a rate that will produce around 215 interpretations by the end of the term in 2003. If the council continues on its current pace, the sixth term will be the most active to date. This pattern suggests a quantitative shift between the fourth term and the sixth term, the period corresponding to rapid political liberalization. The council moved from rendering some fifty interpretations per term to a pace of over two hundred. The interpretations are qualitatively different as well. Of special importance to the present study are those constitutional interpretations that declare laws or administrative actions unconstitutional. Table 5.3 provides more detail on this subcategory of successful petitions for constitutional interpretation.

After the fourth term, the council became increasingly willing to overturn government action, legislation, and other judicial decisions. In the fifth term, the forty-one interpretations striking laws and administrative action overturned a total of ten legislative acts, eighteen decisions by

---

[46] The grand justices and Constitutional Court of the Republic of China (Taipei: Judicial Yuan, 1995), 42.

TABLE 5.3 *Interpretations Concerning Allegedly Unconstitutional Laws/Actions*

	First, Second, and Third Terms	Fourth	Fifth	Sixth
Number of Interpretations	4	29	135	167
Findings of Unconstitutionality	1	5	41	65
Percent Unconstitutional	25	17.2	30.6	38.9

Source: Su Yong-chin, "Summary of Interpretations by Council of Grand Justices," in *Fifty Years of the ROC Constitution* 276 (Taipei: National Assembly, 1997). Sixth term statistics are through 2001.

lower courts, and twenty-one administrative regulations and actions.[47] This diversity indicates the council's increasing independence from both government and legislature, as well as from the ordinary judiciary itself.

The council's growing independence is also shown by a dramatic rise in the number of concurring and dissenting opinions. Table 5.4 shows a significant rise in the number of opinions on the council, a sign of ideological diversity. During the first two terms, when the council was acting as an instrument of political authorities, most interpretations were unanimous. (The third term, where no interpretation was unanimous, is anomalous because of the very small number of decisions rendered.) Some dissent was apparent in individual cases, particularly in the fourth term. But ideological diversity appears to be greatest in the current sixth term, as shown by the low percentage of unanimous decisions. One remarkable feature of this data is the increasing frequency of concurrences beginning in the fifth term. I interpret the rise in concurrences as a sign of the growing *institutionalization* of the council, as well as an indicator of independence. Where a court is merely expressing the will of another political actor, there is little reason to come up with competing justifications for a majority opinion. Such courts are engaged in a kind of translation of political will into constitutional language, and diversity of opinions undermines the coherence of the sovereign command. But where a court is engaged in genuine deliberation and debate, with the capacity for articulating new principles and positions, the reasons behind a decision become extremely important. It therefore becomes rational for individual justices to use their opinions to articulate their constitutional views, both to convince their colleagues of the merits of their position and to plant the seeds of

---

[47] Su Yong-chin, "Summary of Interpretations by Council of Grand Justices," in *Fifty Years of the ROC Constitution* 277 (Taipei: National Assembly, 1997).

TABLE 5.4 *Diversity in Constitutional Interpretations*

Term	First (1948–57)	Second (1958–67)	Third (1967–76)	Fourth (1976–85)	Fifth (1985–94)	Sixth (1994–01)
Constitutional Interpretations	25	8	2	32	149	167*
Dissenting Opinions	0	2	4	25	58	103*
Concurring Opinions	0	0	0	0	10	44*
Percent Unanimous	100	75	0	44	58	48

* *Note:* Sixth Council statistics only include seven years of nine-year term through 2001. An individual interpretation may generate multiple opinions, so the sum of concurrences and dissents is greater than the total number of Interpretations with such opinions.

doctrines that may be developed in future opinions. Where the court is weak as an institution, such opinions make little sense.

The council has shifted from low-equilibrium judicial review to high equilibrium. It is deciding more cases of greater import. It is holding government action and legislation unconstitutional. It is generating public interest and confidence, shown in part by the rapid increase in public petitions in the sixth term. And it is increasingly independent, as indicated in part by growing internal diversity of opinions.

Such statistical data must be supported by qualitative examination of particular cases, because the significance of judicial review is not shown by the mere *number* of cases but also by their impact. The next sections trace in detail how the council has developed from being an instrument of the regime to an independent and active force, regularly able and willing to constrain the government.

Instrument

The early years of the KMT regime on Taiwan were characterized by a state of national emergency, leading to the passage of the Temporary Provisions and the declaration of martial law. The regime continued to hope for a return to the mainland, but military invasion of the PRC became less feasible as time went on. Committed to both a nominal constitutionalism and the preservation of the one-China paradigm, the regime soon faced a problem concerning elections. The National Assembly, Control Yuan, and Legislative Yuan (the "national representatives") were directly elected on the mainland in 1947. As it became apparent in the early 1950s that the KMT would be unable to retake the mainland in time for the next election, the regime was faced with a dilemma. It could sponsor elections in the areas under its control, namely Taiwan and the small island of Quemoy, limiting the electorate to those present there. However, this would have ensured the defeat of the KMT regime, which was perceived as a brutal occupying force by the majority of the Taiwan-born population in the wake of the 2/28 incident. The local electoral option was clearly out.

Another option would be to simply suspend the constitution entirely and cease holding elections. This was undesirable as well, for the KMT was formally committed to constitutional government of a sort. Furthermore, the constitution was so imbued with Sun Yat-sen's thought that it could not simply be overturned.[48] Heavily bankrolled by the United States government, Chiang's claim to legitimacy was based on distinguishing his regime from that of the communist PRC. The KMT's commitment to democracy and constitutionalism were essential elements of this case for distinguishing "Free China" from the PRC.

Just as the government chose to enact Temporary Provisions to preserve a kind of authoritarian constitutionalism, it needed to come up with a constitutional means of suspending elections. The grand justices provided a convenient solution to the problem. The Executive Yuan asked the council to give constitutional sanction to a suspension of elections, and the council obliged in Interpretation No. 31 of January 29, 1954. The council held unanimously that, so long as mainland electoral districts remained in the hands of the communist enemy, elections could be suspended until the territories were recovered. The decision referred to "unforeseen events" that had occurred, forcing the representatives to continue serving to save the constitutional system.

Why did a court decision appear an attractive option to the political authorities? In the narrow political sense, Chiang Kai-shek could be sure of a positive response from the council, for he had appointed all the justices and held indefinite power over their reappointment, because the Temporary Provisions had removed the two-term limit of the presidency. An authoritative pronouncement from the council provided a constitutionally

[48] Along with socialist constitutions in the PRC, the USSR, and Mongolia, the 1947 ROC Constitution was one of the few constitutions to explicitly name a person in the text. To overturn the 1947 Constitution would sever the charismatic tie with Sun that Chiang sought to maintain. In addition, the notion of political tutelage provided some ideological cover for the KMT, suspending elections through nominally constitutional mechanisms.

legitimate means of accomplishing the goal of suspending elections. The legal rationale provided by the council was consistent with the tutelage ideology and laid out specific conditions under which elections would be restored. The regime had secured an authoritative declaration providing it with indefinite legitimacy.

In molding the constitutional order to the needs of the government in the ongoing national emergency, the council was acting as a straightforward instrument of the KMT. The legitimacy of the council suffered accordingly. It is perhaps not surprising that the image of the justices as KMT partisans lingered four decades later.[49] The council did not need any overt threat to comply with Chiang's dictates. The council was part of the mainlander KMT mainstream and as such can hardly have been expected to oppose the interests of Chiang and the mainlander national representatives. From their perspective, holding national elections only on Taiwan would require jettisoning the 1947 Constitution, the product of decades of development of Chinese constitutional thought, along with all its component institutions, including the council. It would also mean the end of the one-China paradigm so essential to justify mainlander rule over an unwilling Taiwanese population.

Discipline and Punishment

Interpretation No. 31 shows the council as KMT instrumentality. Like it, the other early jurisprudence of the grand justices is primarily focused on government organization rather than individual rights, and few interpretations restrain the authority of government in any substantive way. Although the council frequently read the constitution broadly, rendering abstract interpretations and using theories of inherent powers,[50] only once did it declare legislation or administrative action unconstitutional in its first three terms.

As a strategy of judicial legitimation, a focus on separation-of-powers decisions is not risk free, of course. Indeed, to the extent that separation-of-powers issues involve the authoritative allocation of powers to one branch of government versus another, they are zero-sum decisions that can provoke backlash from the political institutions on the losing side. The decision lies within the tolerance zone of one institution and outside that of

---

[49] Mendel, *supra* note 20, at 168.
[50] See, for example, Interpretation No. 3, holding that the Control Yuan has the power to submit draft legislation to the Legislative Yuan despite no constitutional provision to that effect.

another. Indeed, after one early such case, the power of the grand justices was severely constrained.[51] The council was asked to determine which of the various constitutional bodies should be able to send delegates to an interparliamentary conference in Bangkok, with the National Assembly, the Legislative Yuan, and the Control Yuan all claiming to be "legislative" bodies able to attend. All three were elected bodies and had functions sometimes handled by parliamentary bodies in other countries. After the president neglected to mediate the dispute,[52] the question was submitted to the grand justices.

The grand justices were put into a difficult position. As a classic separation-of-powers case, the council was forced to make an either/or choice. There was no easy way to mediate the preferences of the actors. Furthermore, the council was vulnerable to retaliation through formal mechanisms by all three institutions. The National Assembly had the power of constitutional revision and could, at least theoretically, use it to revise the council out of existence. The appointments of the justices required the approval of the Control Yuan, which was also the body with the power to initiate investigations of any government official. Finally, the Legislative Yuan not only approved the annual budget for the Judicial Yuan, but also controlled the council's jurisdiction through ordinary legislation.

Faced with an intractable choice, the council did its best to find a mediate solution, holding that all three branches were equivalent to a parliament. The Legislative Yuan reacted by restricting the jurisdiction of the council through the passage of the Governing Law of the Council of Grand Justices (hereinafter "Council Law"), which remained in force until revisions in 1993.[53] The Council Law restricted the subjects of council interpretation to the "text of the constitution," curtailing the type of broad advisory decision that had just been rendered.[54]

The Council Law also raised the threshold for rendering a constitutional interpretation from that needed for a unified interpretation of

---

[51] Interpretation No. 76 of May 3, 1957.

[52] As he could have using his power under Article 44.

[53] See Martin Shapiro, *Courts: A Comparative and Political Analysis* (1981); Christopher Larkin, "Judicial Independence and Democratization: A Theoretical and Conceptual Analysis," 44 *Am. J. Comp. L.* 605 (1996) for more techniques politicians can use to control courts.

[54] Article 3 of Law Governing the Council of Grand Justices of the Judicial Yuan (promulgated July 21, 1958; available in Major Statutes of the ROC (1990)). Mendel, *supra* note 20, at 175 notes that this means the council could unify several conflicting laws but not interpret the resulting law.

ordinary law. Article 13, paragraph 2, provided that only a simple majority of grand justices present with a quorum of half the members could establish a unified interpretation. This meant that as few as five of seventeen total members could issue a unified interpretation. (There was an informal requirement that twelve justices be seated, which prevents this occurrence.[55]) Constitutional interpretation, on the other hand, was allowed under the Council Law only when approved by three-fourths of those present, with a quorum of three-fourths of the justices.[56] With seventeen total justices, thirteen constitute a quorum and ten are therefore required to carry a vote. Because no more than sixteen justices have been seated at any one time, this means that a minimum of nine justices would be required to interpret a law, if the quorum is met by twelve.

By deciding against the Legislative Yuan, the council had provoked a political response that was to significantly constrain its ability to render constitutional interpretations. This incident illustrates that the political dynamics of discipline and constraint surrounding court decisions operate in authoritarian periods as well as democratic ones. Even in the Leninist regime of the KMT, where all political bodies were controlled by a single, disciplined, hierarchically organized party, institutions had particular goals that conflicted with those of other institutions and sought to aggrandize their own power. The distinction between democratic and authoritarian regimes for constitutional courts is that certain strategies of legitimation are not open to courts under authoritarianism that might otherwise be available. Most obviously, in systems where popular participation is minimal, populist strategies will have little efficacy in shielding the court from political discipline. A rights-promoting strategy is likely to be perceived as violating core interests of the regime. Authoritarian constitutionalism emphasizes the structural aspects of channeling governmental power at the expense of individual rights. The strategies of legitimation open to courts, therefore, are limited to those involving alignment with powerful interest groups and institutions.

[55] Mendel, *supra* note 20, at 171.
[56] Article 13, paragraph 1 of Governing Law; Article 6, paragraph 1 of Organic Law of Judicial Yuan. This provision was modified by the substantial revision of the Governing Law in 1993. Governing Law Article 14 provides that two-thirds of justices present at a meeting with a two-thirds quorum of the full council can render a constitutional interpretation, but that only a majority vote at such a meeting is required to declare a regulation unconstitutional. A uniform interpretation of laws can be rendered by a majority of grand justices at a meeting with a quorum of half the total membership of the council. These procedures distinguish constitutional review of legislation from review of administrative regulations, making the latter easier to strike.

The extent to which an authoritarian regime uses constitutional courts as opposed to other modalities of authority depends partly on exogenous factors, such as the particular ideology of the regime and the relationship with external actors that value the appearance of constitutional constraint. For example, U.S. policy during the Cold War, with its heavy reliance on the distinction between authoritarianism and totalitarianism, was more amenable to those nondemocratic regimes that maintained some commitment to constitutionalism than those that did not. A regime such as that of the KMT, dependent on the American security umbrella, had a much greater incentive to use the courts to justify its rule than, say, the regime in Cuba.

Endogenous factors may also play a role in setting the level of constitutional review activity in an authoritarian setting. A court's willingness to submit to the political dictates of the regime and its skill in justifying regime interests are important factors in giving the authorities a reason to use constitutional law to advance its interests. Playing off the various actors in the complicated governance scheme of the ROC in separation-of-powers disputes provided the primary modus operandi for the council through the 1970s. From the council's perspective, these types of decisions expanded its institutional authority. From the regime's perspective, the council was playing a useful role in clarifying convoluted boundaries.

Despite this role in resolving intragovernmental disputes, the early decades of the council's history are notable for their relatively low level of activity. Following the passage of the Council Law in 1958, the grand justices became less active, rendering decisions of lesser significance and fewer of them. They were classic exemplars of what I have earlier characterized as low-equilibrium judicial review. In several sequences of interaction with the political authorities, the council failed to secure compliance or provoked punishment. Following this repeated pattern, the council became much more deferential.

A key incident in this regard was the council's only finding in its first three terms that a government action was unconstitutional. This case was an early effort to expand judicial control over court administration and was rebuffed by the failure of political authorities to comply. The case considered the question of whether or not judicial administration for lower courts should remain the responsibility of the Ministry of Justice under the Executive Yuan or should be transferred to the Judicial Yuan, which had responsibility for the Supreme Court. The council held in Interpretation No. 86 on August 15, 1960 that the lower courts should be placed under Judicial Yuan jurisdiction. The council, as a component of the Judicial Yuan, sought to expand judges' power over their own administration, often cited as a key element of judicial independence.[57] The government, however, resisted, and did not comply with the council's interpretation until July 1, 1980.[58]

Understanding how the council's level of judicial review moved from a low equilibrium to a high equilibrium requires a conception of the council as a strategic actor at least partly responsible for determining its own fate. The next three sections show how the council systematically extended its purview over three other branches of the government. The first section describes the council's relationship with the other top courts in the Judicial Yuan, the Supreme Court and the Administrative Court. The next section discusses the council's administrative law jurisprudence, through which it increasingly reviews and restrains the actions of the Executive Yuan. The seeds of administrative review were laid before 1986 but subsequently blossomed. The third section shows how the council has avoided the attempt of the Legislative Yuan to maintain exclusive control over its jurisdiction. Together, these three sections paint a picture of a body that has systematically expanded its jurisdiction to ensure the normative supremacy of the constitution and, of course, the council's role in interpreting it.

Building Jurisdiction I: Ordinary Court–Council Relations

A crucial and understudied issue in comparative constitutional studies is the relationship between ordinary and constitutional courts. Several possible political dynamics are apparent in relationships between ordinary and constitutional courts. In some circumstances, both bodies may compete for cases, seeking to maximize their own jurisdiction to expand their power. In other situations, however, the power-maximizing institution might seek to *avoid* certain categories of cases that are likely to provoke political backlash. In such circumstances, courts may play a game of jurisdictional hot potato, trying to characterize a category of disputes as being properly resolved by the other branch. A third possible dynamic is one of alliance, wherein two courts cooperate to promote a legal agenda vis-à-vis another court or political institution. Even this brief discussion suggests the variety of scenarios that might play out between two coordinate court systems.

---

[57] *Judicial Independence: The Contemporary Debate* (Shimon Shetreet and Jules Deschênes, eds., 1985).

[58] Mendel, *supra* note 20, at 172 n.123.

In Taiwan, the grand justices are not at the top of the judicial hierarchy, but a coordinate body with the Supreme Court and the Administrative Court within the Judicial Yuan. Under such circumstances, the relationship between constitutional interpretations and ordinary law is far from straightforward. By statutory omission in the Council Law, the Council of Grand Justices was not entitled to consider the constitutionality of ordinary court precedents.[59] Formally, when the council issued an interpretation it had neither *inter partes* or *erga omnes* effect. Rather, the council was interpreting the norm at issue as an abstract matter, not deciding its application in any particular case. Such interpretations had only prospective effect. When a law was challenged during ordinary adjudication and the council declared it void, the case might be remanded to the original court hearing the matter to apply the council's interpretation. Occasionally, however, a lower court refused to rehear the case. In such a situation, the original litigant had no remedy. These procedural arrangements acted as a substantial disincentive for individuals to bring cases to the council, for there was no guarantee of ultimate relief. This configuration provides an example of how the hybrid status of designated constitutional courts can interfere with the coherence of the legal system. By limiting remedies and discouraging constitutional claims, the Council Law supported low-equilibrium judicial review.[60]

In response to this state of affairs, the council unilaterally extended its purview to precedents of the Supreme and Administrative Courts in Interpretation No. 154, treating them as "laws and regulations" for purposes of the council's jurisdiction. In Taiwan, these courts can designate particular decisions as binding precedents. Unlike a common law system of *stare decisis*, this requires special action by the court. In one case, a petitioner argued that a Supreme Court precedent was unconstitutional because it denied him access to the courts. The grand justices' interpretation held that unless the Supreme Court specifically deemed otherwise in a special meeting, a precedent would be included in the "laws" over which Article 4 of the Council Law provided jurisdiction. The council did not, however, review the particular decision of the Supreme Court that had been challenged. Rather, it contented itself to asserting that it had the

---

[59] ROC law allows for certain, but not all, appellate opinions to count as precedent, in which case they are considered binding on lower courts. Opinions are designated as precedents by special meetings of the Supreme Court. Liu, *supra* note 10, at 16 n.60.

[60] Mendel recommends that the Legislative Yuan confer adjudicatory power on the council. Mendel, *supra* note 20, at 189.

power to do so, as Marshall did in *Marbury*.[61] This strategy ensured that there was thus no opportunity for noncompliance: The council created a new weapon but did not deploy it.

Then, in Interpretation No. 177 on November 5, 1982, the council announced the need for limited retroactivity of its decisions. It first decided an ordinary court precedent was partly unconstitutional and furthermore said that this finding would apply to the very case before it if the appellant applied to Supreme or Administrative Court for a retrial considering the new constitutional interpretation.[62] Before this interpretation, a private petitioner could not benefit from a successful challenge because the ruling would not apply in the instant case. The petitioner would have to move for retrial at the Supreme Court to gain relief. Interpretation No. 177 made the interpretations of the grand justices binding on retrial. This decision, and others expanding council jurisdiction over decisions of the Administrative and Supreme Courts, were crucial for encouraging individuals to use the court system and the council with greater frequency.[63]

A crucial decision in this line of cases was Interpretation No. 242, which was the first Supreme Court precedent to be declared unconstitutional.[64] The case concerned a man who had fled the mainland in 1949 and had left a wife behind. The man had subsequently remarried in 1960 on Taiwan and had a new family. He subsequently learned his first wife was alive. In 1986, while living in Hong Kong, she sued to nullify the later marriage as violating ROC Civil Code provisions against bigamy. The marriage was annulled by the trial court, which noted there was no statute of limitation for annulment of bigamous marriages. The case was eventually affirmed by the Supreme Court. The man and his second wife subsequently brought a petition to the council asking for a statutory limitation on the right to annul the marriage.

The council rejected this argument, but held that the law did not apply to bigamous relationships when the separation was caused by the "national tragedy" (of the separation of Taiwan from the mainland) and where there was no knowledge of survival or communication at the time of the later marriage. To apply the law in such instances would impair the

---

[61] 5 U.S. (1 Cranch) 137 (1803).

[62] *Fa, supra* note 7, at 207.

[63] Other early interpretations that consider the constitutionality of Supreme Court and Administrative Court precedents include Numbers 143, 148, 154, 177, 185, 187, 197, and 201.

[64] The case and its circumstances are discussed extensively in Nigel N. T. Li and Joyce C. Fan, "An Uncommon Case of Bigamy: An Uncommon Constitutional Interpretation," 4 *J. Chinese L.* 69 (1990).

social order of the nation and hurt the interest in family life established during the second marriage. Thus, according to the council, the man and his second wife were not included in the class of persons to whom the Civil Code provision was meant to apply.[65] The council used Article 22 of the constitution, guaranteeing "all freedoms not detrimental to the constitutional order or public welfare," to find that there was a constitutionally protected right to marriage and the family. This was the first time the court had used this open-ended language to create a new constitutional right. This decision allowed the man and his second wife to move for retrial at the Supreme Court, which duly vacated the annulment.

The political logic of this case illustrates several of the themes of this study. For constitutional courts concerned with expanding their institutional dominion, it is crucial to ensure that supreme court decisions as well as ordinary legislation are within the ambit of judicial review. Otherwise, a particular constitutional right may be abused simply because another court has previously heard the case. Furthermore, the style of the decision, using a broad interpretation of text to void the application of a law in a particular case but not the law itself, follows a certain political logic. The court can say to the legislature, your legislation is acceptable, but your commands do not apply in this case. We are not disobeying you; on the contrary, we are following your orders in the way consistent with your true intentions. This is essentially a framing tactic, avoiding a direct challenge to the legislators. It allows the legislature to believe the court is not challenging its will.

Procedurally, Interpretation No. 242 was important as the first exercise of the council's power to review and overturn a supreme court decision.[66]

---

[65] The dissents were of particular interest, one of which agreed with the majority for a distinct reason. Grand Justice Liu applied the least-means test. Thus, in his analysis the statute could have had a limit on the right to bring an annulment action as the petitioners argued, while still advancing the statutory purpose of the deterrence of bigamy. Li and Fan, *supra* note 64, at 72. By failing to advance the legislative goal in the manner least restrictive to citizen's freedoms, the law was unconstitutional. Such an approach is a frequent tactic of constitutional courts. David Beatty, *Constitutional Law in Theory and in Practice* (1995); Nigel T. Li, "The Less-Restrictive Means Principle – A 'More or Less Restrictive Methodology?" Paper presented at Conference on the Evolving U.S. Constitution 1787–1987, Taipei, 1988. Liu's balancing opinion also invoked the U.S. Constitution, claiming that the annulment would constitute a "cruel and unusual punishment" when the marriage had lasted nearly thirty years. Another dissent supported the Supreme Court's judgment. Li and Fan, *supra* note 64, at 73.

[66] Interpretation No. 154 had held that precedents were within the set of laws and regulations subject to council review. Indeed, the Law on Courts, as subsequently amended on December 22, 1989, allowed the Supreme Court itself to decide which

The council could have avoided this by declaring the statute unconstitutional, and indeed the offending provision has subsequently been removed from the Civil Code. Instead, concerned with both substantive justice *and* its own institutional environment, the council chose an approach that ensured the normative supremacy of its decisions over those of the ordinary judicial hierarchy.

After the revision of the Council Law in 1993, Interpretation No. 371 of the Sixth Council in January 1995 greatly expanded citizen access to judicial review by striking provisions that prevented lower-court judges from referring cases to the council.[67] Article 5 of the law said that the Supreme and Administrative Courts, at the top of their respective judicial hierarchies, may adjourn proceedings and refer constitutional questions to the grand justices. These provisions contemplated the lower court deciding the issue and the Supreme Court considering the issue on appeal, suspending the provisions at that point. The justices extended the adjournment provisions to all lower courts and voided those provisions incompatible with their interpretation. Besides empowering lower courts, this interpretation expands citizen access by providing more opportunities for council rulings earlier in the legal process.

This interpretation may prove to be the most important of all interpretations related to structural position of the council. By providing for immediate and direct certification to the constitutional court, the decision empowers lower courts, relative to the top bodies of their judicial hierarchy. Because Taiwan's judicial system, like that of Japan,[68] relies heavily on the promotion of judges through a hierarchy as a means of political control, the extension of constitutional reference power to every judge in Taiwan radically decentralizes the source of referrals to the council and will likely create a new important source of cases for the council to hear. The dynamic is similar to that used by the European Court of Justice (ECJ) under Article 177 (now replaced with Article 234) in extending its power.[69] European national courts, including lower courts, could halt

---

legal judgments would be precedents through a resolution of a supreme court symposium.

[67] Article 5, Section 3.

[68] See J. Mark Ramseyer and Eric B. Rasmussen, "Judicial Independence in a Civil Law Regime: The Evidence from Japan," 13 *J. L., Econ. & Org.* 259 (1997).

[69] Treaty on European Union and the Treaty Establishing the European Community, 37 I.L.M. 56, 125–26 (January 1998). See also Alec Stone and James Caporaso, *From Free Trade to Supranational Polity: The European Court and Integration,* Working Paper (Berkeley: Center for German and European Studies, 1996) and *The European Court*

proceedings to refer questions of European law to the ECJ. This provided lower courts with a vast and expanding new set of legal norms to apply. This amounted to a new set of ammunition to reach decisions that might otherwise be unavailable to them. Previously, conflicting national law would be enforced on appeal by higher courts. So the provision allowing them to use European law had the dual effect of enhancing lower courts' power relative to that of higher courts at the national level, as well as expanding the normative reach of European law as quasi-constitutional law.

Interpretation No. 371 suggests a similar dynamic that may lead to a vast expansion of lower-court referrals to the council. Lower courts can now "constitutionalize" issues when they are unhappy with the precedents of their respective judicial hierarchies. This expands their power relative to the Supreme and Administrative Courts, while at the same time allows the Constitutional Court to undercut the jurisdictional autonomy of those branches. Finally, it suggests that a steady stream of new cases may be brought to the council, essential for the continued exercise of constitutional power.

The decision is also significant because it definitively declares that the council, not the Legislative Yuan, is the ultimate determiner of its own jurisdiction. The rhetoric of the decision shows the increasing power of the international dimensions of the rule of law, as the justices invoked the constitutional review systems in Japan, the United States, and Germany, which they characterized as "modern countries observing the rule of law."[70] The decision also shows the particular importance of Germany as a reference point for Taiwan law. German constitutional procedure has a similar device for so-called concrete norm control through certification of questions from ongoing proceedings.[71] Constitutional law scholarship on Taiwan retains heavy German influence, and this is reflected in the composition of the council: Of nine current grand justices

---

and National Courts, Doctrine and Jurisprudence: Legal Change in Its Social Context (Anne-Marie Slaughter, Joseph Weiler, and Alec Stone Sweet, eds., 1998).

[70] Sean Cooney, "A Community Changes: Taiwan's Council of Grand Justices and Liberal Democratic Reform," in *Law, Capitalism and Power in Asia* (Kanishka Jayasuriya, ed., 1999). The grand justices argued that it is an important function of judicial review to safeguard the constitution and to protect "judges' independent exercise of powers so that they observe only constitution and legislation and are subject to no other interference." Sean Cooney, "Taiwan's Emerging Liberal Democracy and the New Constitutional Review," in *Asian Laws Through Australian Eyes* 173 (Veronica Taylor, ed., 1997).

[71] Donald Kommers, *The Constitutional Jurisprudence of the Federal Republic of Germany* 14–15 (2d ed., 1997).

who have obtained foreign degrees, five have German or Austrian degrees, while four have American degrees.

Building Jurisdiction II: The Uses of Administrative Law

Judicial review of administrative action is sometimes easier to effectuate politically than striking down legislation for unconstitutionality. When a court strikes a piece of legislation, it is challenging the legislature in a very public fashion. It is telling the lawmaker that it is mistaken and that the particular action is unacceptable despite the fact that the majority of legislators have approved it. When striking administrative action, on the other hand, the court is challenging a particular agency with limited democratic pedigree. It can credibly say that it is working on behalf of the sovereign to protect its commands from the subtle subversion by its appointed agents.

Consider also the alternative mechanisms available to different bodies to discipline the council. When it wants to attack a court institutionally, the legislature may respond in one of the various ways discussed in Chapter 3, including passing legislative limitations on court jurisdiction, financial punishment, and many other tools. The executive branch is in a different position. Only certain ministries have direct means of retaliating against courts. The Ministry of Justice, for example, may have some administrative responsibility for judicial administration; the Ministry of Interior may have access to means of physical coercion. But other ministries may have no means of collateral attack. Unless the target of a negative constitutional decision has some such direct instrument of counterattack, it will require political allies in the legislature to impact the court. Other things being equal, this implies that decisions holding administrative actions unconstitutional are easier to "make stick" than those striking legislation. (This does not, of course, mean that such decisions are automatically more efficacious. Executive agencies have multiple techniques of avoiding compliance with judicial pronouncements, including delay, subterfuge, and outright disobedience.)

It is no surprise that administrative law cases were the first substantive terrain in which the council challenged governmental authority. The framework for doing so was set in the early years of the council, in Interpretation No. 38, where the council asserted that it had by implication the power to review regulations for constitutionality, as well as conformity with statutes.[72] This power was developed further in Interpretation No. 137, where the council announced that it has the power to review the interpretations of regulations by executive agencies.[73] The supremacy of judicial power over the executive branch was confirmed in Interpretation No. 216, where the council held that the Ministry of Justice's opinions on constitutionality of laws and regulations were not binding on judges.

Some of the administrative law cases also had the effect of expanding jurisdiction and standing, encouraging the creation of new classes of litigants. For example, Interpretation No. 187, issued on May 18, 1984, overturned a long-held principle of administrative law (drawn from prewar German law) that civil servants had no standing to sue the government. In 1986, Interpretation No. 201 struck down a similar Administrative Court ruling that civil servants could not appeal internal administrative hearings. The council indicated that even when administrative hearings were not required, to hold them without the possibility of judicial appeal was not constitutional.

As liberalization proceeded, the council then began to examine areas typically regulated by the Executive Yuan, following the same incremental strategy that had served it in other cases. One line of cases has concerned agencies acting under extremely loose statutory authority, usually adopted during the period when the Legislative Yuan was a one-party body. Interpretation No. 394, for example, deals with the rules made by the Ministry of the Interior under a statute requiring that "regulations for the administration of the construction industry shall be made by the Ministry of Interior."[74] Under this extremely broad delegation, the Ministry of the Interior had issued rules providing that certain technicians would be subject to administrative reprimand if unable to carry out their responsibilities "as a result of leaving the country or another reason." This was one of several restrictions on freedom of movement used by the regime during the one-party period, but this particular restriction was promulgated by the ministry without clear guidance or instruction from the legislature. The council held that Article 23 of the Constitution, which mandates that rights may only be restricted by law, required that the legislature itself

---

[72] Chiu Hungdah and Fa Jyh-pin, "Taiwan's Legal System and Legal Profession," in *Taiwan Trade and Investment Law* 21, 25 (Mitchell Silk, ed., 1994).

[73] *Ibid.* at 25. Although technically the subject of review was not the regulation but its interpretation, the justices exercised the power as reviewing the statute itself.

[74] Building Law 1938, Article 15; trans. Cooney, in Jayasuriya, ed., *Law, Capitalism and Power in Asia, supra* note 70.

provide clear and specific authorization and guidance to administrative agencies.[75] The provision in question was impermissibly vague. Similar interpretations requiring firmer delegation from the legislature were made for a wide range of other areas of regulatory policy.[76]

Building Jurisdiction III: Avoiding the Council Law Restrictions

The earlier discussions of the council's extension of its jurisdiction over Supreme and Administrative Court decisions and administrative regulations showed that the council acted consistently with our view of it as a strategic institutional actor. The council took an incremental approach, first asserting that it had a power but without exercising it. This allowed other actors in the system a chance to respond and perhaps made the decision to strike a precedent or regulation seem more natural when it finally occurred.

The council utilized a similar gradual approach to expand its jurisdiction in response to Council Law Article 3, the provision limiting the subjects of constitutional interpretation to those actually appearing in the constitution. The council did so with a *Marbury*-like interpretation that appeared to support the Legislative Yuan, but in fact acted to expand the council's jurisdiction beyond what the legislature had mandated. The issue concerned whether or not the Legislative Yuan had the power to create speech immunity for local city council members, so that they could deliberate issues in public without threat of defamation or libel lawsuits. The constitution guarantees freedom of speech but makes no mention of speech immunity, so this case concerned a subject not explicitly regulated by the constitution. In accordance with Article 3 of the Council Law, the council should not have been able to rule on the case, yet it did so in Interpretation No. 165, holding that the Legislative Yuan could create a qualified speech immunity without offending the constitution. It thereby extended its jurisdiction beyond the Council Law in a way that was favorable to the Legislative Yuan.[77]

Once it had begun to erode the edges of Article 3 of the Council Law with Interpretation No. 165, the council continued to push the

---

[75] Constitution of the Republic of China, Article 23; trans. Cooney, *ibid.*

[76] See, for example, Interpretations Nos. 313 (civil aviation), 384 (university curriculum), and 390 (factory inspections).

[77] Mendel, *supra* note 20, at 182.

boundaries in a delicate manner. In Interpretation No. 175,[78] the council found implicit in the constitution that the Judicial Yuan could sponsor legislation in the Legislative Yuan. The constitution holds that the Legislative, Executive, and Examination Yuans can sponsor legislation in certain fields.[79] In an early interpretation, Interpretation No. 3,[80] the grand justices had held that the Control Yuan also had power to propose bills in areas related to its competence. In 1982, the Control Yuan brought a petition to clarify its own ability to sponsor legislation, but the council worded the interpretation so that every yuan could sponsor legislation relevant to its own specific subfield. This had the effect of giving the Judicial Yuan, for the first time, the power to sponsor legislation related to judicial organization, a key element of judicial independence. This provides an example of the "alliance" dynamic between the council and the administrative sections of the Judicial Yuan.

Enforcement: Deadlines for Compliance

As the council expanded its power over various subjects and appellate review power, it turned to the question of enforcement of its judgments. Conscious of early attempts by political branches to ignore interpretations, the council began stipulating that unconstitutional government or legislative action had to be remedied within a particular period of time or the provision in question would be void. This approach has become almost routine for the council since democratization.[81]

As in so many other doctrinal areas related to its power, the council moved gradually. In Interpretation No. 188 (August 1987), the council said that interpretations come into effect on the date of issuance unless otherwise specified. This approach implies that if the Legislative Yuan or governmental actor does not act the law will become null and void. In some cases, however, the council provides a specific date.[82]

---

[78] May 25, 1982.
[79] See Articles 63–72 (Legislative Yuan), 57 (Executive Yuan), and 87 (Examination Yuan).
[80] May 21, 1952.
[81] Yeh Jiunn-rong, "An Analysis of Council of Grand Justices Interpretations Imposing Compliance Deadlines," 6:1 *Proceedings of the National Science Council*, R.O.C. 1–23 (January 1996). See also Yeh Jiunn-Rong, "Changing Forces of Constitutional and Regulatory Reform in Taiwan," 4 *J. Chinese L.* 83 (1990).
[82] For example, in Interpretation No. 218, rendered in August 1987, the council declared that an administrative interpretation of the Ministry of Finance would not be applicable after six months. Similarly, Interpretation No. 224 on April 22, 1988

One such decision involving time limits was Interpretation No. 365, concerning Article 1089 of the Civil Code, pertaining to the guardianship of children. According to the provision, a father's decision concerning guardianship of children took priority over the mother's. This was held to violate the constitution's guarantee of equal treatment without regard to gender.[83] The council ordered that the provision be amended within two years or it would be invalid. This led the Legislative Yuan to reconsider the entirety of the family law provisions in the Civil Code, with substantial participation by women's groups. In this case, the council interpretation supported the demands of an interest group seeking alternative avenues to advance a political goal.

The shift in strategy by the council from issuing demands for compliance, in its early years, toward open-ended provisions allowing for "prompt" enforcement was a sign that the council recognized its strategic constraints. Similarly, the recent and gradual move toward demanding compliance from other political branches is a sign that norms of compliance are taking root. Indeed, as of 1998 no government body had failed to comply with any order from the council, issued after democratization commenced in 1987, to amend legislation or administrative regulations.

THE COUNCIL AND DEMOCRATIZATION

We have so far demonstrated how the council steadily and incrementally expanded its ability to review the constitutionality of supreme court judgments, administrative regulations, and legislative provisions, including those related to the council's own jurisdiction. The council thereby established the normative superiority of the constitution over all provisions of ordinary law. We have not yet examined in depth the substantive ends toward which the council used its power. The council has played an important if understated role in Taiwan's democratization, most prominently through Interpretation No. 261 in 1990. This key decision is discussed in the next section.

---

gave two years for the Legislative Yuan to void certain provisions of the Law on Tax Collection.

[83] Article 7 of the constitution guarantees equality before the law irrespective of gender. See also Cooney, *supra* note 70, at 178.

Interpretation No. 261 and the Return of Taiwan

The council played a relatively passive role in the intense politics of the early democratization period from 1987 to 1990. It was far from clear during this period whether Lee Teng-hui's "reform" faction of the KMT would be successful in its challenge to the conservatives in the National Assembly. There were numerous crises and potential setbacks as the Taiwan-born Lee, who lacked an independent power base in the party at the time of his appointment, struggled against established mainlander factions.

The key source of resistance was the mainlander-dominated KMT group in the National Assembly. The representatives elected on the mainland in 1947 still held office some forty-three years later, thanks to the council's early Interpretation No. 31, which allowed the "old thieves" to remain in power. But the continuing presence of these old members proved increasingly anachronistic as they aged. While it would theoretically be possible for the old thieves to continue to serve until they all died, this would do little to renew the legitimacy of the KMT as a Taiwan-based party. The party needed to find a way to encourage the National Assembly members to retire. The KMT began in 1987 to devise a plan to secure their retirement, including a law to compensate the old representatives passed in early 1990.[84] Nevertheless, it was far from clear the old thieves would retire peacefully. Furthermore, because the Assembly was the body solely responsible for constitutional amendment, it had an effective veto over efforts to abolish it, as well as to undertake other institutional reforms desired by the reformers. The old thieves were the central obstacle to continued liberalization.

Interpretation No. 261, announced on June 21, 1990, overturned Interpretation No. 31 and forced the retirement of the old thieves. This was undoubtedly the most important case in the history of the council and removed the last legal barrier to rapid institutional reform in the ROC.[85]

Because the decision overturned an earlier council case, the rhetoric of Interpretation No. 261 was conditioned by that of Interpretation No. 31. That case had referred to "unforeseen events" that had occurred, forcing

---

[84] Chao and Myers, *supra* note 4, at 154.

[85] My assertion that this was the most important case was corroborated by interviews with law professors, grand justices, judges, and lawyers in Taipei in 1998. In interviews with these members of the legal profession, I asked the respondents for their opinion of the most important case in ROC constitutional history. Each respondent answered without any solicitation that Interpretation No. 261 was the most important.

the representatives to continue serving to save the constitutional system. Had new elections been limited to the "free" areas in 1954, there would not have been enough representatives to fill the National Assembly. Therefore, the old thieves had to keep serving until the second term could be elected. Interpretation No. 261 recalled this account of the initial decision as preserving the "paradigm," but it also noted that regular reelection is needed to reflect the people's will. The conflict was thus framed as being between a formalist constitutionalism adopted in the early 1950s against the needs of the "democratic constitutional system" to respond to newer developments.

The grand justices then turned to textual sources. They noted that none of the legal sources used to justify the extended terms, including Temporary Provision 6, Constitution Article 28(2), and Interpretation No. 31 itself, contains any explicit provision for *indefinite* rule by those elected on the mainland or any prohibition against a new election. Therefore, a decision to reinstate elections would not itself be unconstitutional. In this manner, the council shifted the rhetorical burden of proof onto those who opposed new elections. The interpretation went on to provide for the immediate discharge of those representatives unable to exercise their duties and provided a deadline for the retirement of the others. It then called for a new election in accordance with the "spirit of the constitution."[86]

Interpretation No. 261 thus represented a pragmatic reinterpretation of the one-China paradigm to allow its continued viability. Whereas the structure of the constitution had mandated the extension of the first terms in the early 1950s, the impossibility of recapturing the mainland while the old thieves remained alive made the continued postponement of new elections anachronistic. Furthermore, the "spirit" of democratic constitutionalism suffered. Thus, the constitution required radical reinterpretation in the light of new circumstances, in order to bring the system in line with the people's will.

There is no doubt the decision marked a significant turning point, providing an authoritative pronouncement of the continued democratization of the ROC. The old thieves, whose claim to their seats rested on the legitimacy of the 1947 Constitution, could no longer rely on that document to justify their position. Without the authoritative pronouncement of the grand justices, the democratization process would have remained at a standstill, with the possible consequence that Lee Teng-hui would never

---

[86] The single dissent, by mainland-born Grand Justice Lee Tze-pong, challenged the deadline.

have cultivated his strong position within the KMT, and reform would be delayed indefinitely.

The question of judicial *power* in the decision, however, is outstanding. For it is not obvious on the face of the decision that the grand justices' power was the key factor in facilitating the shift in their stance toward the old thieves. Any evaluation of judicial power should consider three components: the *significance* of judicial decisions, *compliance* with the decisions by losing parties, and *independent input* by a court into the decision. Interpretation No. 261 was undoubtedly a significant decision, and one that secured unchallenged compliance from the affected parties, for the old thieves all retired within the deadline imposed by the council.

The key analytic issue, then, concerns the *independent input* of the council into the case. This decision could not have occurred without the consent of the ruling party and in particular the victory of the reform faction over the older faction within the KMT. The compromise with the old thieves included substantial cash payoffs approved by the legislature. The decision appears to have been part of a several-pronged strategy to ease the old thieves out of power. Indeed, the leading account of democratization during this period asserts that the ruling was under preparation by a KMT committee as early as 1987.[87] This point could not be independently verified, and it seems rather unlikely that the actual text of the interpretation was drafted by the party. However, it is equally apparent that the council would not have taken such a huge step without support from the KMT. Despite some scholars' assertion that the decision provided evidence for increased judicial independence of KMT interests,[88] it is more plausible that the decision reflected the dominance of one faction of the KMT over another. Furthermore, the institutional incentives of the council weighed heavily in favor of the proreform decision, because the lead protagonist in the reform faction was President Lee, who held reappointment power over the council.

The justices appeared to be the voice of democratic renewal, but in doing so they were also siding with the ascendant political authority in the person of Lee Teng-hui. Together, the council and Lee's reform faction worked against the old vision of the KMT by promoting, in many areas, the revitalization of political life on Taiwan. Unlike the series of cases where the council worked to expand its freedom of maneuver, it is

[87] Chao and Myers, *supra* note 4, at 154.
[88] See June Teufel Dreyer, "Testimony Before Asian Affairs Subcommittee, U.S. House of Representatives, Hearings on Taiwan," 1–2 (September 24, 1991).

difficult to untangle the council's substantive preferences from those of the political forces it supported. Although an important decision, Interpretation No. 261 is only an ambiguous illustration of judicial power. It is a key step, however, in the development of high-equilibrium judicial review.

Reclaiming Political Space a Step at a Time

In less prominent areas, the council has been much more active since 1990 in dismantling the tools of authoritarianism and expressing the new values of Taiwan's leadership. The gradual nature of the democratic transition left much old legislation and many administrative regulations intact from the authoritarian period. By striking these one at a time, the council has become the instrument of the new Taiwan. In a gradual transition led by a dominant party, a natural strategy of constitutional courts is to strike the detailed rules that contradict the substantive requirements of democratic constitutionalism. Courts in this way speak for the present against the past.

The council's role in this regard has some parallels with that of the Italian Constitutional Court after World War II. As Mary Volcansek has shown, the Italian court played a crucial role in redemocratizing Italy by striking fascist legislation that remained on the books.[89] By reclaiming, step by step, space for democracy, the Italian court allowed gradual institutional adjustment to the new configurations of power and played a key role in democratization.

The grand justices have played a similar role in Taiwan. This is especially apparent with regard to the Sixth Council's Interpretations concerning the police and military. Several cases have arisen since 1990 where the council held that police action violated criminal procedure rights guaranteed in Article 8 of the constitution. These have been particularly controversial decisions because of the rising crime rate in the ROC that has accompanied liberalization. For example, in Interpretation No. 384 the council struck five articles of the "Antihooligan Law" of 1985. These articles had allowed police to administratively detain without a judicial warrant any persons designated as "hooligan."[90] No judicial appeal of one's "hooligan" status was allowed, and there were special

[89] See, for example, Mary Volcansek, "Political Power and Judicial Review in Italy," 26 *Comp. Pol. Stud.* 492, 498, 504 (1994).
[90] Lawrence Chu, "Legislators Pass Amendments to Hooligan Control Act," *Central News Agency*, December 30, 1996; Cooney, *supra* note 70.

procedures used by police to interrogate and punish such people. These rules were held to violate various provisions of Article 8 even though they were technically administrative rather than criminal in nature. In response, the Legislative Yuan passed new antigang legislation, one day before the deadline imposed by the grand justices. The new law, however, also came under council scrutiny because, even though the power to detain alleged hooligans had been transferred to judicial authorities, it allowed two months of investigative detention without adequate guidelines. In 2001, the council again struck the law and gave the legislature a year to reform it.[91]

Another criminal procedure case relying on Article 8, Interpretation No. 392, concerned the power of prosecutors to authorize detention of civilians without judicial warrants. The prosecutors argued that they had quasi-judicial status and served as a "court" for purposes of the required hearing within twenty-four hours of detention. The council, however, disagreed and insisted that a court means a judicial body and does not include prosecutors. This decision led to a complete revision of the Code of Criminal Procedure.[92]

In December 1997, the council interpreted the conscription restriction in Article 8 of the Military Service Law. Under this provision, men were banned from leaving the country until they completed required military service. The council held that this restriction violated the constitution's guarantee of freedom of movement and emigration.[93] Both the Ministries of Defense and Interior announced they would comply.[94] In another 1997 case, the grand justices held that military trials were subject to appeal before ordinary courts. Given the history of military trial in Taiwan, this subjection of military trial to ordinary courts was a step of great symbolic significance.[95] Then in March 1998, the council held that universities no longer could be required to allow military counselors (*chiao-kuan*) on campuses.[96] These military figures, who numbered about 5,000 and were

---

[91] Interpretation No. 523, March 2001.

[92] Cooney, *supra* note 70.

[93] Constitution of the Republic of China, Article 10.

[94] Deborah Kuo, "Grand Justices Say Conscription Restriction Unconstitutional," *China News Agency*, December 26, 1997, available at http://ww10.sinanet.com/news/1226news/20_E.html.

[95] See *United States Department of State, Taiwan Report on Human Rights Practices* (1993).

[96] Interpretation No. 450 (March 27, 1998). The challenged provision was Article 11 of the Universities Law.

placed in every college dormitory on the island, had been justified as providing order and training to Taiwan's youth, but were also widely viewed as an instrument of political control.[97] The compulsory character of the system was held to violate the constitutional right to freedom of expression in teaching.[98] According to the council, universities should be given the right to choose whether to invite the counselors. This interpretation followed many years of student activism protesting the system. It thus appears that the council, if not leading the society, was giving voice to another demand of Taiwan activists against the military-KMT structure.

As a Leninist regime, the KMT placed special emphasis on the university system, and the council's freedom of education decisions have sought to dismantle the mechanisms of authoritarian control. For example, Article 22 of the University Law Implementation Provisions, issued by the Education Department, allowed the department to mandate required subjects, including certain ideological courses in Sun Yat-sen's thought. In Interpretation No. 380, the council held these provisions unconstitutional as an unreasonable delegation.[99] The legislature, it said, had not authorized or guided the department as to the types of courses that could be required, with the consequence that too much discretion lay with the administrative authorities.

In January 1998, a council interpretation ended the ban on rallies advocating secessionism or communism as a violation of free speech, saying that "effective immediately, police cannot disapprove applications for public rallies advocating secessionism and communism."[100] The council thus demanded that the authorities act in a content-neutral manner when considering censorship, without regard to the particular viewpoint of a potential speaker.[101] The interpretation also, however, reveals something about the current council's substantive views about the advocacy of independence. The continuing illegality of "civic organizations" that advocate independence[102] means that a proindependence political party can

---

[97] Alan Searl, "Legislature Debates Need for Soldiers on College Campuses," *China Times*, April 4, 1998, at 2.

[98] Constitution of the Republic of China, Article 11.

[99] Cooney, *supra* note 70.

[100] *Japan Times*, January 25, 1998.

[101] Indeed, one academic advocate before the court had used precisely this argument. Interview, Fa Jyh-pin, March 31, 1998. The council was sympathetic to the American approach using a permit system with content-neutral time, place, and manner restrictions.

[102] Sean Cooney, "Why Taiwan Is Not Hong Kong: A Review of the PRC's 'One Country Two Systems' Model for Reunification with Taiwan," 6 *Pac. Rim. L. & Pol'y J.* 497, 518 n.123 (1997).

theoretically be banned by the council sitting as the constitutional court. However, given the Taiwanese origin of the majority of council members and this recent decision, it appears that the DPP has little to fear from the constitutional court in this regard.

Labor law has also been an active area for the council. The KMT's "authoritarian corporatism" had included a quasi-state labor organization, the Chinese Federation of Labor (CFL), which was the only legal islandwide labor union. In 1994, twelve unions from state-owned enterprises sought to leave the CFL and form a new union and after being rejected by the authorities went to the Council of Grand Justices.[103] The next year, the council released Interpretation No. 373, allowing teachers to form unions and voiding provisions of the Labor Union Law to the contrary. The constitution protected the right to form unions, according to the grand justices. German and Japanese constitutional law played an important role in the reasoning of a concurring minority.[104]

In all of these areas, the council has not directly challenged the old paradigm, but has systematically removed many of the barriers to discussing and challenging it. The fact that these decisions mainly came after the appointment of the overwhelmingly Taiwan-born Sixth Council suggests that their goal is not merely a matter of reviving the 1947 Constitution adopted on the mainland. Rather, the council appears to be dismantling the systems of mainlander control and developing a new constitutional scheme through case-law, by using broad concepts of a constitutional "spirit" and the practice of other modern democratic nations. In a subtle way, the council is articulating a vision of what the new Taiwan will be about, predicting the direction the society is heading in and hence securing compliance with its decisions.

Political Questions: Challenging the Emperor?

Courts in new democracies are often confronted with cases that they choose not to answer. In many systems, this is facilitated by the development of a "political questions" doctrine,[105] asserting that there are certain questions that courts are institutionally incapable of answering and hence are advisable to leave to the political process to resolve. The

---

[103] *United States Department of State, Taiwan Report on Human Rights Practices* (1996).
[104] Sean Cooney, "The New Taiwan and Its Old Labour Law: Authoritarian Legislation in a Democratised Society," 18 *Comp. Lab. L. J.* 1, 52, 58 (1996).
[105] *Baker v. Carr*, 369 U.S. 186 (1962).

council has leaned toward such a doctrine at some points. For example, in Interpretation No. 328 the grand justices were asked to rule on Article 4 of the constitution, which states that only the National Assembly may change territorial boundaries. This strikes at the heart of the one-China paradigm, but the council ruled it was a political question better resolved through other processes.[106]

The Sixth Council, when confronted with another highly political issue, avoided finding a political question in Interpretation No. 419. The case concerned Lee Teng-hui's vice-president, Lien Chan, who was simultaneously serving as premier. Lien (later the presidential candidate of the KMT) had been premier before the December 1995 election of the second Legislative Yuan and was Lee Teng-hui's running mate in the upcoming presidential elections, the first in ROC history. Lee promised that Lien would serve as premier only through the presidential election, but after winning the election sought to retain Lien as premier. Faced with a potential confirmation battle in the Legislative Yuan, Lee declined to submit the nomination of Lien to the Legislative Yuan. In doing so, he argued that while the Legislative Yuan was entitled to approve an appointment to the premiership, this requirement did not extend to a retention appointment. This sequence of events, however, violated a norm that cabinets resign upon presidential inauguration, so as to give the incoming president an opportunity to nominate his own candidate. Although earlier council interpretations had discussed this norm, its constitutional status was unclear.

The DPP, along with the right-wing New Party, challenged Lien's dual role as unconstitutional, and the Legislative Yuan sent a resolution to the president asking him to nominate a new premier. The legislature then submitted a petition to the grand justices asking them to declare that Lien could not concurrently serve as premier while vice-president.[107] This resolution was supported by all three major parties in the legislature, who sought to throw the political controversy to the courts. Opposing the resolution were the Executive Yuan and the president. The justices considered abdicating the issue by declaring it to be a political question, but instead ruled on the merits in an unusually long and ambiguous decision. There was nothing in the constitution, they held, preventing the vice-president from serving as premier.[108] Furthermore,

---

[106] Cooney, *supra* note 70, at 174.
[107] See Osman Tseng, "Legislature Grants No Honeymoon to President," *Business Taiwan*, June 24, 1996.
[108] Cooney, *supra* note 70, discusses the arguments presented by both sides.

the practice of the premier resigning at the outset of a new presidential term was merely a courtesy and not a constitutional requirement.[109] The resolution of disputes over this norm was not the responsibility of the grand justices, but instead a part of the president's "governing power."[110]

Nevertheless, the majority held that the simultaneous appointment was not in complete conformity with the *intent* of the constitutional document. The constitution clearly implies that the president and premier cannot be the same person, because the former appoints the latter and the latter can in certain circumstances act for the former.[111] The vice-president can succeed to the presidency, and in that event the simultaneous appointment of the vice-president as premier would become unconstitutional. Thus, said the council, it would not be advisable for Lee Teng-hui to retain Lien Chan as both vice-president and premier.

The council did not hold against the president in this case, leading to criticism that the council remained a tool of the mainstream faction of the KMT. On the other hand, the extraordinarily long interpretation was so ambiguous that both the DPP and the Executive Yuan claimed that the ruling supported their position in the immediate aftermath of the decision. The interpretation is notable in the manner it deferred to the president. Although Lien's simultaneous appointment was not found to violate the constitution explicitly, the council invoked the spirit of the constitution in its attempt to convince the president to nominate a new premier. And although the grand justices did not set a deadline, it is noteworthy that within nine months Lien Chan had resigned as premier, after passage of the 1997 constitutional amendments. The direct cause of his resignation was political conflict over the continued high crime rate, as well as the completion of the amendments with the spirit of bipartisanship that they had relied on.[112]

---

[109] The Executive Yuan argued that twice previously, 1958–63 and 1966–72, the vice-president had served simultaneously as premier. In both cases, this involved resignation and reappointment.

[110] See text at note 15, *supra.*

[111] Constitution of the Republic of China, Article 55 (appointment) and Article 51 (premier's temporary acting for president).

[112] Cheng Tun-jen and Lao Yi-shing, "Taiwan in 1997: An Embattled Government in Search of New Opportunities," 38 *Asian Survey* 53, 54 (1998). Indeed, by eliminating the Legislative Yuan's right to approve the premier, the amendments responded to the problem underlying the Lien Chan dispute.

Leading or Following? The Council and Political Reform

A large debate in American constitutional scholarship concerns the capacity of courts to bring about social change.[113] Comparative scholarship can help to address this question by examining environments undergoing rapid social and political change and identifying the precise role of courts in supporting or leading these changes. The history of the grand justices described previously suggests that for the most part the council followed political forces during the initial period of democratization, giving constitutional sanction to those who have emerged on top in intraparty battles. Figure 5.2 presents major reforms since 1986 in both politics and constitutional law.

Figure 5.2 shows that the council only began to engage in tentative activism after Chiang Ching-kuo's tolerance of the formation of the DPP, the first major test of liberalization. This tolerance provided a signal to the council that it might be able to play a more independent role without provoking political punishment. The council responded initially by declaring a regulation unconstitutional, but it still remained quite cautious. Indeed, through the fifth term, the major achievements of the council appear to have been the line of cases incrementally expanding its own power.

Even the great decision forcing the retirement of the first-term national representatives appears to be an instance where the council articulated a consensus that had already developed within the ruling party. This is demonstrated by the fact that it followed extensive attempts to convince the "old thieves" to retire voluntarily, including legislation in February 1989. Only when many had retired voluntarily and the KMT was firmly decided on the issue did the council give constitutional blessing to a decision taken elsewhere.

Only after the appointment of the Sixth Council in 1994 did the council really take control of its own agenda. Since then, it has struck down various barriers to participation and constrained the instruments of the military and party-state. It has served as an important force in the Taiwanization of the constitution, broadening its normative basis to include comparative law and general principles beyond those written in the text in Nanjing in 1946. Indeed, holding up the ROC system to the rhetorical standard of international practice may be the most important

[113] Two key protagonists in this debate are Gerald N. Rosenberg, *The Hollow Hope* (1991), and Michael McCann, *Rights at Work: Pay Equity Reform and the Politics of Legal Mobilization* (1994).

Date	Politics	Grand Justices
May 1986	Chiang Ching-kuo gives speech announcing reform	
Sept. 1986	DPP formed in violation of law; KMT acquiesces	
Oct. 1986		First administrative action declared unconstitutional
July 15, 1987	Martial law lifted	
Jan. 1988	Press and assembly restrictions lifted	
Jan.–Feb. 1989	Revision of law on civic organization allowing new political parties to register; passage of statute on voluntary retirement of "old thieves"	Interpretation No. 242 completes council's efforts to ensure normative supremacy of constitution over ordinary court judgments and strikes a provision of the Civil Code
June 1990		Interpretation No. 261 forces retirement of "old thieves"
Apr. 1991	First stage of constitutional reforms provides for election of second-term national representatives	
May 1991	Termination of temporary provisions; passage of new national security laws	
June 1991	New statutes for police authority to punish misdemeanor, complying with eleven-year-old interpretation of grand justices	
Dec. 1991	Popular election of second National Assembly	
July 1994	Third-stage constitutional reform provides for direct election of president and vice-president	
Oct. 1994		Sixth Council appointed; begins long line of cases dismantling authoritarian structures
Jan. 1996	Lee Teng-hui becomes first directly elected president	
Dec. 1996	National Development Conference	Interpretation No. 419 allows Lien Chan to remain premier
July 1997	Fourth-stage constitutional reform revises political system	Amendments to constitution make appointments nonrenewable after 2003
Aug. 1997	Lien Chan resigns premiership	
Mar. 2000	Chen Shui-bien wins presidential election	
Mar. 2001		Council challenges Chen on nuclear power

FIGURE 5.2. Role of Grand Justices in Political Reform, 1986–2001

contribution the council has made in a country denied a "normal" national identity. In this case, the international rhetoric of the rule of law highlights the distinction between democratic governance on Taiwan and the one-party state on the Chinese mainland.

The historic victory by long-time oppositionist Chen Shui-bian in the 2000 presidential election marked a watershed in Taiwan's politics and the first interparty democratic change in power in Chinese history. Chen's

DPP party, however, did not control the legislature, creating institutional tensions and divided government. These tensions came to a head in a controversy over the government's October 2000 decision to halt construction of Taiwan's fourth nuclear power plant. Chen's party had long opposed nuclear power and with the plant one-third completed announced that construction would be halted on the $5.5 billion plant. The proplant KMT, whose government had initiated the project, was outraged and sought to recall Chen. A serious constitutional crisis loomed.

Faced with an attack from the legislature, the executive sought to defuse the crisis by filing a request for interpretation to the council to the effect that its decision was constitutional. The new situation of divided government, however, gave the council expanded policy space to work in. In a carefully worded interpretation, the council held on January 15, 2001 that the government's decision violated procedural requirements and that the government should have consulted with the legislature before making the decision. It required the government to report to the legislature on the issue and urged the parties to reach a political compromise.

Intense disagreements ensued over the interpretation, with both the DPP and KMT claiming the decision was consistent with their position. The legislature sought to use the decision to embarrass the government. For his part, the president kept quiet, praising the grand justices for mediating between hostile interests. Even though his policy preferences were antinuclear, Chen had no ability to challenge the decision with the threat of recall hanging over him in the situation of divided government. Within a month, the government agreed to resume the project, leading to severe internal disagreement within the DPP and ultimately costing the government billions of dollars in compensation for the work stoppage.

This incident represents a new stage in Taiwan's constitutional politics. The new president and government were constrained from implementing a major campaign promise, with the council playing a crucial role in mediating between the legislature and executive. And by embarrassing the DPP, the council ultimately served the interests of the party that had lost the presidential election, the KMT. The party that had itself governed Taiwan for five decades now was the beneficiary of the political insurance of judicial review.

At the same time, the council prevented a more severe attack on the president in the form of a recall. It transformed a political dispute into a constitutional one, ensuring that neither party exited the constitutional order and that the council would continue to occupy a central place in resolving political conflict. Its carefully worded decision capped a long period of careful strategic action to expand its own power and ensure Taiwan's democracy continued to function as smoothly as possible.

CONCLUSION: THE JUDICIALIZATION OF POLITICS UNDER GRADUAL CONSTITUTIONAL REFORM

The dynamics of the emergence of constitutional review power in Taiwan illustrate the political constraints around the exercise of judicial review in a gradual democratic transition. In the early period of the ROC on Taiwan, the council was somewhat active as an instrument of governmental control, illustrated by the predominance of petitions from the government. Though an agent, the council naturally sought to exercise some independence vis-à-vis its KMT principals. However, the Legislative Yuan was easily able to sanction the court when unhappy with a decision. Subsequent attempts by the council to constrain political power were ignored. Consequently, the council entered a two-decade period of low-equilibrium judicial review. Few cases were decided, of little import.

As liberalization began after the death of Chiang Kai-shek, the court began to assert more and more autonomy. It did not, however, begin to challenge political power until after Chiang Ching-kuo's 1986 speech that marked the beginning of the period of democratization. From that time on, the dominant disciplined party began to transform into a factional entity that sought to control political reform while making continuous concessions to a democratic opposition. The KMT's discipline declined dramatically with democratization. Two new parties split off on the right, and by the end of 2001 the KMT had lost the presidency to the DPP. However, the DPP did not have effective control of the legislature. All this allowed the council more political space in which to work, especially after 1994.

The council has moved into a high equilibrium of judicial review, breathing life into the ROC Constitution. It now regularly challenges administrative action and legislation and has in the process constrained both major political parties and both the executive and legislature. The council has used this power to advance a vision of democratic constitutionalism drawn from "modern countries observing the rule of law." It has in a step-by-step fashion struck many administrative regulations and laws that had been tools of the authoritarian state, particularly using antidelegation arguments to require greater legislative oversight of administrative agencies. None of this would have been possible had the council not laid the groundwork before 1986 with an incremental expansion of its power within the authoritarian constitutional scheme.

6

Distorting Democracy? The Constitutional Court of Mongolia

INTRODUCTION

In contrast with Taiwan's gradual transition, Mongolia presents a useful context for examining the position of a constitutional court created after a clear "constitutional moment." Since 1990, Mongolia's democratization process has been unparalleled in socialist Asia and is as muscular as any postcommunist society in Europe.[1] Several free and fair elections have been held, a new constitution with extensive human rights provisions ratified, and the formerly Leninist Mongolian People's Revolutionary Party (MPRP) has alternated turns in power with younger democratic parties. By any definition of the slippery concept of democratic consolidation, Mongolia has achieved it.[2]

---

[1] See annual discussions by various authors in the January and February issues of *Asian Survey 1990–2000*; *Far East Economic Review Yearbook 1991–2000*; Tom Ginsburg, "Between Russia and China: Political Reform in Mongolia," 35 *Asian Survey* 459 (1995); and Tom Ginsburg and G. Ganzorig, "Constitutionalism and Human Rights in Mongolia," in *Mongolia in Transition* (Ole Bruun and Ole Odgaard, eds., 1996).

[2] See Tom Ginsburg, "Deepening Democracy: Mongolia in 1997," 38 *Asian Survey* 64 (1998). Linz and Stepan define a consolidated democracy as one where "sufficient agreement has been reached about political procedures to produce an elected government, when a government comes to power that is the direct result of a free and popular vote, when this government *de facto* has the authority to generate new policies, and when the executive, legislative, and judicial power generated by the new democracy does not have to share power with other bodies *de jure*." Juan Linz and Alfred Stepan, *Problems of Democratic Transition and Consolidation* 4 (1996). Other possible indicators of consolidation include the likelihood of a reversal of the basic institutions of democracy and evidence of peaceful handovers of political power between political parties (as occurred in Mongolia in 1996). Timothy J. Power and Mark J. Gasiorowski, "Institutional Design and Democratic Consolidation in the

The new constitutional court, called the *Tsets*, initially played an important role in this process, constraining legislative majorities and building up a body of constitutional law in a society where socialist traditions of parliamentary sovereignty had previously held sway. As democratic institutions developed, however, the court was increasingly criticized for making overly political decisions. Ultimately, the court provoked a constitutional crisis and found itself increasingly politicized from outside.

Much of the controversy surrounding the court can be traced back to a single decision in 1996 that thrust the court into the center of heated political battle. This was the decision on the structure of government, issued immediately following the historic electoral victory of the National Democrat–Social Democrat coalition. That electoral victory had ended seventy-two years of continuous rule by the Mongolian People's Revolutionary Party (MPRP), the former communist party that had tried to steer post-1990 reforms. The euphoria of the new parties was shattered when the court ruled that Members of Parliament (MPs) could not accept cabinet posts, forcing the separation of parliamentary and governmental power. With all the major leaders of the young parties having just won election to the parliament, the decision forced profound changes in the politics of the new ruling coalition, in the structure of parliament, and in the electoral system, all of which will be discussed in more detail later in this chapter. In 2000, the court overturned constitutional amendments designed to clarify the system, leading to further attacks on the court's credibility. Only in mid-2001 was the conflict ultimately resolved, with the court acquiescing to changes in the political system.

These events occurred in an environment in which human rights were well-protected, especially compared with Mongolia's immediate neighbors, Russia and China, but also compared with any of the newly independent states in central Asia.[3] A focus on the global spread of rights-consciousness, while it might partially explain the overall protection of rights in Mongolia, does little to elucidate the history of the court and its conflicts with political forces.

The insurance theory and the strategic framework elaborated in the first part of this book provides a better set of tools to understand the

---

Third World," 30 *Comp. Pol. Stud.* 123 (1997). One might also seek to measure substantive liberalization, such as the extent of civil liberties, media freedom, and civilian control over the military. See the annual surveys in *Freedom House, Freedom in the World.* Mongolia scores well on any of these indicators.

[3] See U.S. Department of State, *Human Rights Reports 1992–2000.*

Mongolian court. The institutional design of the court reflected the needs of the MPRP, which maintained a good deal of legitimacy at the time of democratic reforms. This institutional design almost guaranteed conflicts with the parliament. But it was the particular strategic choices by the court that ultimately hurt its credibility and led to political deadlock for a number of years.

This chapter describes the Constitutional Court of Mongolia and its early case-law, focusing particularly on the role of the court in elaborating, and possibly distorting, the separation-of-powers scheme of the 1992 Constitution. The chapter begins with background on Mongolia's constitutional history and recent democratization, then describes the institutional structure of the Mongolian court. Next, it elaborates the key cases in the court's brief history and documents the important role of the court in both rights cases and separation-of-powers disputes. Finally, it tries to embed the Mongolian case in the broader theory of judicial power developed in earlier chapters.

THE *ANCIEN REGIME* AND MONGOLIA'S DEMOCRATIC TRANSFORMATION

Legal Tradition and Political History

Mongolia has a long legal history and her customary law has been characterized by one scholar as the "second great system of law in Eastern Asia."[4] The Great *Yassa* promulgated by Chinggis Khan codified many of these customary principles, and some were subsequently incorporated into the imperial Chinese legal system during the Yuan dynasty.[5] In the seventeenth century, the Mongols were conquered by the Manchus and regained independence only after the fall of the Ching dynasty in 1911.

During some periods of Mongol history, there was a differentiation between judging and administrative authority, but for the most part the two functions were merged in a manner typical of traditional societies. There was thus at least some vague precedent for the autonomy of judging, but three centuries of administration under the Ching dynasty reinforced the imperial Chinese pattern wherein judicial and administrative power

---

[4] V. A. Riasonovsky, *Fundamental Principles of Mongol Law* 5 (1937). See also William E. Butler, *The Mongolian Legal System* 3–18 (1982); V. A. Riasonovsky, *Customary Laws of the Mongol Tribes* (1929).

[5] See, generally, Paul H. C. Chen, *Chinese Legal Tradition under the Mongols* (1979).

were combined in a single set of officials.[6] Furthermore, the legal system contained no notion of a separation between criminal and civil law nor a tradition of rights along the lines of that found in modern liberal ideology.

Mongolia became formally independent in 1911. After a period of political turmoil and competition among various factions, a group of leaders established effective control with the help of the Red Army in 1921. Closely allied with the Soviet Union from that point on, legal and political development in the Mongolian People's Republic closely paralleled that of the Soviet Union, including a period of bloody purges in the 1930s and 1940s. The 1940 Mongolian Constitution was closely modeled on Stalin's 1936 Constitution, and constitutional amendments in 1944, 1949, 1953, and 1959 tracked similar processes in the USSR.[7] In 1960, the dictator Y. Tsedenbal (later known as Mongolia's Brezhnev) initiated the promulgation of a new constitution that gave explicit attention to the "special relationship" with the Soviet Union. The preamble mentions Lenin and the "Great October Socialist Revolution" as well.[8] Mongolia enjoyed the typical form of a "paper" constitution, elaborating an extensive set of nonenforceable rights and providing for a state structure dominated by a vanguard Leninist party.[9] In keeping with notions of parliamentary sovereignty, constitutional interpretation was to be handled exclusively by the Parliament itself.

As Sino-Soviet tensions deepened in the 1960s, Mongolia's utility as a buffer state increased and the Soviets began a massive influx of development funds. This led to extensive social changes, including rapid urbanization, expansion of higher education, and the creation of whole new classes with a stake in the modernization of Mongolian society. Many Mongolians went to the USSR for study, and legal education became more important. An identifiable legal profession emerged, composed of government, lawyers, advocates (defense counsel), procurators, and judges.[10] But the orientation of the entire profession was heavily biased toward the

[6] Martin Shapiro, *Courts: A Comparative and Political Analysis* 20–21 (1981). Note that Manchu rule in so-called Outer Mongolia was more indirect than in China, and local princes continued to wield significant power. Charles R. Bawden, *A Modern History of Mongolia* (2d ed., 1989); Owen Lattimore, *Studies in Frontier History* (1962).
[7] See Robert Worden and Andrea Marles, *Mongolia: A Country Study* (2d ed., 1991); Owen Lattimore, *Nationalism and Revolution in Mongolia* (1955).
[8] Preamble of the Constitution of the Mongolian People's Republic (1960). The text can be found in Robert Rupen, *Mongols of the Twentieth Century* 413 (1964).
[9] See also Giovanni Sartori, *Comparative Constitutional Engineering: An Inquiry into Structures, Incentives and Outcomes* (2d ed., 1996).
[10] Butler, *supra* note 4.

state. Because there was neither private property nor market relationships, there was no need for a private legal profession. "Telephone justice" was common, and politics determined the outcome of any case where it mattered. The notion of an autonomous legal profession led by autonomous judges was simply absent.

Democratic Transition: 1989–1992

Following the dominolike fall of communist regimes in Eastern Europe in 1989, reformers in Ulaanbaatar formed a group called the Mongolian Democratic Union in Ulaanbaatar in December and began to call for the regime to stand down. More groups were formed in the next three months, and the new opposition launched demonstrations and a hunger strike on the main square of Ulaanbaatar.[11] The MPRP was divided over how to respond to the demonstrations. At its Nineteenth Party Congress in March 1990, the party debated whether to respond with force, as had its Chinese counterpart in Tiananmen Square in June 1989, or to launch reforms, as had the regimes in Eastern Europe the previous fall.

The reform group within the party won the day, and the entire cabinet and MPRP Central Committee resigned. Two months later, the parliament announced that it would hold multiparty elections. It amended the constitution to legalize opposition parties, to delete the reference to the MPRP's "leading role" in society, and to create new political institutions: a bicameral Parliament and the new posts of presidency and vice-presidency.

The first multiparty parliamentary elections in Mongolia's history were held in July 1990 and created a new bicameral parliament.[12] As in the socialist era, each house of parliament was called a *Hural*, the traditional name of government assemblies back to the time of Chinggis Khan. The Great Hural was a national assembly elected by districts, as in the nominal elections of the communist period. It was responsible for deciding major affairs of state, appointing the prime minister and the government, and amending the constitution. With an established network in the countryside and significant financial and organizational advantages over opposition parties that had been legalized only months before, the MPRP dominated the elections for the Great Hural. The second house, the Small

---

[11] For more detail on this period, see William Heaton, "Mongolia in 1990," 31 *Asian Survey* 1 (1991); Ts. Batbayar, *Collected Essays* (1997).

[12] Worden and Marles, *supra* note 7, at xxxvi–xxxvii. See also Heaton, *supra* note 11.

Hural, was a standing legislative elected by proportional representation, responsible for passing ordinary legislation in between the sessions of the Great Hural. Opposition parties obtained 40% of the seats in the Small Hural.[13]

The MPRP's strategy of adjustment to new political circumstances appeared to be effective. By calling quick elections, the MPRP ensured it would control the Great Hural and thereby the constitutional reforms. The party agreed to form a national unity government with the opposition parties, and four cabinet posts went to the opposition.[14] P. Ochirbat, the MPRP leader who had presided over the election, was named president and head of state. The Great Hural also appointed a twenty-member multiparty Constitutional Drafting Commission, chaired by President Ochirbat with former minister of justice and leading lawyer B. Chimid serving as secretary.[15] The commission proceeded to examine the constitutions of over one hundred different nations and formed a number of subcommittees to deal with particular substantive problems, such as human rights provisions, state structure, and the judiciary.

Subsequent political and economic reforms were broad-ranging and rapid. The government established a commission to examine the purges of the 1930s and to rehabilitate victims of political trials during that period. It disbanded the secret police and liberalized the media. A privatization program was launched. There was a renaissance of interest in traditional Mongolian culture, repressed under Soviet influence during the one-party period. Chinggis Khan, criticized by the Soviets as a symbol of feudalism, again became a national hero, and the government revived the traditional Mongolian script. The MPRP attempted to distance itself from the years of bloody repression, blaming them on the personal excesses of the dictators Choibalsan and Tsedenbal rather than on the party itself.

The speed and coherence of the reforms reflected in part the legacy of the Soviet period. Unlike the new republics of central Asia, Mongolia's status as an independent and fairly homogeneous country provided her with a strong sense of nationhood. The Soviet alliance was seen as the lesser of two evils, providing a security guarantor against a China perceived to

---

[13] The opposition parties were the National Progress Party (three seats), the Social Democratic Party (three seats), and the Democratic Party (seventeen seats). Two other parties were listed on the ballot, but they failed to obtain the 2% of the vote needed to gain a seat in the Small Hural.

[14] Heaton, *supra* note 11.

[15] Alan J. K. Sanders, "Mongolia's New Constitution," 32 *Asian Survey* 511 (1992).

hold lingering territorial claims to Mongolia. This left the MPRP with much more legitimacy than the discredited communist parties found in some other postsocialist environments.

With the Soviet umbrella gone, the only perceived course for the Mongolian leadership was to reach out as rapidly as possible to western powers, who were seen as providing a "third force" to balance the interests of the giant neighbors in Mongolia.[16] Rapid and real institutional reform was seen as enhancing western interest in Mongolia and thus contributing to security. International factors thus shaped the domestic choice set for reformers and led to a consensus on the basic directions, if not always on the pace, of reform.

Setting the Institutional Framework: The 1992 Constitution

By January 1991, just a few months after the Constitutional Drafting Commission had been formed, four separate drafts of a new constitution were in circulation. By May, these had been consolidated into a single draft, and in June a revised draft was published in the parliament's newspaper, *Ardyn Erkh (People's Right)*.[17] Comments were solicited from the public and channeled back to the commission through local government bodies. The draft was also submitted to a number of foreign experts and was the basis of an international conference held in September 1991 under the leadership of S. Zorig of the Democratic Party.[18] Following this, the draft was revised by the Small Hural and then forwarded to the plenary session of the Great Hural for ratification in November 1991.

The Great Hural had not convened in full membership since it appointed the government shortly after the summer 1990 election. Its members were eager to play a role in the constitutional process and deliberated on the draft for seventy-six days (probably the longest legislative session in the seventy-year history of the Great Hural), forcing many changes. Some of the issues subject to debate were symbolic ones, such as the official name of the country and the insignia on the flag. However, debate also centered on such crucial questions as the structure of government and the wording of human rights provisions, and the Hural revised the

---

[16] See especially S. Bayar, "Mongolia's National Security Challenges," *San Francisco: Center for Asian Pacific Affairs Report No. 16*, at 1 (September 1994). Bayar discusses the historic search for a "third force" to offset reliance on the two neighbors. See also Lattimore, *supra* note 7.

[17] See Sanders, *supra* note 15.

[18] Zorig was later brutally murdered in 1998 in an incident that attracted international attention.

draft several times over the course of its session. The MPRP demanded a presidential system in keeping with its tradition of strongman leadership, while opposition forces, knowing they had few candidates with the seniority and name recognition to win that post in the short term, wanted a parliamentary system. If there was to be a president, the reformists preferred that it be an indirectly elected position. The MPRP's advocacy of presidentialism during constitutional debates was ironic in light of its socialist-era formal commitment to the supremacy of parliament.

After two months of intense deliberations, the Great Hural ratified the constitution in January 1992. One author close to the process suggested that the shape of the compromise was such that reformers gave in on issues of political structure to secure their gains with regard to human rights and property ownership.[19] The final version of the new constitution called for a mixed political system with a split executive. The president would be the head of state with the power to veto parliamentary legislation in whole or in part. The presidential veto can be overturned by a two-thirds majority of the State Great Hural.[20] The prime minister serves as the head of the government, nominated by the majority coalition. The prime minister's nominations for the cabinet are subject to approval by the State Great Hural.[21] The transitional bicameral parliament was replaced by a unicameral body, the State Great Hural, reflecting the view that quick legislative action was needed to help the country deal with the severe economic crisis. The constitution called for the formation of new political institutions, including a National Security Council, a new body called the General Council of Courts to oversee judicial administration and provide for judicial independence, and a constitutional court.[22]

The Constitutional *Tsets*[23]

During the constitution drafting process, there was widespread agreement on the need for some sort of constitutional oversight body.[24] There

---

[19] H. Hulan, "Mongolia's New Constitutional Regime: Institutional Tensions and Political Consequences," 3 *Mongolian J. Int'l Aff.* 42 (1996).

[20] Constitution of Mongolia, Article 33(1).

[21] Constitution of Mongolia, Article 39(2).

[22] Constitution of Mongolia, Articles 33(10) (National Security Council), 49(3–4) (General Council of Courts), and 64–67 (constitutional court).

[23] Although the body is called the *Tsets* in Mongolian, it will be referred to throughout this chapter as the constitutional court for simplicity, except where context requires the original term.

[24] This had been discussed in Mongolia since 1990, after the USSR adopted its own constitutional court.

were different views about where the authority should reside. Some jurists wanted to adopt the decentralized model of judicial review along the lines of America or Japan, wherein every judge has the power to evaluate constitutional issues. Others argued that because Mongolia's legal system is structured along the lines of the continental system, the "centralized" model of judicial review found in Germany and other European countries was more appropriate.

The drafters of the constitution rejected the American model fairly early in the process. In part, this choice simply reflected the civil law origins of the Soviet-inspired legal system and the lower status of civil law judges relative to their common law cousins. As elsewhere in other postcommunist societies, this low status was compounded in Mongolia by the legacy of political control of the ordinary judiciary and socialist "telephone justice." The low level of trust in the judiciary continues to this day. For example, in a 1997 survey of levels of confidence in major political and government institutions, 74.7% of respondents had "low confidence" in the judicial system.[25] This was the lowest rating for any governmental institution in the survey.

Even having made the decision to create a designated body for constitutional oversight in accordance with the centralized model, a number of issues remained to be resolved. Foremost was whether the new body was a part of the judiciary or not. Although it was not to be called a court, the early drafts nevertheless included discussion of a constitutional council in the provisions on the judiciary.[26] However, the final version set up a body called the *Tsets* as a distinct power of government with a separate chapter of the constitution.

Tsets does not mean court, but is the name for the referee in traditional Mongolian wrestling: The image the word evokes is not of a court upholding the rights of individuals against the government, but of a neutral force mediating between heavyweight political institutions. The drafters of the Mongolian Constitution could have called the body a court, but chose not to do so. Like the *Conseil Constitutionnel* in Fifth Republic France, the name of the body itself symbolizes the ambiguity of grounding constitutional review between law and politics.[27]

---

[25] Sant Maral Foundation, opinion survey of 1,000 households, November 1997. This percentage includes respondents with either "rather low" or "very low" confidence in the judiciary.

[26] Draft, State Yassa of Mongolia, June 1991, Article 62.

[27] Christian Dadomo and Susan Farran, *French Substantive Law* 147 (1997).

The early drafts contemplated that the *Tsets* would be a six-member body with nine-year terms.[28] The final draft inverted these numbers and set up a nine-member body with six-year terms. Members are nominated by each of three institutions, the president, the State Great Hural, and the Supreme Court, with each institution nominating three members.[29] All nominations are subject to approval by the State Great Hural. The early versions called for membership by former presidents of the country, as per the French *Conseil Constitutionnel*.[30] Later versions scrapped these provisions. Members of the court were required by the constitution to be at least forty years of age, and "experienced in politics and law."[31] There was no explicit requirement of legal training, again paralleling the French model rather than the German or American model of judicial review.

The early drafts of the constitution envisioned relatively narrow access to judicial review that could be invoked only by request of the State Great Hural itself or the president.[32] This narrow scope resembles that of the French *conseil* as originally provided by the 1958 Constitution, the body with the most limited access in Europe at the time of its creation.[33] The final draft expanded standing to include the prime minister, supreme court, and the prosecutor general. Most crucially, it allowed the court to decide disputes on "its own initiative on the basis of petitions and information received from citizens."[34] The expansion of access to include ordinary citizens reflected the suggestion of numerous foreign advisors.[35]

[28] *Ibid.* Article 62(2). In the six-member model, two members were to be appointed by the president, two by the State Great Hural, and two by the Supreme Court.
[29] Constitution of Mongolia, Article 65(1). This model of selection was identical to that adopted in Bulgaria. Most reforming countries chose to have Constitutional Court members selected by Parliament, with some presidential role (nomination or approval). For more on different models of constitutional adjudication adopted in Eastern Europe, see George Ginsburgs, "The Constitutional Courts of Eastern Europe," 18 *Rev. Cent. & E. Eur. L.* 6 (1992).
[30] Draft, State Yassa of Mongolia, June 1991, Article 62(6) allowed former presidents who had not been convicted of a crime to serve until age sixty-five. The French system allows former presidents to serve for life. Alec Stone, *The Birth of Judicial Politics in France* (1992).
[31] Constitution of Mongolia, Article 65(2).
[32] Drafts, May 1991, June 1991, on file with author.
[33] Note that the French have since expanded access to the tribunal. See Stone, *supra* note 30. The Mongolian draft constitution did not specify whether the questions were to be limited to abstract review of pending legislation (as in the French case) or whether they could include already-passed legislation.
[34] Constitution of Mongolia, Article 56(1).
[35] See, for example, the unpublished reports provided by the United Nations Human Rights Center, *Report on Draft Constitution* (Geneva, 1991), and Martin Shapiro,

In particular, the major international conference convened by Zorig appeared to bolster the opposition position in favor of expanded access consistent with the insurance theory.

The court was established late in 1992 after passage of implementing legislation during the Small Hural's final session.[36] The court decides constitutional challenges to legislation, other decisions of the State Great Hural, presidential decrees, government decisions, international treaties to which Mongolia is a party, and decisions of the Central Election Commission, as well as serving as a court of first instance for certain cases involving high officials.[37] In form and function, the court is fairly similar to the German Constitutional Court, with several important distinctions: First, ordinary courts have no ability to certify questions to the Mongolian Court in the course of ongoing legal proceedings, and the constitutionality of ordinary court decisions cannot be questioned before the *Tsets*.[38] Second, there is no requirement that ordinary citizens petitioning the court show concrete legal injury or exhaustion of other remedies.[39] These two provisions had important downstream effects. The distinction in the constitutional scheme between law and politics, and the insulation of ordinary legal cases from constitutional review, was subject to later criticism from human rights advocates. On the other hand, the open-standing provisions, without requiring concrete injury or efforts to exhaust other remedies, meant that the court provided an easily accessible alternative forum for those political forces that had been defeated in the legislative arena. Unsurprisingly, this would ultimately lead to the politicization of the court.

A further distinction is that the Mongolian Court has no explicit ability to declare political parties unconstitutional, in contrast with the German Constitutional Court[40] and the Council of Grand Justices in Taiwan. Because the Mongolian transition was a negotiated one in which the former Leninist party played an active role, there was relatively little pressure

---

"Comments on the Draft Constitution of Mongolia" (unpublished manuscript, The Asia Foundation, San Francisco, 1991).

[36] Law of May 8, 1992.

[37] Law on *Tsets* Procedure, Article 21(2).

[38] Cf. Donald Kommers, *The Constitutional Jurisprudence of the Federal Republic of Germany* 14–15 (2d ed., 1997).

[39] *Ibid.* at 15.

[40] See Basic Law, Article 21(2), stating that parties seeking to "impair or abolish the free democratic basic order or to endanger the existence of the Republic shall be unconstitutional."

to abolish the party and consequently not much attention devoted to the notion of "illegal" political parties.[41]

The evolution of constitutional design illustrates the basic logic elaborated in Chapters 1 and 2. A majority MPRP drafting committee, headed by an MPRP president, drafted a document with a French-style constitutional council. This model, designed to resolve conflicts between president and parliament, served the interests of a prospective strong president. It had minimal public access and thus few opportunities for minority parties to challenge government action. However, in subsequent debates opposition parties were able to elicit support from the international community to lobby for a more open constitutional design. The final scheme was open to citizen petition and thereby allowed access to prospective losers in the legislature. Drawing on international resources, small parties effectively demanded "insurance" in the form of an open court.

Although they won on access, smaller parties were not completely successful in creating a *strong* institution, because of the complicated relationship between the Constitutional Court and the State Great Hural (Parliament). This requires an explanation of hearing procedures, as elaborated in the court's procedure law. Upon receiving a request or petition, the chairman of the court assigns it to a member to evaluate whether it contains a valid constitutional claim within fourteen days. *Petitions* are claims from the citizens, whereas *requests* come from designated government agencies empowered to ask the court for a decision (president, ministers, procurator, and Supreme Court). If the member who initially reviews the petition or request finds that it does not contain a constitutional issue or finds that the claim is somehow otherwise improper, the claim is sent back to the petitioner with an explanation. The petitioner, or another court member, could then appeal to a three-member panel of the court as to the first member's finding that no constitutional issue pertains.[42] If the three-member panel *does* believe the claim contains a valid constitutional issue (or if the initial member so finds), the court institutes proceedings and hears the case in panels of five at a public hearing. The result of these proceedings is called a *finding* or *judgment*.

Judgments are not immediately binding but are sent to the State Great Hural for consideration. The Hural must adopt a resolution to recognize

---

[41] For an analysis of the various approaches taken by democracies to "antidemocratic" parties, see Gregory H. Fox and Georg Nolte, "Intolerant Democracies," 36 *Harv. Int'l L. J.* 1 (1995).

[42] Law on *Tsets* Procedure, Article 21(4).

the judgment within fifteen days.[43] If the Hural rejects the judgment by a simple majority, the court must then consider the law *en banc* and can definitively declare the law unconstitutional with a two-thirds majority of its own, or six of nine members.[44] This is called a *decision* and has immediate legal effect. The *en banc* sessions are also held if new circumstances are found to be relevant to a previously decided case and a majority of court members request a reexamination.[45]

The procedures of the court are presented graphically in Figure 6.1.

The distinctive feature of the scheme is that the court shares the function of constitutional interpretation with the State Great Hural. Court findings do not have immediate effect *erga omnes*, but require implementation by the Hural to take effect. The democratically elected legislature is supreme in the constitutional design of the system, being the "highest organ of state power."[46] This primacy may reflect residual socialist notions of parliamentary sovereignty, as Mongolian lawyers trained in Leninist political theory sought to reconcile democracy with constitutionalism. In fact, this institutional pattern had a late communist progeny: The Czechoslovak and Yugoslav Constitutional Courts that were adopted in the waning years of communist rule (chiefly to resolve problems related to federalism) featured similar interplay between legislature and court in effecting decisions of unconstitutionality. In the People's Republic of China, the National People's Congress retains the supreme power of constitutional interpretation, as the Hong Kong Court of Final Appeal learned the hard way in the late 1990s.

The scheme sets up the basis for games of power between the Hural and the court. The key factor for the court is its internal cohesion, that is its ability to override a parliamentary veto of its judgments by garnering a two-thirds majority. Internal politics within the court and dynamics of its interactions with the parliament are crucial here. Imagine, for example, that each member of the court served as the loyal agent of her nominating institution. In that case, three members of the court would always vote with the parliament. But the other six members, if united, would be able to sustain a judgment over the objection of the parliament and issue a final, binding decision with a two-thirds vote.

[43] Law on *Tsets* Procedure, Article 36(2).
[44] Constitution of Mongolia, Article 66(3); Law on the *Tsets*, Article 18(4).
[45] Law on *Tsets* Procedure, Article 30.
[46] Constitution of Mongolia, Article 20.

Constitutional Court Procedure

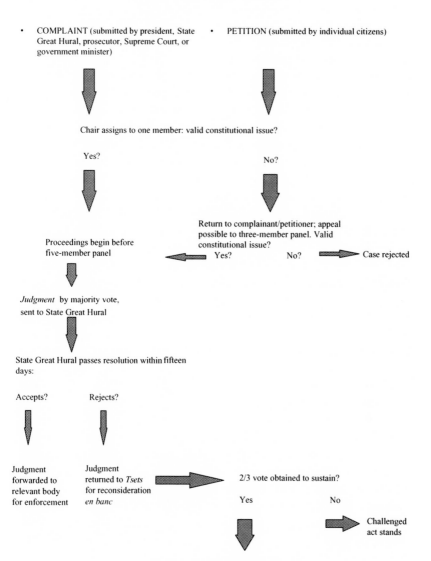

- COMPLAINT (submitted by president, State Great Hural, prosecutor, Supreme Court, or government minister)

- PETITION (submitted by individual citizens)

Chair assigns to one member: valid constitutional issue?

Yes?

No?

Return to complainant/petitioner; appeal possible to three-member panel. Valid constitutional issue?

Proceedings begin before five-member panel

Yes?   No?   Case rejected

Judgment by majority vote, sent to State Great Hural

State Great Hural passes resolution within fifteen days:

Accepts?   Rejects?

Judgment forwarded to relevant body for enforcement

Judgment returned to *Tsets* for reconsideration *en banc*

2/3 vote obtained to sustain?

Yes   No

Challenged act stands

Decision issued; challenged act null and void

FIGURE 6.1. Procedures of Constitutional Review in Mongolia

The Hural, however, has a number of weapons that can be deployed against the court to encourage defections from its opposing bloc. The Hural may amend the Constitutional Court Act and the corresponding procedure act by simple majority.[47] The Hural has the power to amend the constitution with a three-fourths vote.[48] Perhaps most important at a day-to-day level, all nominations to the court are subject to parliamentary approval. By refusing to vote on a new nomination, the Hural can manipulate the composition of the court if a member resigns, so that there are only seven or eight members rather than nine. With seven members, the Hural only needs two votes to prevent a two-thirds override by the court. The Hural can also threaten members with the possibility of refusing to reappoint them. Knowing that the Hural must approve reappointments, individual members may be reluctant to vote to overturn the Hural's refusal to accept a court judgment. This may be true even where a member originally voted with the majority to issue the judgment.

The Hural also has an important role in enforcing the judgments of the court. Decisions passed by a two-thirds majority of the court have direct and immediate effect. But judgments passed by five-member panels of the court require further action by the responsible body to take effect. Those designing the system thought that it was proper, for example, for the Hural to itself formally reverse its own action in the event of unconstitutional legislation. The same is true for other bodies that violate the constitution.

This design assumes that the Hural will indeed comply with the court judgment by voluntarily abrogating its earlier act. The procedure requiring confirmation of judgments, however, can create legal complications. Suppose that the court decides a law is unconstitutional and announces a judgment to that effect decided by the five-member panel. The Hural then has fifteen days to accept or reject the judgment. Ideally, the Hural accepts the decision and voids its own law. Alternatively, the Hural can reject the decision and force the court to reconsider. The result will either be a two-thirds vote overruling the Hural and upholding the judgment, in which case it has immediate legal effect, or a failure to obtain the two-thirds vote, in which case the challenged law stands.

---

[47] See Chapter 5 for an example of such behavior by the Legislative Yuan on Taiwan.
[48] Constitution of Mongolia, Article 69. An alternative procedure allows for the Hural, by a two-thirds vote, to propose a national referendum to amend the constitution. Constitution of Mongolia, Article 68. This referendum would be decided by majority vote.

However, suppose the Hural accepts the judgment but does not take the appropriate action to void the relevant laws. The court has no general power to void laws unless it sits in the *en banc* session after a rejection by parliament. Hence, the challenged law will stand despite being adjudicated as unconstitutional. A similar result will occur if the Hural does not formally act to either accept or reject the judgment. This potentiality became reality in early 2000, as will be described shortly. The possibility of inaction by the State Great Hural does not appear to have been contemplated by the designers of the system, but, to the extent they were MPRP loyalists, it ultimately served their interests.

Membership of the Court

Initial nominations to the court were made in the spring of 1992, and the State Great Hural approved all the initial appointments. At the time of initial appointments, the Hural and presidency were controlled by MPRP candidates and the Supreme Court had not yet undergone the process of reappointing its membership after the adoption of the new constitution. This configuration had the consequence that most of the Constitutional Court members came from the MPRP. Only D. Chilhaajav, a geologist and member of the Democratic Party who had served in the Small Hural, was from the opposition. One reason was that the opposition had few candidates who met the age requirement to become court members. Again, institutional design appeared to be manipulated to serve the interests of the MPRP.

There are two categories of Constitutional Court members. Standing members serve full-time as court members. Nonstanding members continue to work at their ordinary jobs and are paid for their court work on an hourly basis. There is no other difference in the duties, responsibility, or power of the two categories of members.

Table 6.1 lists the members of the court through mid-2000.[49]

Information on internal politics among the justices is extremely difficult to obtain, because decisions are unsigned and published only in summary form upon issuance. The court's files are unavailable to the public. Members interviewed for this study report that there are no jurisprudential differences attributable to their appointing mechanism, but it is impossible to verify that this is indeed the case.

---

[49] This information was constructed from interviews with the secretary of the court in Ulaanbaatar in December 1997.

TABLE 6.1 *Constitutional Court Members Through 2000*

Name	Term	Appointed by	Profession
G. Sovd* (chair)	1992–98	President	Director, Institute of State and Law
G. Nyamdoo*	1992–95	State Great Hural	Diplomat
N. Jantsan*	1992–00	President	Professor, MP
Dangasuren*	1992–93	Supreme Court	Supreme Court
D. Chilhaajav	1992–98	State Great Hural	Geologist, MP
J. Byamba	1992–00	President	Researcher, Institute of State and Law
Choijamtsan	1992–94	Supreme Court	Procurator
Ts. Tsolmon	1992–97	State Great Hural	Supreme Court
L. Baasan*	1992–00	Supreme Court	Professor
J. Byambajav*	1995–00	President	Advocate, Judge, MP
Ch. Enkhbaatar	1995–00	Supreme Court	Director, Institute of State and Law
S. Jantsan	1993–00	Supreme Court	Professor

* standing member (L. Baasan became standing in 1993). In June 2001, Ts. Sarantuya and Ch. Dashnyam joined the court.

According to the constitution, the members are to elect a chairman from among themselves who will serve for a three-year term.[50] The chairman may be reelected once, but it is unclear whether a chairman reappointed to the court after serving six years can again be elected as chairman. The first chairman of the court was G. Sovd (b. 1930), the country's most senior lawyer, a former Supreme Court justice, and former director of the Institute of State and Law, foremost legal research center in the country. Like other elites of his generation, he was educated in Mongolia and later in Russia, taking a doctorate in law from Sverdlovsk. MPRP membership was essential to succeed in his career. Although it would be simplistic to suggest that the MPRP connection accounts for any particular decision, the world view of Sovd was undoubtedly shaped by his position as a very senior lawyer in the socialist system.

Some observers have suggested that Sovd was in a strong position to influence others on the court until his retirement in 1998.[51] This influence resulted from both institutional and personal factors. Institutionally, the chairman is in charge of assigning cases and selecting panel members and thereby has some steering power over the agenda, even if he cannot

[50] Constitution of Mongolia, Article 65(3).
[51] Interview with staff member of the Constitutional Court, December 7, 1997.

personally control the cases that are accepted by the court. He also has administrative control of the court's material resources, such as they are. Furthermore, the court's procedural law provides that the members of the court speak in age order after the presenting member.[52] This norm enhanced the power of Mr. Sovd, the oldest member of the court, for he was always either first or second speaker in any case discussion. Mr. Sovd's personal prestige also enhanced his power in the small, densely networked world of the Mongolian legal profession. As the country's most senior lawyer and a longtime law professor, Sovd had been a mentor to virtually all of the other senior lawyers in the country, including the "father of the Constitution" B. Chimid, many MPs, and Supreme Court justices. Sovd's presence on the court, in and of itself, enhanced its legitimacy as a legal body.

Sovd was replaced as president in 1998 by N. Jantsan, a longtime MPRP member who had served in Parliament. Jantsan had less prestige than Sovd, and his tenure as president has been marred by continuing controversy around the Separation of Powers Decision described as follows. No doubt he bears some of the responsibility for inducing a backlash against the court.

KEY CASES

First Cases: Testing Grounds

Upon its formation in 1992, the court was immediately flooded with petitions from the public. Most of the petitions, however, did not deal with constitutional issues per se.[53] Rather, the public perceived that the court would fulfill a kind of general ombudsmanlike function of advocating for citizen's rights. This misunderstanding was likely rooted in the changes in the role of the procuracy, the socialist-era institution responsible for supervising government action and protecting rights. The "general supervision" function of the procuracy was a distinctive feature of socialist law, but had been taken away during legal reforms of 1992 and 1993.[54] The power of general supervision placed the procuracy at the apex of the legal

---

[52] Law on *Tsets* Procedure, Article 29.2
[53] Interview with member of the Constitutional Court, June 8, 1993.
[54] See Tom Ginsburg, "The Transformation of Legal Institutions in Mongolia 1990–93," 12 *Issues and Studies* 77 (June 1994). For more on general supervision, see Harold Berman, *Justice in the USSR* (1963).

system and allowed it to supervise all government agencies as well as the criminal justice system. Citizens were used to a single hierarchical body having overall responsibility for the law, and in the absence of a clear "one-stop" body to ensure legality of government action, turned to the Constitutional Court to play this role. This was natural, given the wide publicity accorded the constitutional process, and citizens apparently believed the court could do more than it could because many of the petitions did not clearly concern constitutional issues.

The first case the court heard was in 1992 in response to a petition from a citizen in Selenge Aymag, protesting that the administrative reorganization of the *somon* (county) units had been implemented without taking into account public opinion. According to Article 57(3) of the constitution, "revision of a territorial units shall be considered and decided by the State Great Hural on the basis of a proposal by a respective local Hural and local population. . . ." The court upheld the citizen's argument that this provision required the State Great Hural to consult with local citizens as well as the local Hural before reorganizing administrative bodies. The government duly initiated such consultations where they had not been undertaken.

Other constitutional courts have used issues of local-central relations as a relatively uncontroversial way of establishing their legitimacy in the early years of their development. The *somon* case recalled a famous decision of the German Constitutional Court, the *Southwest State* case of 1951 where the Constitutional Court struck down a 1950 federal statute authorizing the reorganization of three southwestern states pending outcome of a referendum. This case was viewed as a major step in the legitimation of judicial review in Germany.[55] Of course, such federalism concerns likewise dominated the early history of the U.S. Supreme Court.[56] Mongolia's unitary government deprives the Mongolian court of the issues of federalism so useful in establishing judicial review, but the logic of focusing on constraining local authority in favor of central government institutions remains powerful.

Another early case to come before the court concerned the series of tax laws passed by the State Great Hural in the fall of 1992. The Hural elected the previous summer was controlled overwhelmingly by the MPRP that held seventy-one out of seventy-six seats. The president argued that a provision in the tax law delegating tax power to local governments

---

[55] See Donald Kommers, *supra* note 38, at 45.
[56] See Chapter 4.

constituted an unlawful delegation of legislative authority.[57] This reflected the new, urban parties' distrust of the local governments that were dominated by MPRP *apparatchiks*. Citing the principle of "no taxation without representation," President Ochirbat vetoed portions of the law. However, the Parliament refused to accept the president's veto in its entirety and, utilizing its power under Article 33 of the constitution, was able to overturn the veto with a two-thirds majority.

The president and opposition forces, having lost in the parliamentary forum, took the matter to the court. There, a five-member panel agreed with the president's argument and sent the law back to the Hural by issuing a judgment of unconstitutionality. The parliament, however, rejected the court judgment by a majority vote. Accordingly, the case was sent back to the court to hear *en banc*. The full panel of the court then voted five to four to uphold its decision over the Parliament's rejection, but the Law on the Constitutional Court required a two-thirds majority of the court.[58] The controversial portions of the tax law stood despite being rejected by a majority of the constitutional oversight body. This case prompted some members of the court to argue for a change in the court law to allow the court to uphold a law with a simple majority rather than a two-thirds supermajority.[59] Such a change was not included when the Constitutional Court Procedure Law was passed in 1997, however.

Citizen Petitions and Rights Jurisprudence

From its rather cautious early decisions, the Mongolian court expanded the number of cases it heard in the years leading up to 1997. Table 6.2 shows that demand in the form of more petitions expanded as well, and this provides one simple indicator of impact for a constitutional court in the early years of democracy. If the court is not seen as an effective forum for advancing political and legal claims, plaintiffs are not likely to bring actions to it. On the other hand, if the court is viewed as welcoming plaintiffs' claims, it is likely that the number of claims it is called upon to hear will expand until it reaches some equilibrium level.

The importance of the court became clear immediately after the lopsided victory of the MPRP in parliamentary elections in 1992. In that

---

[57] Interview with member of the president's staff, June 9, 1993.
[58] See text at note 44, *supra*.
[59] Interview with member of the Constitutional Court, June 8, 1993.

TABLE 6.2 *Caseload of the Mongolian Court, 1992–1997*

Year	Number of Petitions/Requests	Number of Issues	Number of Decisions	Number Accepted by SGH
1992	30	68	1	1
1993	77	118	5	4
1994	79	118	17	5
1995	41	77	15	
1996	84	267	27	7
1997*	54	210	8	

* first nine months only

Source: Unofficial statistics of the Constitutional Court. Later data unavailable.

election, the MPRP dominated, taking seventy-one out of seventy-six seats in the parliament despite getting under 60% of the popular vote.[60] During the next four years, the court served as a check on the power of the parliament. It often sided with the president in the increasingly frequent interbranch disputes between President Ochirbat and the conservative State Great Hural.

One man in particular, the Social Democrat and former Small Hural member B. Lamjav, deserves much of the credit for activating the Constitutional Court through citizen petitions. After failing to win election to the new Great Hural in 1992, the former mathematician took a position within the Social Democratic Party. He then began a campaign of sending petitions to the *Tsets*. Whenever a law contradicted his reading of the text of the constitution, Lamjav would file a petition. He was responsible for bringing the cases leading to the major constitutional decisions during the period of MPRP dominance, 1992–96, and many observers jokingly claimed that the court was working for Lamjav during this period. His petitions had a high rate of success: The secretary of the court estimated that 60% of his petitions were accepted and 80% of those were successful.[61] Although precise data are not available to verify this point, there is no doubt that Lamjav has been the most important claimant before the court. As so frequently happens, opposition forces were able to use the court to restrain the legislative majority.

[60] The culprit was an election law that heavily biased rural areas. There was no evidence of fraud, but rather of miscalculation on the part of the opposition forces who assumed they could gather a significant portion of the twenty seats in Ulaanbaatar.

[61] Interview with staff member of the Constitutional Court, December 4, 1997. This could not be confirmed because the court does not release information on particular cases that come before it. Lamjav himself keeps no systematic records.

Lamjav's claims concerned both rights and structural issues. One important case involved the highly controversial issue of land ownership. Article 5(2) of the constitution provides for state recognition of private-property rights. Article 16, the provision elaborating human rights and freedoms, provides for a right of acquisition, possession, and inheritance of movable and immovable property.[62] The 1994 Civil Code, however, does not elaborate these rights clearly, but Article 100.4 says the state retains ownership of all land until another law is passed. Meanwhile, a 1994 Land Law provides for long-term, nontransferable leasehold interests, but does not allow for private land ownership. Lamjav took the position that the legislative failure to issue laws providing for a right to own land constituted a suspension of a basic human right articulated in the constitution. Under Article 19(2), constitutional rights may only be suspended by law during a state of emergency. The court, however, disagreed with Lamjav's view and said that only affirmative suspensions of rights in a national emergency constitute violations subject to Article 19 protection. Failure to legislate does not constitute an affirmative suspension of rights.

In another case, the court responded to police abuses. During a strike by teachers for more pay in 1995, a policeman walked into the strike headquarters, set down his coat, and left. A week later, it was discovered that the coat had a tape recorder in it that had recorded the conversation of the union leaders. The Constitutional Court censured the police by holding that its actions violated constitutional protections of privacy.

The Court and the Supreme Court

The court's ability to play an active role in rights protection is limited by a "design defect" in its formal jurisdiction, one that we have seen before in the Taiwan context. Article 66 of the constitution states that the Constitutional Court jurisdiction extends to laws, decrees, and decisions of the State Great Hural, government decisions, and international treaties. It does not mention Supreme Court cases. The Constitutional Court has read this provision to hold that Supreme Court cases were not reviewable by the court. In coming to this conclusion, the court relied on Article 50(2) of the constitution, stating that Supreme Court decisions are final. Both the

---

[62] Constitution of Mongolia, Article 16(3).

chairmen of the Supreme Court and Constitutional Courts believed this provision means that judicial decisions should not be subject to further review by any other body.[63]

Some have argued that this position unnecessarily limits constitutional review. Under this interpretation, an individual's rights, including those elaborated under Article 16 of the constitution, may be denied simply because an ordinary court has looked at the matter.[64] If an ordinary court violates a constitutional right through one of its decisions, that decision will not be reviewable.

There is also the potential for problems when both court systems abdicate responsibility for a particular matter, hoping the other system will take care of it.[65] After all, ordinary courts are not empowered to consider constitutional matters. The Supreme Court has held that constitutional rights can only receive protection from ordinary courts if the rights have been incorporated into ordinary legislation. This results in a kind of hermetic separation between constitutional and ordinary law that may result in severe lacunae. For example, the constitutional right to a lawyer in criminal trials can only be raised in ordinary criminal court proceedings as a violation of the Criminal Procedure Code, not as a constitutional violation.[66] Should a suspect not be given access to an attorney, and should the Supreme Court fail to grant relief on the basis of the Criminal Procedure Code, the refusal cannot be heard by the Constitutional Court because of the lack of any explicit authority to review ordinary court cases. The suspect's constitutional right will have been violated with no

[63] Compare Chapter 5, which discusses Interpretations Nos. 154 and 242 by the grand justices of the Judicial Yuan of the ROC, coming to the opposite conclusion, with Chapter 7, which discusses continuing conflicts in Korea over this issue.

[64] G. Ganzorig, "The Relationship between the Constitutional and Supreme Courts of Mongolia," 7 *J. East Eur. L.* 667 (2000).

[65] See also Peter Krug, "Departure from the Centralized Model: The Russian Supreme Court and Constitutional Control of Legislation," 37 *Va. J. Int'l L.* 725 (1997).

[66] Article 45 of the Criminal Procedure Code provides that defense counsel is entitled to participate in the case from the moment of detention or interrogation. Note that this is less expansive protection than that granted in Article 20, which states that a "suspect" has a right to defense counsel. Although one must be informed of being a suspect within twenty-four hours of becoming a suspect, any counsel retained would not be allowed to participate in the case until a formal interrogation or detention. See Edwin Tollefson, "Compliance of the Mongolian Criminal Code and Criminal Procedure Code with International Norms of Human Rights," unpublished manuscript, *United Nations Center for Human Rights* 37 (October 1996). There is no system of state-funded legal assistance at these early stages of legal proceedings, so this "right" is routinely violated in the case of indigent suspects.

remedy. This is especially likely if the Criminal Procedure Code provides less protection than the constitution requires.

The Constitutional Court's reluctance to intervene in such matters essentially means that there is a set of rights protected by neither court system. This leads to inconsistent administration by the ordinary courts, whose personnel vary widely in terms of their awareness of the constitution and human rights instruments. For example, one Supreme Court justice revealed that he regularly remands criminal cases where the self-incrimination privilege is violated in the investigation stage.[67] Other judges, however, do not do so. Thus, enforcement of one's constitutional privilege against self-incrimination in criminal investigations will be exclusively dependent on which Supreme Court justice is reviewing the appeal. The Constitutional Court will in no case step in.

This gap between the jurisdictions of the Supreme and Constitutional Courts was reflected in a challenge to a statute designed to compensate families of those killed in the bloody purges of the 1930s. In most cases, those accused lost their property as well. The government initiated a program to rehabilitate victims of the communist purges and in 1993 enacted a decree authorizing financial assistance to families of those who suffered repression. One group of victims' family members sought to challenge the partial compensation offered by the government as a violation of constitutional guarantees of the right to inherit property and to be compensated for damages.[68] The Supreme Court found that this issue fell within the jurisdiction of the Constitutional Court, while the Constitutional Court maintained it was an ordinary judicial matter and did not fall under its jurisdiction. The case fell into a legal limbo, where it remained.

This significant gap in constitutional protection is a direct reflection of the ambivalent position of the court operating between law and politics. It forms a kind of "legal questions" doctrine that allows the Constitutional Court to abdicate a potentially important role in protecting individuals. This notion of a separation between ordinary and constitutional law is an unusual one; far more common among other constitutional courts is reference to a variant of the political-questions doctrine. This provides the court with the pragmatic ability to identify certain cases as being the proper subject of action by other branches of government. The Mongolian court has also made use of this doctrine, as the next section discusses.

---

[67] Interview with Supreme Court justice, December 2, 1997.
[68] Constitution of Mongolia, Articles 16(3) (property) and 16(14) (damages).

Political-Questions Doctrine

Besides performing a judicial review function, the court has some juris-diction as a court of first instance for cases involving constitutional viola-tions by high officials, or legal grounds for impeachment of the president or prime minister, or recall of members of Parliament.[69] One example of the court avoiding a politically sensitive matter involved the case against former Prime Minister D. Byambasuren, who led the transitional gov-ernment from 1990 to 1992. During this period, traders in the central bank lost the country's entire foreign exchange reserves, totaling more than $80 million, in speculative trading. The former prime minister was charged with abuse of his governmental position for allowing the specu-lation to occur, and an argument was made that this was an impeachable offense that ought to be heard by the Constitutional Court. The Supreme Court had earlier heard the case of several of the currency traders them-selves and repeatedly tried to refer the case to the Constitutional Court, despite the lack of any formal power to do so. The Constitutional Court, however, eventually rejected the case because it did not contain a consti-tutional issue.

Another instance in which the court appeared to invoke a variant of a political-questions doctrine came immediately after the stunning loss of the MPRP in June 1996 parliamentary elections, when the MPRP de-manded that it be given the vice-chairmanship of the parliament. The democratic coalition resisted, and the MPRP left the chamber, obstruct-ing the quorum required to hold a vote on the appointment. Both parties appealed to the court for support of their respective positions. But the court decided that it had no authority to decide such a purely political question.

THE COURT AND THE SEPARATION OF POWERS

The political importance of the court has been most apparent in its ex-tensive involvement in separation-of-powers issues. These include inter-branch disputes between the president and the State Great Hural, disputes between the government and the judiciary about judicial independence, and disputes over the fundamental character of the political system. We treat each type of dispute in turn.

---

[69] Law on the *Tsets*, Article 8(3.5).

Interbranch Disputes

Though himself an MPRP product, President Ochirbat had assumed a liberal, proreform stance since his ascension to the highest executive post in May 1990. Unlike the more conservative, rural wing of his party, he was deeply involved in trying to resolve the country's economic crisis and dealt regularly with international donor institutions. Because of his increasingly liberal stances, he was eventually disowned by the more conservative wing of the MPRP during the presidential campaign in 1993, when the MPRP selected as its candidate L. Tudev, the conservative journalist and editor of the party newspaper *Unen*. Sensing an opportunity, the democratic opposition chose Ochirbat as its candidate. The advantages of incumbency proved sufficient for Ochirbat to win the presidential election. Although there were no reports of fraud, the Constitutional Court fined the head of the Central Election Commission before the election for endorsing Tudev publicly.[70] Despite this incident and reports of media bias toward the MPRP, Ochirbat won easily, initiating a period of divided government that has persisted, with a brief one-year exception, to the present.

Ochirbat was a crucial ally for the court in constraining the parliamentary majority.[71] He vetoed eighteen laws during his tenure, and many of these laws, as revised, were subsequently challenged before the Constitutional Court.[72] In the various refinements that were required to secure presidential cooperation and Constitutional Court approval of the vetoed laws, the Hural became aware of the need to take into account the views of other institutions in developing legislation. A pattern of constitutional dialogue developed wherein constitutional and legal development became the collective activity of the major political institutions, mediating extreme tendencies on the part of any one and contributing to democratic stability.[73] By occasionally striking legislation, the court encouraged democratic discourse.

---

[70] The *Tsets* has jurisdiction over the constitutionality of decisions of the central election authorities. Law on the *Tsets*, Article 8(1), section 6.

[71] Ochirbat also played an important political role in mediating crises in 1994 over the media law and in 1996, when the MPRP walked out of parliament to prevent the new democratic powerholders from appointing a government.

[72] *Mongol Messenger*, June 18, 1997, at 3.

[73] For more on the concept of constitutional dialogues, see, for example, Louis Fisher, *Constitutional Dialogues* (1988); Neal Devins, *Shaping Constitutional Values* (1996); Sally Kenney et al., eds., *Constitutional Dialogues in Comparative Perspective* (1999).

In April 1997, the court was confronted with the question of whether incumbent President Ochirbat, who had been in the office since 1990, could stand for another term of office in May 1997.[74] A citizen believed that Ochirbat's reelection would violate the constitution's Article 31(7), which provides that the president can be reelected only once, and challenged his registration as a candidate by the Central Election Commission. Ochirbat had been elected twice before, but only once under the 1992 Constitution. His ascension to the presidency during the transition period in 1990 resulted from an election by the Great Hural that itself had just been directly elected for the first time. The court found that the first election, held under amendments to the 1960 Constitution, and the second election, held under the 1992 Constitution, were for distinct offices, and thus the prohibition of a second term would not affect Ochirbat until 1992.[75] This case was inspired by an article by Lamjav and shows the court allying with the president again.

Judicial Independence

The court also became involved in an ongoing separation-of-powers dispute about judicial independence. The constitution provided for a General Council of Courts to protect judicial independence, take care of judicial administration, and serve as a disciplinary body for judges. As in many countries, it was believed that this body should include representatives of judges as well as other branches of government.[76] A 1993 Law on Courts provided for a mixed membership and allowed the membership to elect the chairman. When the new parties took power in 1996, one of their first acts was to amend the Law on Courts so that the minister of justice would serve *ex officio* as the chairman of the general council. This was perceived by members of the judiciary to be an attack on judicial independence, especially surprising from the so-called democratic forces. The Democrats maintained that control over judicial administration was necessary in the

---

[74] See "Mongolia: Constitutional Court Dismisses Challenge to President Standing Again," *BBC Monitoring Service – Far East* (BBCMS, BBCFE), April 28, 1997, available in NEXIS, NEWS Library, ALLNWS File.

[75] A number of post-Soviet republics have had to face similar issues.

[76] For more on the composition of the general council, see Ginsburg, *supra* note 54, at 95–97. The composition roughly reflected the pattern in the Spanish *Consejo General del Poder Judicial*. The Spanish body has twenty-one members, twelve of whom are judges approved by a three-fifths majority of both houses of Parliament. The Mongolian body has twelve members, seven of whom are judges.

face of the low popularity of the judiciary and continuing accusations of judicial corruption.[77] The Democrats found support in the German system, wherein judicial administration is handled by the ministry of justice in a nonpartisan manner. The German system, however, is the exception rather than the rule among established democracies in terms of executive control of the judicial administration.[78]

The Constitutional Court has heard at least two cases related to judicial independence. In 1993, following the passage of the Law on Courts, Supreme Court Justice G. Ganzorig brought a case asserting that disciplinary decisions of the general council ought to be appealable to a court of law, in accordance with the right of all citizens to judicial hearings under Article 16(14) of the constitution. Judges, it was argued, are no different than ordinary citizens and ought to be able to appeal administrative decisions depriving them of a job. The Constitutional Court disagreed and held that the right to a hearing did not extend to appeal of a judicial disciplinary decision by the general council.

This decision could be read as supporting or hindering judicial independence, depending on one's characterization of the general council and one's concept of judicial independence. One influential view of judicial independence distinguishes three strands: independence from the parties to a case, independence from influence by other members of the judiciary, and independence from politics.[79] Mongolian judges emphasized the latter aspect in their successful fight over the 1993 Law on Courts and ensured that their representatives constituted a majority of general council members. The chief justice is an *ex officio* member and each caucus of the three levels of the judicial hierarchy (trial courts, appeals courts, Supreme Court) also elects two members, so judges constitute seven of twelve members of the council. The chief justice was promptly elected by majority vote as chair of the general council. So the general council looked increasingly like a body designed to allow judges to control their own discipline and administration. If one emphasizes that component of judicial independence involving freedom from undue influence by political branches of government, a decision weakening appeal rights from the general council's finding may be seen as enhancing judicial

---

[77] See text at note 25, *supra.*

[78] See, generally, Shimon Shetreet and Jules Deschênes, *Judicial Independence: The Contemporary Debate* (1985).

[79] Owen Fiss, "The Right Degree of Independence," in *Transitions to Democracy in Latin America: The Role of the Judiciary* 55–57 (Irwin P. Stotzky, ed., 1993).

independence by strengthening the judges' capacity to control their own administration.[80]

From this perspective, however, the minister of justice's recent ascendance to the chairmanship of the general council may mean that the government is in fact exercising *more* control over the judiciary. Strengthening a disciplinary body chaired by a member of government may weaken judicial independence. Two alternative characterizations of the general council, emphasizing either its leadership or its composition, lead to two different analyses of the impact of the decision on judicial independence.

An inverse interpretation follows if one emphasizes that judicial independence also involves freedom from undue influence by other judges and the judicial hierarchy. If the general council is a body to maintain control over judicial administration by the leadership of the courts, the Constitutional Court's decision seems to compromise judicial independence. By allowing the disciplinary body broader power, the decision strengthens the leadership's power over individual decision makers and thus compromises the second aspect of judicial independence. But if the general council is a neutral body, the decision advances judicial independence by allowing easier discipline of judges who violate standards of independence.

Certain groups of judges have been particularly eager to challenge the minister's reassertion of control over judicial administration. The Mongolian Group for the Independence of Judges and Lawyers, associated with Ganzorig, brought a constitutional petition concerning the minister of justice's nomination of a Supreme Court judge to serve on a working group to draft legislation on banking reform. The petition asserted that by forcing judges to take part in nonjudicial work, the minister violated the independence of the judiciary, and that judges, as a separate branch of government, are not subject to cabinet orders to participate in particular activities. Here the Constitutional Court upheld the claim, angering the minister of justice.[81]

The court's jurisprudence on these two judicial-independence decisions shows its preference for separation-of-powers cases over those involving individual rights. It refused to read broadly the constitutional right to appeal to a court, perhaps because of its general reluctance to mingle its jurisdiction with that of ordinary courts. When confronted with an

[80] *Ibid.*
[81] Interview with Supreme Court justice, December 4, 1997.

attempt to involve judges in broader quasi-legislative duties, however, the court sided with the ordinary judiciary. The two decisions appear to share a focus on the formal separation of government functions.

The Character of the Political System and the Separation of Powers

Social Democrat and frequent constitutional complainant B. Lamjav was one of the heroes of the opposition because of his continual challenges of MPRP-sponsored legislation between 1992 and 1996. His dedication to the constitution earned him the rancor of his party associates, however, following the 1996 parliamentary election that brought the National Democrat–Social Democrat coalition to power. Lamjav, though a member of the coalition, filed a petition to the court to prevent the coalition from filling the cabinet with members of parliament, relying on a provision in the constitution that "members of parliament shall have no other employment."[82]

The issue concerned the nature of the political system established by the 1992 Constitution. Was it a presidential system where the cabinet is unrelated to the parliament? Or a parliamentary system, wherein the government is formed by the leading parties in parliament? The court was called on to resolve a tension that had been lingering at the core

---

[82] Constitution of Mongolia, Article 29. The question of Lamjav's motivation is puzzling. He is a senior member of the Social Democratic Party; at one time, he was considered a potential presidential candidate for the party; and he was a professor of R. Gonchigdorj, the speaker of Parliament. He is also considered to be a person of great intellect, with the highest levels of integrity and devotion to the constitution. Some observers suggested that he filed the petition when it became clear that he would not be offered a cabinet post, hoping that by narrowing the competition he might be more likely to secure a post. Such a motivation would have failed to anticipate the tremendous anger directed at Lamjav by his own party after the decision that was seen to undermine the coalition's historic transition to power. Others suggested that Lamjav's motives were to benefit the coalition by forcing it to distribute power more broadly. A third possibility is that Lamjav saw himself as a strict constructionist and simply believed that the constitution required the separation of parliament and government. This is Lamjav's own claim about his motivation (interview, December 5, 1997). In this view, he brought the case in an effort to enhance the separation-of-powers concept in the Mongolian constitutional structure and to uphold the internal consistency of constitutional provisions. One question left outstanding by this account, however, is why he had waited to file his petition until immediately after the election, when he had been aware that the previous MPRP government was also violating the provision by having MPs in cabinet positions. Lamjav did divulge that he had noticed the constitutional issue a year before bringing the claim.

of the political system since the establishment of the 1992 Constitution with its many codified compromises. The split executive was a source of confusion and created interinstitutional conflicts, illustrated by Ochirbat's frequent use of the veto power and the tension between the president and government after 1992.

Lamjav's petition asked the court to sort out the nature of the political system once and for all. The leading figures on both sides turned out to argue their respective positions. Initial arguments were made by MPRP lawyer S. Tumur for the petitioner and Speaker of Parliament and Social Democrat leader R. Gonchigdorj for the coalition. Tumur, who had served as a staff lawyer for the Constitutional Drafting Committee, argued that the system was basically presidential because it had a directly elected head of state. His opponent Gonchigdorj had been chairman of the Small Hural that adopted the first draft of the constitution in 1991, and he argued that the drafters had intended a parliamentary republic along the lines of the United Kingdom, with a merely symbolic presidency (as in Israel, Germany, and Italy). What had the drafters actually intended? As mentioned earlier, the system was the result of a complex compromise. This was not an issue of overwhelming clear agreement.

The difficulty of determining the meaning of such a fundamental issue as the structure of the political system calls into question assumptions about the clarity of constitutional change. The adoption of the Mongolian Constitution was an almost fairytale example of a "constitutional moment." The drafting committee included members of all parties. There were extensive deliberations and wide public distribution of the draft for comment. Difficult points were resolved by a national assembly freely elected specifically for that purpose. Even though Mongolia enjoyed a clear and defining constitutional moment, unlike so many other new democracies (Poland, Hungary, Chile, and Taiwan, to name a few examples), and even though the Mongolian constitutional drafters were still alive and able to report on their deliberation, there was no agreement on what "they the people" meant at the time. This would seem to counsel against the wisdom of viewing constitutional politics as of a different order than ordinary politics.

The court initially found in favor of Lamjav, holding that parliamentary deputies could not hold cabinet posts. This provoked the rancor of the democratic coalition and forced it to develop a new government lineup, requiring a scramble to find qualified persons to fill the cabinet. The coalition's leadership accused the court of acting in a politically motivated fashion and called for more "scientific" methods of constitutional interpretations, such as a detailed inquiry into the *travaux préparatoires* of the constitutional drafting committee.[83]

One leader called not for punishing the institution, but for lawyers to serve as staff legal advisors to the members of the court. He suggested that the current structure of the court, with several part-time members, could not physically handle the number of petitions sent to it. This is a novel form of imposing discipline on a constitutional court. Rather than trying to punish the court directly – for example, by reducing the material budget or amending its jurisdiction – he proposed improving internal monitoring on the court. The presence of more lawyers may constrain discourse by making it more legal and less political.

This proposal for professionalization was mild compared to the subsequent developments. The State Great Hural was controlled, for the first time, by the new parties, and they were given an opportunity to accept or reject the court's judgment. They rejected it, leading to a reconsideration of the case by the full panel of the court. A second round of arguments was held. National Democratic Party lawyer and Member of Parliament B. Delgerma argued that the parliamentary model had been adopted as a reaction to the socialist "presidential" system and the overconcentration of power in the hands of a single individual. She further argued that, regardless of the intentions of the drafters, Mongolian democratic practice had already established the parliamentary character of the democracy, since the MPRP had formed the government with members of parliament during the first postconstitutional election in 1992.

At the simplest level, the MPRP's counterargument seemed to involve a syllogism: (1) America and Mongolia are both democracies; (2) in America, the presidential system does not allow for MPs to take cabinet appointments; (3) therefore, Mongolia should not. This view obviously failed to take into account the distinction between the head of state and the chief executive. The U.S. president combines both roles, but this is the exception rather than the rule in global democratic practice. Mongolia's president has few executive functions and is named as head of state in the constitution.[84]

The competing position, advanced by the coalition, cited democratic practice in Germany, Japan, and Britain, where ministers are always MPs. It would be antidemocratic, according to the coalition, to allow persons who had run and lost in elections for district-based constituencies to

---

[83] Interview with senior member of the coalition, Ulaanbaatar, December 5, 1997.
[84] Constitution of Mongolia, Art. 30(1).

become ministers. Furthermore, as a practical matter, all the party leaders had been electoral candidates. Unlike the U.S. system, where there is a separation between party leadership and electoral candidates, Mongolian democratic practice after 1990 required that party leaders stand as candidates.

The court was unconvinced by this position. After a second round of deliberations, the court upheld its earlier judgment to the effect that MPs could not join the cabinet without resigning their seats. Although there is little evidence of the considerations that led the court to this position, we can comment on the merits of this "separation decision" from a comparative perspective.

Rule-of-law considerations would appear to weigh against the court's decision. The rule of law is, of course, a complex ideal capable of multiple formulations, but most definitions at their core emphasize the ability of actors to order their affairs to rules that are general, knowable, and performable.[85] Coming as it did right on the heels of the election, the court's ruling fundamentally altered the rules of the political game after all the political forces had detrimentally relied on the previously binding rules. In this sense, the rule articulated by the court was neither knowable nor performable before the decision. And although it was phrased in general terms, the negative impact of this decision was felt on only one side of the aisle, as the MPRP was not in a position to form a government. The court provided the ultimate form of insurance to the MPRP: putting its opponents into disarray after the MPRP lost a major election.[86]

---

[85] William Eskridge and John Ferejohn, "Politics, Interpretation, and the Rule of Law," in *Nomos XXXVI: The Rule of Law* 265 (Ian Shapiro, ed., 1994). The classic formulation is found in Lon Fuller, *The Morality of Law* 46–91 (1964). Fuller defines the rule of law as encompassing obligations that are, general, well-publicized, prospective, clear, not contradictory, susceptible of compliance, stable, and enforced in the manner suggested by their terms.

[86] After forcing the new democratic government to separate the cabinet from the legislature, the court became embroiled in another major controversy. Although the coalition had greatly expanded its network in the countryside before its victory in the 1996 elections, its ranks were still fairly thin. It did not have strong candidates to run for the thousands of seats up for grabs in the October 1996 elections for local hurals, and the MPRP won most of these elections handily. The power of the local Hurals was quite limited, because almost the entire public budget is set by the central government. However, one of the few powers of the local Hurals was to nominate the governors of localities. The constitution allows the prime minister to reject these candidates a single time. The local Hural may then nominate the same or another person to serve as governor, after which the prime minister must accept the candidate. The MPRP quite naturally nominated its own people for governorships in

Proponents of separating the government from parliament had deployed a form of purpose analysis. Lamjav argued that the constitution had different articles for the government and the Hural, showing its intent that the two be separated. In contemporary Mongolian practice, Lamjav asserted, the two powers were indistinguishable. Severing the link between the parliament and government would serve the *purpose* of the constitutional order, namely to effect a separation of powers.

We thus see two competing conceptions of the democratic system wielded by protagonists before the court. Objectively, the decision is difficult to justify. The June 1991 draft of the constitution contained a provision, Article 32, that states "Members of the State Great Hural cannot concurrently occupy the posts of . . . members of the government." But this text was explicitly rejected in the final version in favor of the Article 29 text stating that members may not hold posts "other than those assigned by law." The founders thus considered and rejected a complete separation between the two powers. Attributing rationality to the drafters and engaging in the always risky business of determining legislative intent, it appears that Mongolia's constitutional founders intended to allow MPs to join the government, but subject to ordinary legislation defining the terms under which they may do so. In the absence of such legislation, the court was faced with an interpretive problem, whether to read the original text literally or to rely on more purposive strategies of constitutional interpretation. The court took the former route.

The decision appears antidemocratic by insulating the government from popular criticism, by most definitions a key element of democracy. The prime minister, who is unelected, is the most powerful executive; the president, who is directly elected by universal suffrage, has mere veto power and no control over the government. The legislature can control the government by threat of dismissal and may then form another government. But this is an extreme weapon that would likely lead to confusion within the majority party in the legislature, with the possible result that

---

those regions where it won the Hural elections. Prime Minister Enkhsaikhan rejected these candidates, as he was allowed to do, and demanded that the Hurals nominate representatives drawn from the coalition. However, the local Hurals renominated MPRP candidates in many cases. Enkhsaikhan tried to reject these renominations and demanded the issue be sent to the court for a determination. The court found in favor of the local Hurals, and Enkhsaikhan threatened to ignore the decision. In the end, however, the nominees were installed as governors by the prime minister. The court thus issued two major decisions against the democratic forces within four months of their 1996 victory.

the opposition could form a governing coalition. This weapon was rendered even more unattractive for the legislature in 1996 because of the fact that the other top candidates for prime minister were all sitting in the parliament and would have to convince their colleagues that it was worthwhile to resign a seat in order to accept the prime ministership. The coalition's majority was only one seat more than necessary to secure a quorum, so it was unlikely any coalition member could resign a seat.

The court decision rejects the ordinary European practice of forming the government out of parliament. The European model facilitates a routine kind of parliamentary oversight that exists when cabinet members sit daily with members of parliament and are subject to regular questioning in the legislative arena. To be sure, Mongolian cabinet members may still be called to testify in front of parliament, but the link between the two institutions is more tenuous.

Why would a court seek to enforce a strict vision of the separation of powers, placing it even above the democratic accountability of government as a constitutional goal? One possibility is that, where legislature and executive are closely tied and held by the same party, the court's capacity to articulate its own policy views is more constrained. At this level of analysis, the Mongolian case is about the court ordering the internal relationships among governmental institutions in such a way as to expand its own freedom of action. By exacerbating tensions between government, whose decisions it is frequently called on to review, and the parliament, which wields a variety of weapons and has the ability to reject court decisions, the Constitutional Court may have sought to ensure that its decisions would stand more easily after the decision to separate government from parliament.

If the *effect* is to expand judicial latitude by diffusing power, the decision also dovetails nicely with traditional justifications for judicial review. It sides with the electoral losers, and it decreases the ability of the new rulers to exercise dominance. By helping a political party after it had been trounced in the polls, the court contributed to a balance of political forces. The judges could also help the MPRP, where many of the members had connections.

Political Impact of the Separation Decision

The decision had profound effects on subsequent politics. The decision was made after the nomination and approval of Prime Minister M. Enkhsaikhan, who had been chairman of the coalition and leader of the successful election campaign. Enkhsaikhan had not run in the parliamentary election. In the immediate aftermath of the separation decision, the coalition had to decide whether leaders who had won parliamentary seats would resign them to take ministerial posts. The coalition had fifty out of seventy-six parliamentary seats, while the MPRP held twenty-five. One seat was held by the United Traditional Party, whose representative aligned himself with the MPRP in the immediate postelection period. Should fourteen MPs resign to take ministerial positions, the coalition majority would become thirty-six to twenty-five, with the fourteen seats of Parliament to be filled in by-elections.[87] There was a real risk that the coalition would lose its historic majority. (The coalition subsequently reorganized the government to reduce the number of ministries to nine. If only nine MPs resigned, even if the MPRP won all the seats contested in by-elections, the coalition majority would be ensured.) In any case, even a single-seat loss to the MPRP would further jeopardize the ability of the coalition to obtain a quorum of two-thirds of the membership: As it was, they were one seat short, and the swing voter from the United Traditional Party had helped the MPRP deny a quorum by joining a walkout during hearings to appoint the vice-speaker of the Hural. In light of these considerations, the coalition decided to comply with the decision and to form the government exclusively with non-MPs.

One of the tensions exacerbated by the separation decision was that between the prime minister and other members of his coalition. In the aftermath of the decision, the democratic coalition found itself in the odd position of having its most powerful leaders ineligible for ministerial posts. With the coalition forced to give ministerial positions to second-line leaders, many top leaders were left as mere MPs. Without distributing ministerships, *de facto* power within the coalition could not match formal structure. When the decision was announced, Enkhsaikhan had urged coalition members not to resign their parliamentary seats, arguing that such a precedent would distract MPs from their parliamentary duties, might make the public angry, and would turn parliament into a ministers' training ground. Enkhsaikhan was able to satisfy members of his coalition that consultation between parliament and government would be a sufficient mechanism to advance policies together, and he was able to put together a cabinet of second-line coalition members who had either not run for parliament or not won. The effect of promoting a second-line

---

[87] Parliament had not yet clarified what would happen if a member vacated a seat.

cabinet, predictably, was to strengthen the prime minister's control of government, and many said he began to exert the same autocratic tendencies as his MPRP predecessors.

The insulation of the government from parliament certainly weakened democratic accountability. Neither the chief executive nor any member of his cabinet had won an election. This strange result seems antidemocratic and suggests the title for this chapter. The usual principal-agent problems that exist between parliament and government in a parliamentary system were exacerbated by the lack of mechanisms for the parliament to discipline the government and by the social and institutional distance created when cabinet members are not legislators. There was no opportunity for day-to-day policy debate, with the prime minister defending his policies before the public. Rather, government members had to be summoned to the parliament and appear there as outsiders on an infrequent and extraordinary basis.

In response to the lack of ministerships, the coalition put powerful members into committee chairmanships. Initial committee chairmanships included both top leaders and lesser leaders appointed to satisfy certain constituencies, such as women and herdsmen. They did not, however, reflect political balance between the two main coalition partners. The initial coalition agreement between the National Democrats and Social Democrats called for a democratic prime minister and a Social Democrat as speaker of the Hural. Ministerships would be divided among the two major parties, but the parliamentary committees would be headed by National Democrats. The Social Democrats grew increasingly unhappy with these arrangements, because their founding leader B. Batbayar had neither cabinet post nor committee chairmanship. Meanwhile, the MPRP began intensive efforts to woo the Social Democrats to leave the government coalition and form a new government with the MPRP. With fifteen seats, the Social Democrats formed the decisive bloc between the two large parties. The MPRP attempted to break the coalition by splitting the Social Democrats from the National Democrats (and later even offered ministerships to National Democrats as well).[88]

This intracoalition tension was revealed in mid-1997, when the Social Democrats demanded committee chairmanships from the National Democratic Party. In response, the parliament created two new committees by splitting portfolios. The coalition's internal problem of distributing

---

[88] Interview with member of parliament, December 8, 1997.

power among parties was resolved for the moment, but the structural problems in the relationship between parliament and government remained. The entire parliament had become backbenchers as a result of the separation decision, and the leadership of the parties was effectively shut out of government decision making. In response to complaints of lack of influence, the coalition set up a number of councils to bring together parliament and government members concerned with particular policy areas.

All in all, the effect of the separation decision was to weaken parliament and strengthen the government by insulating it. Subject to neither electoral nor parliamentary oversight, the government was eventually accused of large-scale corruption, disenchanting voters with the democratic forces.

One predictable result of the weakening of parliament was a decline in coalition discipline. Party leaders are able to discipline followers when loyalty can be rewarded, with ministerships the ultimate potential reward. Without the ability to offer prospective benefits to the backbenchers, parliamentary leaders have much less ability to discipline them. As positive political theory would predict, discipline in the State Great Hural began to decline after the separation of the government from parliament. One example was the 1997 Law on Privatization of urban housing. President Ochirbat vetoed the bill, meaning that a two-thirds vote of the State Great Hural would be required to effect an override. The coalition, with fifty out of seventy-six votes, would be able to secure an override with the help of B. Dashbalbar, the lone parliamentary representative of the United Traditional Party, who had begun to side with the coalition on occasion. However, a Social Democrat MP defected, forcing a revision of the law to gain the assent of President Ochirbat. In early 1998, another example of lack of discipline emerged in debates regarding a draft media law. Both the sponsor and most vocal opponents of the bill were from the National Democratic Party.[89]

In summary, there were several tensions in the political system that were either directly caused or exacerbated by the separation decision. These include the structural tension between parliament and government, latent political tensions within the coalition leadership itself, as top leaders were left without formally powerful positions, and tensions within each party

[89] "Parliament Discusses Press Laws," *BBC*, January 23, 1998, available in NEXIS, NEWS Library, CURNWS File. The sponsor of the bill was E. Bat-uul, former leader of the National Democrats. Fellow National Democrat H. Hulan was the most vocal critic.

as leaders lost the ability to discipline backbenchers, leading to a rise in district-based political entrepreneurship on the part of MPs.

Response and Restructuring

In late 1997, parliamentarians began to send informal feelers to see if the president would veto an attempt to modify the election law to facilitate the replacement of vacated parliamentary seats by members of the same party.[90] This was likely a covert threat to the prime minister, for once the issue was resolved of what would happen to vacant parliamentary seats, the prime minister would be subject to pressure to replace certain weak ministers with stronger members of the coalition. Furthermore, the parliamentary power of dismissing the government would become a real threat, because the top aspirants for the prime ministerial job would no longer be hindered by virtue of their membership in parliament.

After a year of insulated government, Enkhsaikhan was pressured to consult more frequently with his coalition. By involving the president in their internal power struggles, the coalition MPs also gave the president leverage over the prime minister, for he could threaten to allow the bill through and effectively negate the Constitutional Court decision. This was a bizarre twist on the design of the presidential veto power. In a parliamentary system, the veto power is usually anticipated to restrain the program of the government, by allowing the president to block legislation. With the parliament now using the legislative power to restrain the government, the president was able to wield his veto power to become a mediating institution between government and parliament.

Soon thereafter, on January 15, 1998, the parliament passed a bill to allow members of parliament to serve in the cabinet. The coalition then decided to replace the Enkhsaikhan government with a new one formed out of the parliament, led by former journalist Ts. Elbegdorj. This

---

[90] Others have proposed modification of the electoral system to achieve similar goals. One such system under consideration would allow voters to choose both a representative and a party on each ballot, combining majoritarian districts with proportional representation elements. If any candidate wins 50% of the vote, he or she will represent that district; if no candidate receives 50%, the seat would be distributed by proportional representation at the national level. The party lists will be used to fill these seats as well as those of any MPs that resign their seats. Presumably, this would mean that some districts will be represented by persons appointed by the parties after the election. Apparently, if this system had been used in the 1996 parliamentary elections, the MPRP would have won forty-one out of seventy-six seats instead of twenty-five. Interview with prominent political activist, December 8, 1997.

government, however, was weak and fell within three months, initiating an eight-month period of caretaker government that ended in December 1998 with the appointment of J. Narantsaltsralt as the new prime minister. Meanwhile, Lamjav brought a challenge to the new legislation, and the Constitutional Court duly followed the thrust of its original decision in holding the act unconstitutional.[91] Although this judgment was rejected by the parliament, the full bench of the court subsequently upheld the original decision. Again, the result was political chaos, with the MPRP demanding the resignation from parliament of cabinet members and the democratic coalition speculating about early elections.[92]

With ordinary legislative channels precluded as a means of repairing the political system, parliamentarians turned to a constitutional amendment. Mongolia's first-ever constitutional amendment was passed in December 1999 with the support of all major political parties. The amendments sought to resolve the issue by providing that ministers could serve concurrently as MPs. The amendment was sent to the president, who promptly vetoed it even though it had been supported by members of his own party. Among the grounds given was the lack of consultation with the Constitutional Court, which is alleged to have a role in constitutional amendments. This argument was based on Article 68, section 1 of the Constitution, which provides, *inter alia*, that the Constitutional Court can propose constitutional amendments. The president also suggested the State Great Hural should have consulted with the seventeen political parties not represented in it, along with the president, the National Security Council, and the government, before passing the amendment. This tortured interpretation of the constitution relied on a reading of the power to propose amendments as including a right to consultation over any proposed amendment.

The president's veto, however, was overridden by the State Great Hural in January 2000, prompting an appeal to the Constitutional Court on the validity of the constitutional amendments. On March 15, the initial bench of the court ruled that the constitutional amendments were themselves incompatible with the constitution, particularly the separation-of-powers principle.

According to the procedural law of the Constitutional Court, it was now up to the Hural to accept or reject the court decision. The Hural,

---

[91] "Constitutional Court Ruling," *BBC*, December 2, 1998, available in NEXIS, NEWS Library, ALLNWS file.
[92] *Ibid.*

however, chose to take no action at all. Without a rejection by the Hural, the court could not issue a final decision *en banc*. This is precisely what the Hural wished. Despite the public criticism and three formal requests by the Constitutional Court, the Hural delayed its consideration until parliamentary elections in June.

Those elections resulted in an overwhelming victory by the MPRP, which took seventy-two out of seventy-six seats in the State Great Hural. The issue of how to form a government was again at the fore. After an "interpretation" of the status of the court ruling by the Hural, the MPRP declared that it was able to form a government out of parliament, as if the controversial amendments to the constitution had survived. The court had stood firm and as a consequence had provoked the parliament to completely ignore it and claim the power to authoritatively decide the constitutional issue.

On July 28, 2000, over four months after the court's decision and nearly four months after the expiration of the period required by law for consideration of such a decision, the State Great Hural finally debated the Constitutional Court ruling, but avoided a formal rejection. By a vote of sixty-two to two, it stated that the Constitutional Court had heard an issue outside its jurisdiction – namely, the constitutionality of a constitutional amendment. But the Hural acted not by issuing a formal resolution reacting to the court decision as required by law, but rather by issuing a short note in its record indicating that it considered the issue finalized. The Constitutional Court expressed its dissatisfaction with this action, and on August 1, 2000 it sent a letter demanding an official resolution. The court also asserted that the State Great Hural had authorized itself to interpret the constitution, which should be the exclusive job of the Constitutional Court.

The same day, Speaker of the Hural L. Enebish replied to the Constitutional Court chairman, stating that the parliament had concluded that any resolution accepting or rejecting the court's decision would be considered an acceptance of the illegal action of the Constitutional Court in ruling a constitutional amendment unconstitutional. One influential member of the Hural, Ts. Sharavdorj, suggested merging the Constitutional Court with the Supreme Court, asking rhetorically whether Mongolia needed two high courts.[93] Moreover, he mentioned the possibility of recalling those members of the Constitutional Court that had been appointed by

[93] *Zuuny Medee* (newspaper), March 28, 2000

the State Great Hural despite the fact that there is no such formal mechanism of recall. These remarks can be seen as a tacit threat to the court.

Constitutional Court Chairman N. Jantsan reacted in a newspaper interview, saying that the State Great Hural violated the constitution by refusing to render a formal resolution, because the Hural had intended to prevent the Constitutional Court from hearing the issue. There should not be any confusion about whether the issue was under the jurisdiction of the Constitutional Court, said Jantsan, and only the court is capable of determining the extent of constitutional court jurisdiction. Therefore, the court must review the matter and issue a final decision. Otherwise, the Hural would never render any formal resolution if it disagreed with a constitutional court ruling, allowing parliament to avoid the supervision of the Constitutional Court and undermining the procedural scheme laid out in the constitution.

On October 29, 2000, the court reconsidered the constitutional amendment and *again* ruled that it was unconstitutional. It relied on procedural grounds, specifically Article 68.1 that states that amendments to the constitution may be initiated by certain designated bodies. The court read these as being exclusive, implying that a constitutional amendment initiated by State Great Hural on its own was not constitutional unless the legislature consulted with the Constitutional Court and the president. Seven members of the court were present and voted.

The MPRP government was now in a dilemma. The prime minister and four members of the cabinet were themselves members of the State Great Hural. Giving up the parliamentary seats would force a by-election, but that was not completely out of the question given the huge MPRP majority. Nevertheless, the MPRP responded by initiating another constitutional amendment with exactly the same text as had already been adopted – and rejected – the previous year. The proposed amendment was presented simultaneously to the State Great Hural, the president, and Constitutional Court, seeking to avoid the charge that the initiators had not followed proper procedures. In a sense, they were daring the Constitutional Court because the court had, in its final rejection, relied on procedural grounds rather than the provision in the constitution that says that members can have no other employment outside Parliament.

The amendment passed by a vote of sixty-eight to zero with four members protesting the session by not attending. The president, however, vetoed the amendment, forcing the State Great Hural to reconsider the amendment. The Hural then mustered the necessary two-thirds vote to overturn the president's veto. Intensive discussions ensued, and finally, the third time it had heard the issue, the court agreed that the amendments were indeed constitutional. The amendments were signed in May 2001. The democratic integrity of the political system had been restored, and the court had backed down in the face of repeated pressure and political noncompliance with its formalist approach.

The tortuous story of the Mongolian Constitutional Court and its game of political hot potato with the president and parliament illustrates the dangers for courts in new democracies when they cannot avoid overtly political issues. Although the court had several opportunities to defuse the situation by giving in to parliamentary wishes, it never took the opportunity to do so and in this manner extended the constitutional crisis for nearly five years. The court's reading of the constitution was dubious and formalistic, both in terms of the underlying issue about the formation of the government and with regard to the procedure for constitutional amendments. Ultimately, the court contributed to its own marginalization, as the focus on the separation of powers and its inability to obtain parliamentary compliance has discouraged others from bringing cases.

This is not to say the court was the only source of the crisis. The president's reading of the constitution was itself bizarre. The behavior of the State Great Hural in failing to respond to the court decision of unconstitutionality was not contemplated by the constitutional drafters and appears to have hurt the constitutional order. At a minimum, the Hural violated its own organic law by failing to consider the issue within fifteen days and then issuing a ruling either accepting or rejecting the Constitutional Court decision. The Hural's finding that the court ruling was itself illegal was a clear signal to the court to back off, but one the court failed to respond to.

THEORY AND THE MONGOLIAN CASE

The Mongolian case sheds light on several of the theoretical issues laid out in earlier chapters concerning the establishment and expansion of judicial review in new democracies. Foremost among the issues considered in this comparative project is why the institution of a constitutional court is adopted in the first place and why it takes the shape it does. Chapters 1 and 2 emphasized the importance of electoral uncertainty as a motivating factor for choosing to set up an independent judiciary in a democracy. Where constitutional designers believe that they may not control the political institutions of government, they are likely to set up a court to serve as an enforcement body protecting the constitutional bargain from encroachment. Where designers believe that they will retain a dominant position in government, they will seek stronger power for the political branches and will forgo institutional constraint in favor of parliamentary sovereignty.

The Mongolian situation was somewhat in between. Although it was fairly legitimate for a communist party, with a strong base of support in the countryside, the MPRP knew it might lose elections. It also needed opposition support for the constitutional bargain.

Certainly, the new parties would have to have been quite optimistic to believe they would be able to overcome the MPRP's natural political advantages in the short run. With an established party machine, large membership, and a deep network in the countryside, the MPRP was in a position to become a dominant party along the lines of what Lucien Pye has called "one-and-a-half party" systems found elsewhere in Asia.[94] Fear of an MPRP comeback is what motivated the new political forces to push for speedy adoption of the constitution. Expecting to be out of power gave them incentive to push for open access to constitutional review.

On the other hand, the MPRP's position in the constitutional scheme was also uncertain. It created a directly elected presidency with an age requirement that most oppositionists would be unable to meet. This gave the MPRP a likely veto power over new legislation. But it also led to a need for constitutional adjudication. In any system of separated powers, it is natural to ask for an arbiter to delimit the respective responsibilities of each institution and maintain the "purity" of the separation scheme. The drafters certainly received what they bargained for in the jurisprudence of the Mongolian court that has placed the separation of powers above all other constitutional values.

Why not rely on ordinary courts to perform the review function? The Mongolian drafters considered and rejected this option. There was little confidence in the abilities of the ordinary judiciary, a low-status profession, to undertake the important task of constitutional review. Other segments of the legal profession were not held in particularly high esteem either, as the entire criminal justice system was heavily biased toward the state and the private legal profession was minuscule. There was, and is today, little discussion of the rule of law in the popular press, and judges are widely believed to be corrupt, with civil cases auctioned to the highest bidder. In such an environment, it would have been remarkable if the

---

[94] Lucien Pye, *Asian Power and Politics: The Cultural Dimensions of Authority* (1985).

constitution drafters had entrusted ordinary judges with the constitutional review function.

It is important not to overemphasize the capacity of actors to engage in rational *ex ante* choices in such environments. Several times in Mongolian political development, parties took action expecting a particular outcome that failed to materialize.[95] The saga of parliamentary election law illustrates this point. Immediately after the passage of the constitution, the Small Hural debated and passed a law governing elections to the new State Great Hural to be held in June 1992. The four-party opposition agreed to a single-member district, plurality system, but then proceeded to run multiple candidates in each district. The results were straight out of Duverger. By not coordinating their candidates, opposition parties drew support away from each other, and the MPRP won seventy-one out of seventy-six seats with only 56% of the popular vote. During the next parliamentary election in 1996, the opposition formed a coalition to coordinate candidacies in the individual districts. It nevertheless demanded that the electoral system include some component of proportional representation, thinking this would increase its chances of gaining seats. The MPRP predictably refused to modify the system, believing that its rural network would lead to victory. But the coordination by the opposition proved sufficient to overcome organizational disadvantages, and they won elections in 1996.

A similar example of such institutional miscalculation occurred during constitutional design. The MPRP was the proponent of a strong presidency because it had a number of senior and popular figures, while the new, younger political forces favored a strong Parliament. But the new forces were decimated in the first postratification parliamentary elections. Meanwhile, the MPRP's President Ochirbat began to distance himself from his party's parliamentary majority. He more frequently used the veto and sought to preserve some semblance of political balance in the face of the MPRP's overwhelming parliamentary majority.[96] Frustrated with Ochirbat's performance, the MPRP dropped him as a candidate in

---

[95] Similar instances can be found in other postsocialist contexts. In Hungary and Bulgaria, opposition forces in roundtable talks anticipated that the communists would control the presidency and hence gave it few powers. Opposition leaders then won the offices. Mark Brzezinski, *The Struggle for Constitutionalism in Poland* 242 n.2 (1998).

[96] This illustrates the importance of the institutional approach. Although our account has emphasized parties, there are important cleavages that exist between institutions controlled by the same party.

the first presidential election held in 1993. He ran and won on the opposition ticket.

The general point is that poor information in states of political disequilibrium characterizes new democracies. Examples abound from other contexts. Even where information is accurate, other players may not act as predicted.[97] In the Mongolian case, parties chose positions in the debate over institutional design based on certain expectations of future performance. Within eighteen months, the institution that each political force had promoted was controlled by the other side. Disequilibrium means outcomes are harder to predict. In the context of such uncertainties, the incentive to adopt a constitutional court resembles a minimax strategy on the part of all parties and factions to secure political gains. By controlling the power of the state in conditions of political uncertainty, the constitutional drafters minimize the maximum damage they could suffer in the event they lose electoral power. Constitutional review provides insurance against electoral loss. Decentralized access to constitutional review makes sense as a way of ensuring that the power to constrain government can be invoked easily. And without a tradition of private law or a culture of legal constraint on powerholders, ordinary judges could not be trusted with this function.

The system initially worked as anticipated, as both political forces have been able to gain victories at the court when they were out of power. However, the Mongolian system contains an explicit mechanism for politicians to express their dissatisfaction with the Constitutional Court, namely their power to accept or reject the initial judgments of the court before enforcement. This led to increasing constitutional difficulties as the MPRP established an overwhelming majority in the parliament and increasingly rejected the court's decisions.

To understand how this has worked in fact, we return to the caseload statistics presented in Table 6.2. The statistics indicate a troubling increase in the frequency of parliamentary refusals. Judgments were accepted by the Hural most of the time until 1994, even though the parliament was controlled by the MPRP's conservative faction. Perhaps in the early years, the prestige of the constitution prevailed over raw power considerations,

---

[97] To take one example only, the Polish constitutional drafters of 1921 were concentrated in the parliament and expected that the dominant political figure Jozef Pilsudski would win the presidency. They designed a weak institution. The weakness induced Pilsudski not to run, contributing to political instability in the early 1920s. Brzezinski, *supra* note 95, at 28.

but by 1994 the Hural began to refuse court decisions more frequently. Eventually, it appears that refusal became a matter of course, for in 1995 the Hural did not accept a single judgment of the court. This obviously makes a final decision more difficult to obtain and has led to a lower equilibrium level of judicial review.

According to the chairman of the court, the relationship with the State Great Hural is the single greatest problem facing the court.[98] The State Great Hural appears less and less willing to defer to the court's view of the constitutional text and allegedly is now refusing to accept even the most straightforward judgments. As the court's decisions are less frequently accepted, it becomes a less attractive place to bring disputes. The caseload statistics in Table 6.2 indicate that the court is less likely to receive petitions when it is being ignored by parliament. Because the court has only been in operation for six years, there are not enough data points to demonstrate this statistically. Nevertheless, a regression analysis modeling the number of petitions as a function of the previous years' rejection rate by parliament shows a correlation in the predicted direction (albeit at an insignificant level of $t = -.48$). "Punishment" by the political body appears to reduce the demand for dispute resolution.

CONCLUSION

The Mongolian case illustrates how the court has provided a forum for electoral losers. During 1992–96 and again after 2000, the Mongolian Hural has been dominated by one party to an extent seldom seen in democratic politics. During this period, the MPRP had a sufficient majority to unilaterally modify the constitution and could pass legislation easily. However, the president provided a counterbalancing force, as he used his veto liberally to constrain the parliamentary majority. This led to a number of interbranch disputes wherein the court generally sided with the president. The court's rights jurisprudence also developed during the early years of its existence, pushed by frequent petitions from NGOs formed by the opposition forces. Those who lost in the legislature went to the court.

The minoritarian habit proved hard to kick, however, and the court made a major decision hampering the new parliamentary majority

---

[98] Interview with G. Sovd, December 4, 1997. This statement is all the more remarkable because almost every other public institution in Mongolia would likely respond to such a question with a discussion of the material difficulties caused by the transition to a market economy.

in 1996. In the wake of the separation decision, the new parties who had been the court's best clients until 1996 became its fiercest critics. Even Lamjav began to quiet his invocation of the court, perhaps chastened by his own party's criticism of him for bringing the petition to separate government and parliament. Unable to secure parliamentary compliance with its ruling on the 1999 constitutional amendments, the court appears to be moving from a high equilibrium toward a lower level of judicial review. On balance, the court has not played the stabilizing role that it could have had it been willing to develop mediate solutions to the great political controversies it faced.

The Mongolian case illustrates the tension between a court's need to build up institutional power and the pressure to play the insurance function for political losers. If the court is too aggressive in pursuing the latter in the short term, it may undermine its own power over the medium and long term. On the other hand, if it is too cautious for fear of provoking political backlash, it will fail to fulfill its role as a political insurer and will be only a marginal player. Navigating this tension is the task of courts in new democracies. The Mongolian story illustrates the danger of miscalculation.

7

Rule by Law or Rule of Law?
The Constitutional Court of Korea

INTRODUCTION

The two previous case studies of Taiwan and Mongolia traced the growth of judicial power in the shadow of dominant Leninist parties. In both cases, the dominant party was able to maintain substantial influence on the constitutional court in a democratic era, even as the preferences of the party evolved to reflect the changing rules of the political game. Korea presents a very different context for democratization because the prior regime was a military dictatorship. This type of regime has a different capacity for influencing a court under conditions of democratization, as argued in Chapter 3. Unlike dominant parties, military authoritarians have difficulty translating their power into democratic constitutional schemes. Their only threat is to exit the constitutional order completely. The Korean case therefore illustrates the difference between political party and military regimes in setting the stage for judicial review.

Unlike Taiwan and Mongolia, Korea's democratization process is sometimes characterized as incomplete. Whereas local scholars and politicians in the former two countries celebrate the successful transformation to democracy, scholars of Korean politics focus on the imperfections of its democracy, using such terms as *procedural democracy*, *partial democracy*, and *electoral democracy* to reflect their ambiguity.[1] By any objective

[1] For a good discussion, see David I. Steinberg, "The Republic of Korea: Pluralizing Politics," in *Politics in Developing Countries: Comparing Experiences with Democracy* 369–416 (Larry Diamond et al., eds., 1995); see also David I. Steinberg, "Korea: Triumph amid Turmoil," 9 *J. Democracy* 76–90 (1998); and Robert E. Bedeski, *The Transformation of South Korea: Reform and Reconstitution in the Sixth Republic under Roh Tae Woo, 1987–1992* (1994).

measure, however, Korea has made great strides since 1988 in reestablish-ing representative institutions, expanding protection of civil rights and political liberties, and transferring effective power from the military to civilians. The 1998 presidential inauguration of long-time dissident Kim Dae-jung marked a significant milestone in this regard.

The performance of the Constitutional Court in constraining political power illustrates the robustness of Korean democracy. In the years since its establishment in 1988, the court has systematically sought to expand its jurisdiction to make itself accessible to the public, has created new unwritten constitutional rights, and has actively promoted freedom of ex-pression.[2] The court has constrained political power in key cases and has engaged in continuing dialogues with other political institutions about the limitations on government power necessary to healthy democratic func-tioning. And the court has done so in a most unlikely context, where legal authority was traditionally subservient to political control. One leading analyst notes that the judiciary today "is far more autonomous than it has been at any time in Korean history."[3]

The success of the court has to a great extent resulted directly from the interplay of politics and structure, illustrating the interaction of in-stitutional and political factors. The court was created at the moment of launching of democratization and thus embodied a consensus toward lib-eralization of Korean politics and at least a formal commitment to the rule of law. More importantly, the particular political configuration of Korean democratization, with a military intent on withdrawal from active politics and three major civilian political forces more or less evenly balanced, has prevented any one force from dominating the court. In addition to these political and institutional factors, the careful jurisprudence of the court itself has played a role, as it has been able to assert itself into important political questions without provoking backlash.

This chapter traces the development and early jurisprudence of the Korean Constitutional Court and explores how it has contributed to nascent norms of constitutionalism and the rule of law in a political en-vironment traditionally imbued with personalism. The chapter will also address the crucial question of how institutional incentives can encourage a shift from personal to legal authority at the highest levels of the political system. This issue is of concern not only to democracies in Northeast Asia,

---

[2] For particular discussion of freedom of expression, see Youm Kyu-ho, "Press Free-dom and Judicial Review in South Korea," 30 *Stan. J. Int'l L.* 1 (1994).

[3] Steinberg, "The Republic of Korea," *supra* note 1, at 400.

but to the many countries seeking to enhance the rule of law to promote "good governance" and economic development.[4]

THE KOREAN LEGAL TRADITION AND
THE AUTHORITARIAN PERIOD

Korea has long enjoyed a Confucian tradition, with an attitude of distrust toward litigation and a preference for internalized norms as a means of social ordering.[5] The Korean legal tradition began to undergo intensive modernization during the Japanese colonial period (1910–45). During this period, Korea was imbued with the particular Japanese adaptation of Western European law. Korean judicial structure, legal education system, and substantive law were all copied directly from Japan. The civil law tradition is thus the starting point for any analysis of Korean law, but not the only source of influence. The end of World War II marked Korea's independence and the beginning of a three-year occupation by U.S. military authorities. American influence on the legal system became increasingly important after 1945, particularly in constitutional law.[6] Many substantive legal doctrines were imposed by the occupying authorities or borrowed from American models. As in Japan, however, the anticommunist politics of the U.S. occupation prevented a complete purge of lower-level legal officials and bureaucrats, and substantial Japanese influence remained in place. The judiciary has thus been seen as rather conservative and formalistic since at least the early 1950s.

Since independence in 1945, Korea has had six republics. None of the eight constitutional amendments before 1987 was openly discussed or debated but rather reflected the prerogatives of the ruling forces of the

---

[4] See, for example, Lawyers Committee for Human Rights, *Halfway to Reform: The World Bank and the Venezuelan Justice System*, at 11–12 (1996) for a discussion of recent programs in this regard by multilateral development banks in Latin America. See also *Good Government and Law: Legal and Institutional Reform in Developing Countries* (Julio Faundez, ed., 1997).

[5] For example, Steinberg, *The Republic of Korea, supra* note 1, at 397. For discussions of the role of Confucianism in Korean law, see Hahm Pyong-choon, *The Korean Political Tradition and Law* (1987); Yoon Dae-kyu, "New Developments in Korean Constitutionalism: Changes and Prospects," 4 *Pac. Rim L. & Pol'y J.* 395 (1995); Yoon Dae-kyu, *Law and Political Authority in South Korea* (1990); Choi Dae-kwon, "Informal Ways vs. the Formal Law in Korea," paper presented at Research Committee on the Sociology of Law, Tokyo, 1995.

[6] Ahn Kyong-whan, "The Influence of American Constitutionalism on South Korea," 27 *S. Ill. U. L. J.* 71 (1998).

day. Even the 1987 Constitution, which initiated political liberalization in response to the demands of the public, enjoyed a relatively closed process of adoption, carried out by the various political factions behind closed doors. Public input and discussion were minimal, although the opposition parties did play a role for the first time in Korean history.

Of the six republics, only the brief Second Republic and the current Sixth Republic have been democracies in any kind of complete sense, though electoral institutions remained functional throughout the postwar period. The basic pattern, extant during the First, Third, Fourth, and Fifth Republics, was a kind of corrupt bureaucratic authoritarianism, formally legitimated by regular but manipulated elections, with military generals occupying the presidency at the center of the system. These strongmen had little interest in tolerating an independent rule of law with the capacity to check their power.

While the regime types have varied, there have been certain constants in postwar Korean politics. Gregory Henderson claims Korean politics can be understood as a vortex, with all power at the center.[7] The presidency has remained squarely at the center of politics. Other constants include a deepening, and occasionally violent, regionalism, the centralized state, and highly personal concepts of power.[8] Another fixed feature of modern Korean governance has been the instrumental use of law. The authoritarian rulers of Korea have continuously relied on law to implement their programs and legitimate their authority. Law has been a tool of the rulers, not a constraint on them. Of particular importance were the National Security Act and the Anti-Communist Act, which criminalized anyone who praised, encouraged, or supported communist or antistate organizations. These laws severely limited the efficacy of formal constitutional guarantees of freedom of expression.[9] The authoritarian state used the continuous and real threat from North Korea to justify internal suppression of dissent.

The Supreme Court routinely upheld these laws when challenged. Some scholars attributed this passivity to a judicial culture affected by a preference for unanimity, consensus, and mediation over confrontational adjudication.[10] Another traditional explanation would focus on the strong influence of continental legal thought, in which judges are seen as expert

[7] Gregory Henderson, *Korea: Politics of the Vortex* 242 (1968).
[8] Steinberg, *The Republic of Korea, supra* note 1, at 370.
[9] Yoon, *supra* note 5, at 171–76.
[10] This is the famous argument of Hahm, *supra* note 5.

functionaries of the hierarchically organized governing bureaucracy. Probably most important, however, were the political constraints on courts.

Each of Korea's authoritarian republics included some provision for constitutional review. The First Republic (1948–60) bifurcated constitutional review between a Supreme Court, with the power to adjudicate the constitutionality of administrative regulations, and a Constitutional Committee with the power to review legislation. The latter was composed of the vice-president of the country, five Supreme Court justices, and five legislators, and was therefore as much a political organ as a legal one. This form of centralized review was adopted after extensive consideration of the American decentralized model of judicial review. Ultimately, the U.S. model was rejected because of the distrust of the judges who had served the Japanese colonial regime.

The Constitutional Committee's procedures could only be invoked by an ordinary court presented with a constitutional question in the context of a concrete case. Because it required a two-thirds majority to decide cases, this structure gave the appointees of the judiciary and the legislature mutual vetoes over findings of unconstitutionality, and hence it was highly improbable that it would develop into an effective constraint on legislative power. Indeed, the Constitutional Committee reviewed only seven cases in its eleven-year history, striking two statutes that designated lower courts as the final appellate authority for certain violations.[11] As such, the committee can be seen as siding with the superior levels of the judicial hierarchy at the expense of administrative expediency or empowering lower courts. As constitutional decisions, however, these did not constrain the substantive preferences of the authorities; they merely ensured that the procedures used to adjudicate cases were consistent across different areas of law and were consistent with the hierarchical structure of the administration of justice.

As the 1950s drew to a close, President Rhee Syng-man aged and grew increasingly authoritarian. Rhee eventually was forced into retirement by student demonstrations and pressure from the United States. The short-lived Second Republic (1960–61) was a period of chaotic postauthoritarianism and was Korea's only democratic regime until the 1987 constitutional reforms. The Second Republic included in its constitutional

---

[11] The two laws were the Agricultural Land Reform Act, Article 24(1), which allowed final appeal to the Court of Appeal, and the Special Decree for Criminal Punishment Under Emergency, Article 9(1), providing for the district court as the only court of original jurisdiction for certain crimes, without appeal to the Supreme Court. Yoon, *supra* note 5, at 154.

amendments provisions for a German-style constitutional court, but this body was never established.[12] However, the provisions had a longer-term impact, as numerous institutional design features from the second Republic were incorporated into the design of the Constitutional Court in the Sixth Republic, including the appointment mechanism, the six-year terms, and the two-thirds voting requirement. In contrast with the earlier Constitutional Committee, the Constitutional Court members were explicitly required to maintain political neutrality and were prohibited from joining parties. As such, the institutional design began to move in the direction of autonomy for constitutional adjudication.

In 1961, the Second Republic fell in a military coup, and the Third Republic (1961–72) was established under General Park Chung-hee. Park ruthlessly suppressed dissent and purged supporters of earlier regimes, but his rule set the stage for economic takeoff by creating an autonomous, powerful, and relatively clean bureaucracy.[13] The combination of authoritarian rule and export-oriented industrial policy produced the "Korean miracle." In many ways, Korea is still confronting the legacy of Park's program of economic and social modernization accompanied by tight political control.

The Third Republic had a U.S.-style decentralized system of judicial review, but the judiciary used its power sparingly. Toward the end of the Third Republic, however, the Supreme Court challenged political authority and provoked a backlash that contributed to the downfall of the entire constitution. The incident arose when a lower court struck Article 2(1) of the Government Compensation Law, a provision that excluded military personnel from certain forms of compensation normally available to those who suffered injury from government action.[14] The court held that this provision violated the constitutional guarantee of equality. This was controversial because, as a militarized state, compensation to active servicemen for injuries sustained in training or war could impose a severe cost on the state budget. The executive branch feared the financial consequences of the decision.

The case was appealed to the Supreme Court. Anticipating an unfavorable decision at the Supreme Court level, the political authorities amended Article 59(1) of the Judiciary Organization Act in July 1970 to raise the

[12] Ahn, *supra* note 6, at 86.
[13] See the discussion in Hilton Root, *Small Countries, Big Lessons: Governance and the Rise of East Asia* at 18–31 (1996). See also Alice Amsden, *Asia's Next Giant* (1989).
[14] Yoon, *supra* note 5, at 185.

voting threshold required to declare a law unconstitutional from a simple majority to two-thirds of all justices. This obviously would have hampered the future exercise of judicial review and, more importantly, sent a signal to the judiciary that the executive was willing to interfere with its institutional autonomy to achieve the result it desired. Despite this clear signal from the politicians, the Supreme Court upheld the lower court's decision that the Government Compensation Law violated military personnel's constitutional right to equal treatment. The court also struck the statutory amendment raising the vote threshold as a violation of the separation of powers, arguing that majority rule was a "basic principle of judgment."[15] If the constitution did not provide otherwise, held the court, the political authorities could not raise the threshold for a judicial decision through ordinary legislation. This was the only instance of the Supreme Court striking a statute during the Third Republic.

President Park was furious at this decision and the audacity shown by the court in resisting political interference. Judicial review was thus at the center of events leading up to the establishment of the Fourth Republic, known as *Yushin*, in 1972. This round of constitutional amendments centralized power in the presidency and specifically gave President Park the power to renominate all judges, which he subsequently used to exclude every judge who had voted to strike down Article 2(1) of the Government Compensation Law. The constitution was also amended to incorporate the provision denying compensation to military personnel who sustain injuries in active duty. In this way, by inserting the *status quo ante* into the text of the constitution itself, Park overruled the court, but accompanied this overruling with a counterattack on the institution.[16]

In reaction to Park's negative experience with the decentralized system of judicial review, the *Yushin* Constitution assigned constitutional review power to a constitutional committee, where it remained for the duration of the Fourth and Fifth Republics (1972–81 and 1981–88).[17] The Constitutional Committee was a nine-member body, with three members each appointed by the president, National Assembly, and chief justice. This scheme effectively gave the president (who controlled the dominant party in the National Assembly) a veto over a declaration of unconstitutionality. Questions could only be referred to the committee by the Supreme

---

[15] Yoon, *supra* note 5, at 186.
[16] Constitution of 1972, Article 26(2).
[17] Yoon, *supra* note 5, notes that popular pressure for an American-style judicial review system was rejected in the 1980 constitutional debates. See ibid. at 168.

Court, so access was quite limited. Not surprisingly, the committee was never called on by the Supreme Court to use its power during those years.

In summary, judicial review in its various institutional forms had marginal impact during the early years of postwar Korean history. The exercise of judicial power was so minimal as to be almost nonexistent, and it can be characterized as a low-equilibrium, prostrate form of judicial review. When courts began to exercise the power to constrain the state in the early 1970s, they were subject to counterattack and overruling in the form of the *Yushin* Constitution. President Park's first counterattack, raising the decision threshold, appeared to be formally constitutional, but the Supreme Court struck the legislation, prompting a higher-order counterattack in the form of constitutional amendments that emasculated the court. By insisting on challenging the sovereign on a matter of some political importance, the court contributed to the deepening of authoritarianism in the *Yushin* period and lost the power to exercise judicial review.

THE 1987 CONSTITUTIONAL AMENDMENTS AND DEMOCRATIZATION

Judicial review provides a means of legitimating authority as well as limiting it. By failing to empower even a low-equilibrium form of judicial review, the Fourth and Fifth Republics failed to enhance their own legitimacy over time. The effects were felt particularly strongly by President Chun Doo-hwan of the Fifth Republic, who took power in a military coup in December 1979 after Park was assassinated by his own Central Intelligence Agency director. The subsequent massacre of civilian protesters at Kwangju some months later further eroded the regime's legitimacy and continued to haunt Korean politics through the election of Kim Dae-jung in 1997.

Chun desperately lacked legitimacy from the beginning and sought to gain it by presenting his regime as a transitional one. It would follow procedural forms of constitutionalism and prepare the way for an eventual return to civilian power. This strategy may have bought the regime some time, but it also ensured continual pressures to move faster than the regime was willing to. The key issue for the opposition was constitutional revision to create a presidential system of government with a directly elected president.

The Chun government found its electoral support slipping in the 1985 National Assembly elections and pressure for constitutional reform began to build. In 1986 and 1987, student protests became much more active, and the United States indicated that it would not overlook violent suppression of the students as it had in 1980.[18] Chun announced there would be constitutional revision. Then on April 13, 1987, he decided to suspend debate on constitutional reform.[19] This galvanized the opposition, gave new momentum to the student protests that had been losing steam, and drew in the recently emerged middle class.[20]

Protests escalated after Chun picked military colleague Roh Tae-woo as his successor on June 10, 1987. On June 29, Roh issued a declaration announcing political liberalization, including new parliamentary elections the following year, direct election of the president, and amnesty and a restoration of political rights for prominent dissident Kim Dae-jung.[21] A corner had been turned; democratization would proceed.

As in Taiwan and Mongolia, the international environment was a crucial factor in the decision to democratize. The position of the United States as external guarantor of the regime, as well as the principal training ground for political thinkers, meant that the regime was vulnerable to external pressure to democratize. Indeed, the February 1987 signal by the United States that it would not countenance repression was no doubt a key factor in delimiting Chun's options for responding to escalating demonstrations.

Subsequently, the three main political parties agreed to constitutional amendments. The key reform was direct election of the president, who had traditionally served as the center of the Korean political system.[22] Roh's declaration, however, promised other reforms, including greater freedom of the press and labor and resumption of local government elections. Constitutional amendments were agreed upon in October 1987 by representatives of the three main parties in the National Assembly, and many reflected political compromises without apparent rationale.[23] One result of this closed-door process is the scarcity of data on the 1987 adoption of constitutional amendments. This makes scholarly analysis of the

[18] The message was delivered in the form of a speech by Assistant Secretary of State Gaston Sigur in February. Steinberg, *The Republic of Korea, supra* note 1, at 385.
[19] John Kie-chang Oh, *Korean Politics* 95 (1999).
[20] Han Sung-joo, "South Korea: Politics in Transition," in *Democracy in Korea: Its Ideals and Realities* 49 (Choi Sang-yong, ed., 1997).
[21] The text of the declaration can be found in Bedeski, *supra* note 1, at 169–70.
[22] Bedeski, *supra* note 1, at 45. Kim Dae-jung's party supported the creation of a new office of vice-president, so as to dilute presidential power and give Kim the opportunity to gain support from another region by having a running mate.
[23] For example, the five-year term of the presidency. See Ahn, *supra* note 6, at 98.

constitution-writing process quite difficult and additionally means that original intent is not a viable interpretive strategy for a court seeking to interpret terms of the constitution.

Why did the ruling party agree to direct election of the president? The conventional wisdom is that this was the central issue for the opposition and that their demands could no longer be resisted.[24] In fact, the regime may have foreseen that the institutional design was to its own benefit. The political configuration was such that a single candidate supported by a united opposition could have easily defeated the ruling party of Roh Tae-woo. Nevertheless, regional and personality differences divided the opposition supporters of Kim Young-sam and Kim Dae-jung. It was thus predictable that the two would ultimately split the opposition vote, and they proceeded to do so in the 1987 presidential election, when Roh triumphed with only 36.6% of the vote.[25] The decision to reform appears to have been a rational choice by the regime. Knowing it had an excellent chance to convert its authoritarian rule into electoral power in a reformed game, the ruling party agreed to reforms and was able to accomplish the difficult trick of transforming itself from a military power into a civilian force. Clearly, the ruling party "won" at constitutional revision by having the president elected by simple plurality and without provision for a vice-president. The lack of a vice-presidency, in particular, made it harder for the opposition to unite into a single ticket.

The political dynamic of the constitutional bargain, with three parties of nearly equal strength, was crucial in the institutional design. In such a circumstance, none of the three leaders could predict that he would win the presidency. In fact, the likely result was that each would see himself as the loser in the first election. One response to this situation was to limit the presidency to a single five-year term. This would permit the office to be held for a limited period by each of three leaders, a situation that has in fact occurred since 1987. A second response was to create a constitutional court to ensure that the bargain is kept by the other protagonists. In this sense, the political configuration of three equally strong parties provided an ideal environment for political insurance.

In the years following the 1987 election, democratization advanced significantly, despite Roh's military background and association with Chun.[26] Many political rights were restored, and the military decisively

---

[24] Oh, *supra* note 19, at 93–95.
[25] *Ibid.* at 95.
[26] See, generally, Bedeski, *supra* note 1.

moved out of politics during this period, a remarkable achievement. In 1992, long-time opposition leader Kim Young-sam was elected president, the first president without a military background since the brief Second Republic. Democratic performance under Kim Young Sam was criticized, and some abuses of rights remained, including continued use of the National Security Law, tight control over organized labor, and detention of political prisoners. But there was no doubt that the system was evolving in ever more liberal directions.[27]

The political environment of the Sixth Republic retains its strongly presidential character. The president appoints the prime minister with the approval of the National Assembly and appoints other cabinet members on the prime minister's nomination. The president also is the head of his political party, which, until the administration of Kim Dae-jung, always controlled the National Assembly. The vast majority of bills – some 80% according to a senior staff member of the National Assembly – come from the presidential administration, but this is likely to change under conditions of divided government.[28]

One of the most important constitutional amendments adopted in 1987 concerned the reestablishment of a constitutional court. It appears that the decision to adopt a designated court was the result of a compromise between the ruling party and the two opposition forces. The ruling party was strongly against giving the power of constitutional review to ordinary judges and even argued for limiting constitutional interpretation to the National Assembly.[29] The opposition, however, thought that basic rights needed protection somehow. Ultimately, the ruling party proposed a designated constitutional committee, and the opposition accepted so long as it would be a court with jurisdiction over direct constitutional complaints.

Why did the parties agree to a designated constitutional court? The Supreme Court itself may have been reluctant to take on the power.[30] The official commentary to the constitution notes that the creation of a special constitutional court is in part designed to avoid "the politicization

---

[27] Steinberg, *The Republic of Korea, supra* note 1, at 393.
[28] Interview with senior member of National Assembly research staff, March 29, 1998.
[29] See *The First Ten Years of the Korean Constitutional Court* (Constitutional Court of Korea, 2001).
[30] Compare *The First Ten Years of the Korean Constitutional Court, supra* note 29 (Supreme Court sought the power of judicial review), with James West and Yoon Dae-kyu, "The Constitutional Court of the Republic of Korea: Transforming the Jurisprudence of the Vortex," 40 *Am. J. Comp L.* 73, 76 (1992) (Supreme Court did not want the power).

of the courts of law due to their involvement in constitutional contro-versies."[31] This argument for separating constitutional issues reflects the ruling party's view that a centralized body is more responsive, easier to influence, and perhaps more predictable.[32] The constitutional complaint, however, ensured open access for those who thought they would lose the elections, the two opposition forces. The bargaining dynamic of the ruling power wanting centralization and the opposition wanting access was the same as in the Mongolian constitutional negotiations discussed in the last chapter.

Modeled closely on the Federal Constitutional Court in Germany, the constitutional adjudication system of the Sixth Republic marked a break with the immediate past. However, few observers expected the court to have the impact that it has had.[33] The court quickly served notice that it intended to take its role as guardian of the constitution seriously. Indeed, in its very first case, the court struck a provision of the Special Act on Expedited Litigation that held that the state could not be subject to pre-liminary attachment orders.[34] The court insisted that the constitutional guarantee of equality under the law requires civil procedure provisions to apply similarly to the state as to private citizens or corporations. In doing so, the court struck directly at the philosophical underpinnings of the *dirigisme* that had been at the heart of the postwar Korean political economy. In many other areas, as well, the court has had a dramatic im-pact. An examination of the institutional structure of the court will help in understanding this impact.

---

[31] James M. West and Edward J. Baker, "The 1987 Constitutional Reforms in South Korea: Electoral Processes and Judicial Independence," 1 *Harv. Human Rights YB* 135 (1988).

[32] *The First Ten Years of the Korean Constitutional Court, supra* note 29.

[33] Interviews with staff members of the Constitutional Court and constitutional law scholars, Seoul, February–March 1998. See also West and Baker, *supra* note 31. One author claims that some observers did not even expect the court to issue a single judgment in accordance with the ineffective supervision practiced by its immediate predecessor, the Constitutional Committee of the Fifth Republic. Peter Holland, "Towards Constitutionalism: The First Term of the Constitutional Court of South Korea," in *Asian Laws through Australian Eyes* 146 (Veronica Taylor, ed., 1997). The fact that there were originally two categories of justices, standing and nonstanding, also reflected an expectation that the workload of the court would be light. See West and Yoon, *supra* note 30, at 79; Yang Kun, "Judicial Review and Social Change in the Korean Democratizing Process," 41 *Am. J. Comp. L.* 1 (1993).

[34] Constitutional Court of Korea, *A Brief Look at the Constitutional Justice in Korea* (1996) (hereinafter, *A Brief Look*).

THE CONSTITUTIONAL COURT: STRUCTURE AND OPERATIONS

The Constitutional Court was established by the Constitutional Court Act of 1988.[35] Under Article 111(1) of the 1987 Constitution, the court has the following jurisdiction: (1) adjudicating the constitutionality of a law upon the request of a court; (2) impeachment; (3) deciding on the dissolution of unconstitutional political parties; (4) resolving jurisdictional disputes among state agencies and local governments; and (5) hearing public petitions relating to the constitution as prescribed by law. Of these, adjudicating the constitutionality of laws and constitutional petitions have been by far the most important; there has not to date been a single case related to either impeachment or the dissolution of a political party.[36]

The jurisdiction of the court, including the power to review legislation and to hear constitutional petitions, is essentially copied from that of the Federal Constitutional Court in Germany. Unlike the German court, however, the court cannot perform abstract review at the request of designated government agencies. Although the court has some role in resolving jurisdictional disputes between organs of government, this differs from abstract review. Indeed, Article 61(2) of the Constitutional Court Act restricts this form of review to those cases where the act or omission of the responding agency "infringes on or is in obvious danger of infringing on" the petitioning agency's authority. This is decidedly not abstract review in the pure form, but requires a showing of at least a threat to a concrete interest.

This form of jurisdictional dispute is further limited to disputes between branches of the government, between local and national government, and among local governments. There is no provision, for example, for the Constitutional Court to hear disputes between ministries or executive agencies.[37] Presumably, the strong political authority of the presidency is sufficient to resolve such disputes when they arise in the Korean context. Furthermore, local autonomy has historically been quite underdeveloped in Korea, where the first full-fledged local elections did not occur until 1995.[38] This underdevelopment is particularly noteworthy in comparison

---

[35] Law No. 4017 (1988).

[36] For a discussion of the legal requirements for the exercise of constitutional court jurisdiction over these two categories of cases, see West and Yoon, *supra* note 30, at 85–88.

[37] *Ibid.* at 91.

[38] Oh, *supra* note 19, at 152–54.

to federal states such as Germany or Austria, the countries whose systems of constitutional adjudication influenced the Korean institutional design. It is therefore not surprising that jurisdictional disputes have been seldom brought before the court, with only a few cases filed since the court was founded in 1988.

We can distinguish between two kinds of demand for judicial review. The sovereign seeks to use judicial review to legitimate its authority, as well as to resolve disputes among various agencies that may threaten the coherence of policy formation and execution. The other source of demand for judicial review is plaintiffs who seek to constrain the exercise of government power. The jurisdiction of the Constitutional Court of Korea reflects both kinds of demand; however, to date actual demand for judicial review has come mostly from plaintiffs through the petition process or through referrals by ordinary courts in the course of litigation, rather than from the sovereign. This is a key precondition for high-equilibrium review.

Article 45 of the Constitutional Court Act provided for a dichotomous decision as to constitutionality. The court in its early years adapted from the German system various other categories of decision that the court can render. First, the court can hold an act unconstitutional (*Verfassungswidrig*), voiding the act immediately. The court can find the act to be nonconforming with the constitution (*Unvereinbar*), in which case the National Assembly may be required to amend the act in the near future; the court can find a part of the act unconstitutional, in which case the offending provisions are severed and voided; the court can find the act constitutional but applied in an unconstitutional way ("unconstitutional limitedly"); and the court can find that the act is conformable limitedly (*Beschränkete Verfassungskonforme Auslegung*), that is, constitutional as long as it is interpreted in a certain way, as in the instant case. Finally, of course, the court may uphold the act as constitutional (*Vereinbar*).

These various gradations of declarations of constitutionality and unconstitutionality place the court in dialogue with the legislative branches and executive agencies. The court need not openly challenge legislative authority, but rather can send a signal to the legislature demanding or suggesting revision. The court can also provide guidance for enforcement agencies as to how to apply the law to avoid constitutional defect. These intermediate findings, falling short of a complete voiding of the law or action in question, force the political authorities to reconsider their initial decisions in light of constitutional interpretation. While the findings do not guarantee compliance, they throw the ball back into the court of the politicians. The court also has reduced risks from any failure to secure compliance: Because the politicians may have some period to comply, their failure to do so will be apparent only after some months, when the issue may have less political salience. The attractions of these mechanisms are amply illustrated in the Korean case, as the Constitutional Court has recently become more inclined to use the noncomformable finding than to declare a law unconstitutional.

As in the German system, any person who asserts that her or his constitutional rights have been infringed by government action or inaction may directly petition the court for relief.[39] There are two separate grounds for such petitions. Article 68(1) of the Constitutional Court Act allows petitions, after all available legal remedies have been exhausted, by citizens whose rights have been infringed by unconstitutional state action. Most of these cases have involved allegations of abuse of prosecutorial discretion when prosecutors do not indict.[40] Article 68(1) cases predominate because decisions of ordinary courts (to whom plaintiffs must turn to exhaust legal remedies) are excluded from the jurisdiction of the Constitutional Court. Article 68(2) concerns cases where a party has unsuccessfully sought referral by an ordinary court under Article 41 of the Constitutional Court Act and leads to a stay in ongoing litigation pending the Constitutional Court judgment.[41] This system is designed to partially remedy the lack of jurisdiction over decisions of ordinary courts. If no such petition right existed, ordinary court processes would be completely unreviewable by the Constitutional Court.

The court is composed of nine justices, who are appointed by the president upon nomination by various institutions. Three are nominated by the National Assembly, three are nominated by the chief justice, and three may be appointed by the president himself. The head of the Constitutional Court is appointed by the president from among the justices, with the consent of the National Assembly. Justices must be forty years of age, be qualified as attorneys, and must have served for fifteen years as a judge, prosecutor, attorney, government lawyer, or law professor.

When seven or more justices are present, the court has a quorum or full bench. At least six votes are required to declare a law unconstitutional, to dissolve a political party, to accept a constitutional complaint,

---

[39] Constitutional Court Act, Article 68(1) (hereinafter "CCA").

[40] Ahn, *supra* note 6, at 77; see also West and Yoon, *supra* note 30, at 101–2 (noting that in some cases the prosecutors reconsidered decisions not to indict). Some argued this showed the traditional autonomy of the prosecutors' office. *Ibid.* 102 n.108.

[41] CCA, Article 68(2).

or to overrule a previous precedent of the Constitutional Court. As in Germany, constitutional complaints are originally heard by a smaller bench of three justices that must decide whether or not a constitutional issue exists and whether procedural requirements have been satisfied.[42] *Amicus* briefs and interventions by third parties with a legally cognizable interest are allowed, and interest groups are increasingly active in using these techniques.

Because of the strong centralization of Korean politics, the president in fact can control the appointment of at least four or five justices of the court. An unwritten norm allows the parliamentary opposition at least one appointment from the three selected by the National Assembly. The president himself appoints three members, and his party in the National Assembly can appoint one or two more depending on its strength.[43] Because of the two-thirds supermajority requirement to strike a law, the president's appointees have an effective veto on finding laws unconstitutional. This reflects the general predominance of the president in Korean political structure.[44]

The tenure of constitutional court justices is six years, during which period they may not join any political party nor engage in political activities. The term is renewable, although like other judges constitutional justices must retire at age sixty-five.[45] Justices can only be removed upon impeachment or imprisonment for a crime.

PERFORMANCE OF THE COURT: QUANTITATIVE DATA

The court has been quite active in its first two terms of operations, becoming involved in numerous politically sensitive cases and frequently striking legislation. In its first full year, 1989, the court found legislation and government action wholly or partially unconstitutional in 38% of the cases in which it rendered a decision on the merits.[46] To be sure, the vast majority of cases filed were settled or dismissed;

---

[42] These procedural requirements include exhaustion of other legal remedies, representation by an attorney, and time limitations. CCA, Article 72.

[43] In 1987, Roh's party appointed one, because the opposition was composed of two main parties. In 1992, Kim Young-sam and Roh Tae-woo had merged into the ruling Democratic Liberal Party. It appointed two members, and the single opposition party appointed one.

[44] See, generally, Hahm Sung-deuk and L. Christopher Plein, *After Development: The Transformation of the Korean Presidency and Bureaucracy* (1997).

[45] The president of the court can sit until age seventy. CCA, Article 7(2).

[46] Extracted from Constitutional Court statistics.

TABLE 7.1 *Caseload of the Constitutional Court through September 2001*

	Constitutionality of Law	Competence Dispute	Article 68(1) Constitutional Complaints Subtotal	Article 68(2) Constitutional Complaints Subtotal	Total Article 68 Constitutional Complaints	Total
Total Cases Filed	414	15	5,787	915	6,702	7,131
Dismissed by Small Bench	98	2	2,387	72	2,459	2,459
Withdrawn			179	27	206	306
Full Bench Decisions:						
Ruled Unconstitutional	68		23	125	148	216
Nonconformable	24		6	32	38	62
Limitedly Unconstitutional	8		6	18	24	32
Limitedly Constitutional	7			20	20	27
Constitutional	164		3	435	438	602
Revoked (Administrative Action)		2	139		139	141
Rejected		3	2,040		2,040	2,043
Dismissed	18	5	665	79	744	767
Miscellaneous			2	1	3	3
Total decisions on merits:	271	5	2217	630	2847	3126
Number Partial/Fully Struck	91	2	174	160	293	451
Percentage Partial/Fully Struck	37	40	8	31	12	14

Source: Extracted from Constitutional Court statistics. In keeping with Korean convention, merits cases include rejections but not dismissals. Partially/fully struck includes all decisions but "constitutional" and "rejected."

nevertheless, the threat of the court finding an act unconstitutional was sufficiently serious that the government became increasingly irritated. As might be expected, political forces sought to punish the court by limiting jurisdiction, most prominently in 1992, when the ruling party proposed to restrict the court's jurisdiction to cases of interbranch disputes.[47] This proposal by the ruling party was withdrawn due to strong public pressure.[48]

Table 7.1 describes the court's caseload through nearly twelve years of operations.

Of the 3,126 cases it has decided on the merits, the court has found 451 of them, or 14%, unconstitutional in whole, in part, or in the application. The percentage of laws struck has been much higher, some 37%. By striking laws early in its first term, the court induced an increase in filings to the court during the second term, as Table 7.2 demonstrates. The first row on the table represents those cases arising under Article 111(1) of the constitution, where the issue is referred to the court by an ordinary court in the course of ongoing proceedings. The second and third rows represent constitutional complaints from the public, as described in Article 68 of the Constitutional Court Act.

Court filings have been high and have generally increased over the course of its operations, as Figure 7.1 demonstrates. Although the court rejects or dismisses most complaints, the court often decides for the complainant when it does accept a constitutional petition. This illustrates the difficulty of using strike rates as a comparative tool, as the definition of the relevant pool of cases is likely to vary across institutional environments. It *is* possible to use this data to evaluate change in a particular court's performance over time, however.

Petitions under Article 68(1) of the Constitutional Court Act have been the single largest source of cases for the court, although the vast majority of these petitions are rejected by the court. The court has used Article 68(1) regularly to review the decisions of prosecutors not to prosecute, constraining the discretion of what was formerly the highest-status component of the Korean legal profession. However, the impact of Article 68(1) review has been somewhat limited by the uncertain legal effect of a finding of unconstitutionality. Some prosecutors interpret the finding as an instruction to reinvestigate the case; others, including scholars and

---

[47] Ahn, *supra* note 6, at 76.
[48] Yang Kun, "Judicial Review and Social Change in the Korean Democratizing Process," 41 *Am. J. Comp. L.* 1, 8 (1993).

TABLE 7.2 *Filings to the Constitutional Court*

Type of Filing	88	89	90	91	92	93	94	95	96	97	98	99	00	01 (Through September)	Total
Unconstitutionality of law	13	142	71	9	24	17	10	17	23	15	18	18	12	25	377
Petition 68(1)	25	268	230	233	313	301	286	395	431	433	528	784	857	703	4,227
Petition 68(2)	1	15	60	22	54	67	50	64	96	90	107	120	96	73	746
Total	39	425	362	264	392	385	347	476	552	538	657	924	968	802	5,361

Source: Extracted from statistics of the Constitutional Court. Total is greater than the sum of the filings on the table because it includes filings brought under other provisions of Article 111 of the constitution, including competence disputes among governments. 2001 statistics are nine-month statistics.

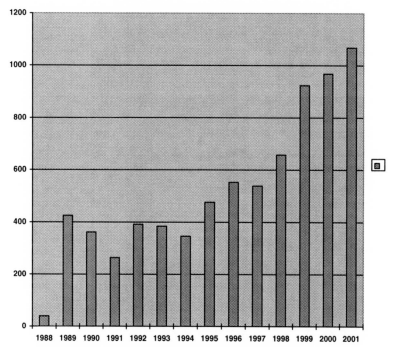

Note: 2001 number is an estimate based on nine-month statistics.

FIGURE 7.1. Total Filings by Year

activists, see it as an order to prosecute. As a result, findings of unconstitutionality do not always lead to prosecution.[49]

Constitutional complaints under Article 68(2), where a party challenges the failure by an ordinary court to refer a case to the court, are far more likely to be heard on the merits than 68(1) petitions, and the chances of success are higher for those that reach the merits stage. Roughly 30% of such petitions have resulted in a whole or partial finding of unconstitutionality.

The number of referrals by ordinary courts in the course of ongoing litigation has varied dramatically from year to year, as have the number of decisions. Indeed, one factor in the relatively low "strike rate" of overall cases under the court's first term was an anomalous year in which a large number of court referrals were found to concern a law that was eventually upheld.[50]

[49] Chang Yook-seok, "Prosecutor's Discretionary Power in the Republic of Korea," 49 *UNAFEI Resource Material Series* 69, 77 (1997).

[50] In the course of this study, I was unable to find a respondent who could explain this seemingly anomalous result.

One sign of institutionalization of a court is the practice of dissent. Dissenting opinions only make sense when a judge sees a real possibility of shifting the position of the court over time. Only when jurisprudential battles potentially matter will judges in the minority seek to engage in them. Constitutional Court justices in Korea have filed dissenting opinions from the outset, but the practice became particularly identified in the first term with the single justice nominated by opposition parties in the National Assembly, Byon Chung-soo. In the second term of the court, this role shifted to Justice Cho Seung-hyung, another Kim Dae-jung appointee. Although statistics are not kept by the court, these two have been particularly vocal in dissent and frequently used foreign constitutional practice to bolster their positions.

IMPACT IN KEY AREAS OF LAW

As demonstrated above, the Constitutional Court has regularly struck government action and legislation on behalf of private plaintiffs and ordinary courts. The court's impact cannot be measured by numbers alone, however. This section will focus on several key cases to show the depth of the court's impact on Korean law and society.

New and Unenumerated Rights

One sign of the court's boldness has been its willingness to create new constitutional rights by reading the text of the document quite broadly. Article 37(1) of the constitution explicitly grants the court the power to protect unenumerated rights.[51] Interestingly, the court has preferred to read existing rights quite broadly rather than to use this open-ended provision. In this sense, it has acted like the U.S. Supreme Court vis-à-vis the Ninth Amendment, which on its face would appear to allow the court wide latitude in creating new rights.[52]

In 1991, the Constitutional Court read Article 10, which grants citizens a right to pursue happiness, to include a right to freedom of contract.[53] The case involved a legislative requirement that certain building owners

---

[51] The text reads: "Freedoms and rights of citizens shall not be neglected on the grounds that they are not enumerated in the Constitution."

[52] For a discussion, see, for example, Louis Henkin, *The Age of Rights* 96 (1996). See also Charles L. Black, *A New Birth of Freedom: Human Rights, Named and Unnamed* (1998).

[53] Ahn, *supra* note 6, at 89. See, generally, Lim Jibong, "The Pursuit of Happiness Clause in the Korean Constitution," 1 *J. Korean L.* 71 (2001).

carry insurance, and the court struck the provision as interfering with the freedom of contract. Another instance came in 1989, when the court found an implied "right to know" based on several clauses of the constitution.[54] The court subsequently strengthened that provision by referring to the Universal Declaration of Human Rights.[55]

The court has also used a provision in the constitution providing for due process of law in criminal procedure quite broadly and has said that "due process is a unique constitutional principle, not limited to the criminal procedure.... [T]he principle requires that not only the procedures be described by the law, but the law be reasonable and legitimate in its content."[56]

From an American perspective, these decisions evoke *Lochner v. New York*, which used a notion of substantive due process to find a constitutional guarantee of freedom of contract.[57] Unlike the *Lochner* court's judicial activism, which reacted to the first inklings of the modern regulatory state, the Korean court's activism comes in the face of a statist economic policy that is entrenched and pervasive. Arguably, it is more radical for a court to find a freedom of contract in the Korean context than in the turn-of-the-century United States, where laissez-faire economic doctrine prevailed.

The Court and the Political Process

One effective strategy of courts is to diffuse political power in the face of threats to concentrate it. This countermajoritarianism serves not only to protect the democratic process, as is conventionally argued. Diffusing political power also serves to widen the court's latitude for substantive decision making and thus enhances judicial power. Consistent with this approach, the Korean court has consistently sided with political minorities in cases involving electoral law. For example, a minority party challenged the Local Election Law of 1990, which required large deposits of money from candidates. This provision served as a strong disincentive for minority parties to field candidates. The court found that the party had standing and that the provision in question violated the constitutional guarantee of equality.

---

[54] Ahn, *supra* note 6, at 89.
[55] *Ibid.*
[56] April 28, 1993, 93 HonBa 26, 6–1, KCCR 355–56. Translation by Ahn, *supra* note 6, at 109.
[57] 198 U.S. 45 (1905).

Similarly, in 1989 the court struck Article 33 of the National Assembly Members Election Act, which required a higher deposit from independent candidates than from those affiliated with a party. In its decision, the court identified the right to vote and to run for office as core democratic freedoms that could not be granted unequally.[58] In 1992, the court struck provisions in the same law that provided party-based candidates advantages over independent candidates in campaign appearances and leafletings. The court found that these provisions limited the constitution's guarantees of equality of opportunity and of the right to hold public office.[59] The court thus rejected a party-based view of democratic governance.[60]

The court in 1995 found several provisions of the electoral law to be "nonconforming" because of excessively disproportional representation for rural districts compared with urban ones. As in Japan, Korean districting has been designed to maximize the influence of rural areas at the expense of urban voters. Relying in part on Japanese, German, and American cases, the court set an explicit limit of 1:4 disproportionality between urban and rural districts.[61] In an instructive contrast with similar cases before the Japanese Supreme Court, the National Assembly amended the election law to conform with the court's decision.[62]

The Court and Kwangju: Issues of Retroactive Justice

The court has also been heavily involved in sensitive political issues, including those concerning retroactive justice for the bloody Kwangju incident of May 1980, where military personnel slaughtered hundreds of

[58] See Constitutional Court of Korea, *Constitutional Justice in Korea* 24 (1993).
[59] Article 11 and Article 25.
[60] In doing so, the court may have paid attention to German precedent. Article 21 of the Basic Law recognizes the role of political parties in democratic governance. The German Constitutional Court has repeatedly used this provision to regulate the functioning of parties. But the court has also upheld the right of independent candidates to receive state funding for campaigns as do parties. 41 BvergGE 399 (1976), cited in Donald Kommers, "Building Democracy: Judicial Review and the German *Rechtstaat*," in *The Postwar Transformation of Germany* 94–121 (John Brody, Beverly Crawford, and Sarah E. Wiliarty, eds., 1999).
[61] 1995, Case Nos. 224, 239, 285, 373.
[62] Cf. *Kurokawa v. Chiba Election Commission* 30 Minshu 223 (Sup. Ct. G.B., April 14, 1976), where the court declared that the Diet had failed to correct unconstitutional levels of malapportionment and declared the system illegal, but refused to invalidate it or the election held under it. See discussion in Chapter 4. See also William Somers Bailey, "Reducing Malapportionment in Japan's Electoral Districts: The Supreme Court Must Act," 6 *Pac. Rim L. & Pol'y J.* 169 (1997).

nonviolent protesters.[63] The incident occurred when authorities ordered elite troops to Kwangju, the home province of veteran opposition leader and later President Kim Dae-jung, to suppress a protest they characterized as a North Korean–inspired communist revolution. No credible evidence to support this assertion has ever emerged, and most observers believe that the protesters were mostly nonviolent students.[64] Presidents Chun Doo-hwan and Roh Tae-woo, both military generals at the time, were strongly implicated in the incident, as well as in the coup of December 1979 that had brought them to power. The alleged revolt served as the basis for the conviction and death sentence of Kim Dae-jung and polarized Korean politics for the next decade and a half.

Many believe that President Kim Young-sam, who became the first civilian to assume the office in 1992, had agreed not to pursue claims against Roh and Chun as part of the deal that allowed him to take power and democratization to proceed.[65] Early in his term, prosecutors had investigated the two generals and dropped all charges related to treason during the 1979 coup or the deaths in the 1980 incident at Kwangju. This failure to prosecute was challenged in the Constitutional Court through a petition under Article 68(1), and the court was asked to toll the statute of limitations, whose fifteen-year period for prosecution would soon expire. In January 1995, the Constitutional Court upheld the tolling of the fifteen-year statute of limitations against the two men during their presidencies, on the grounds that the constitution expressly provides that sitting presidents may not be prosecuted for any crimes other than insurrection or treason.[66] For rule-of-law reasons, however, the court would not allow retroactive application of the tolling to include offenses for which the statutory period had already expired. On its face, this decision would have rendered the 1979 coup d'état unprosecutable. Other crimes, however, including those related to the Kwangju incident, would remain prosecutable for several more years.[67] This decision served notice

---

[63] The precise facts of the incident are hotly disputed, including the number of dead, estimates of which range from the official figure of 191 up to 2,000. See, generally, *The Kwangju Uprising: Shadows over the Regime in South Korea* (Donald Clark, ed., 1988).

[64] See James M. West, "Martial Lawlessness: The Legal Aftermath of Kwangju," 6 *Pac. Rim L. & Pol'y J.* 94 (1997).

[65] Kim Young-sam joined Roh's party and a minor party led by Kim Jong-pil to form the Democratic Liberal Party in 1990.

[66] West, *supra* note 64, at 105.

[67] Ahn, *supra* note 6, at 95, notes that this contradicted an earlier decision in which the court had strictly limited tolling to specific statutory grounds.

that efforts to bring the two men to justice would have to conform to the dictates of the rule of law. However, the court did not force the prosecution to prosecute Chun and Roh by declaring the exercise of prosecutorial discretion unconstitutional.

The case continued to remain in legal limbo, but political controversy followed with vocal protests and petitions demanding prosecution of the two former leaders. Meanwhile, the ruling Democratic Liberal Party, created by an alliance between Kim Young-sam and Roh, foundered at the polls. Furthermore, in October 1995 the public learned of a massive fund in Roh's possession that had allegedly come from political "donations." Kim Young-sam began to reconsider his earlier position to avoid prosecuting the two men, believing that he might gain political advantage from pursuing the two in the face of mounting popular pressure.[68] Some also speculate that Kim, himself implicated in the slush fund scandal, may have sought to distract attention from himself by shifting the focus onto Roh and Chun. Subsequently, prosecutors considered reopening the case at the direction of Kim Young-sam.

Meanwhile, in late 1995 the Constitutional Court was preparing to rule on a second Article 68(1) petition for failure to prosecute, this one brought by relatives of victims. Perhaps responding to leaks that the court would force prosecution by overturning the earlier decision,[69] the prosecutors announced they were reopening the case with regard to both the 1979 coup and the 1980 Kwangju massacre. This flew in the face of the earlier Constitutional Court decision on the statute of limitations, which had rendered the coup unprosecutable. To circumvent the decision, the prosecutors found that the offenses in question had lasted continuously from the coup itself through the lifting of martial law on January 24, 1981.

The leaks about the impending court decision had forced the hand of prosecutors. The leaks, however, had been false. When it became apparent that the court was in fact prepared to rule that the charge of treason related to the coup could *not* be prosecuted because the statute of limitations had expired, the petitioners withdrew the petition to avoid an adverse finding.[70] The court subsequently declared the case moot before it could announce its decision.

---

[68] Oh, *supra* note 19, at 172.

[69] See C. W. Lim, "Student Clash with Riot Police over Kwangju Massacre," *Agence France Presse*, November 27, 1995, available in NEXIS, NEWS Library, NON-US File.

[70] The court's decision implied that the coup was prosecutable, in contrast with the position of the prosecutor's office.

The National Assembly, under the solid control of Kim Young-sam's party, then announced that it would pass special legislation to facilitate the prosecutions. In December 1995, sixteen years after the coup d'état, the National Assembly passed two laws providing that the statute of limitations would not bar prosecution and stipulating that the protests at Kwangju were not an uprising but a democratization movement.[71] Immediately, the laws were challenged by lawyers for Chun and Roh in the newly initiated case and referred to the Constitutional Court by the trial court hearing the prosecution of the two ex-presidents. The trial judge asked the court to clarify whether the statute violated the prohibition against retroactive legislation in Article 13 of the constitution. For a third time, the court would hear a case related to the prosecution of Roh and Chun and again appeared to face a choice between the political pressures of the day and upholding the values of the rule of law.

In its February 16, 1996 judgment, the court upheld the controversial acts, although a majority of justices dissented. (Six votes are required to find a law unconstitutional.) In dissent, five justices wrote that the acts would be unconstitutional if applied to persons for whom the statute of limitations had run prior to the passage of the act. The court did not specifically discuss whether the various offenses with which Roh and Chun were charged would be covered by the statute of limitations, saying that the application of the statute in individual cases was a matter of ordinary law.[72] However, the dissenting opinion suggested that the acts had been passed after the expiry of the statutory period for the 1979 coup and furthermore only covered the Kwangju incident because of the court's decision on tolling a year earlier. With this analysis, the unusual majority dissent highlighted Kim Young-sam's failure to take action against Chun and Roh early in his presidency, when the statute of limitations would not have been an issue.[73]

The court's decision allowed the prosecutors to proceed with the case in local court. The lower court was able to consider the legality of the coup because of the prosecution's awkward argument that the coup extended through the expiry of martial law. Ultimately, both men were found guilty. Chun was sentenced to death and Roh to twenty-two years in prison. Both sentences were reduced on appeal, and the men

---

[71] The Act on Non-Applicability of Statutes of Limitations to Crimes Destructive of the Constitutional Order and the Special Act on the May 18th Democratization Movement.

[72] West, *supra* note 64, at 124.

[73] *Ibid.* at 125.

were subsequently pardoned through the initiative of President-elect Kim Dae-jung in December 1997.

The performance of the Constitutional Court through this series of decisions is ambiguous, but on balance reflects the court's independence as well as its institutional sophistication. On the one hand, the court ultimately allowed the prosecution to go forward and in this sense can be seen as bending to the dictates of a popular political movement. Apparently, the court was prepared to prevent the prosecution in December 1995, before the plaintiffs withdrew their case. Its mooting of that case after the withdrawal allowed the political process to continue. However, the dissenting opinion issued by a majority of the justices questioned the dubious legislation of the ruling party by calling attention to the rule-of-law values of consistency and predictability in criminal justice. Special legislation would be acceptable, but not if applied to those for whom the statute of limitations had already expired, a category that by 1996 included everyone involved in both the 1979 coup and the 1980 Kwangju incident. The court thus avoided a direct challenge to the dominant political interests, but at the same time managed to focus on issues of legality and caused maximum embarrassment to President Kim through dissent.

The court's rhetorical strategy, invoking a wide range of international materials, is also of interest. International practice itself is not very clear on issues of retroactive justice.[74] The court cited two German statutes that had suspended statutes of limitation to facilitate prosecution of Nazis after World War II and East Germans after German reunification. The court also cited an international treaty to which Korea was not a party, the 1968 UN Convention on the Non-Applicability of Statutory Limitations to War Crimes and Crimes Against Humanity.[75] Reliance on these nonbinding sources appear to be part of an appeal to some international notion of the rule of law rather than to any specific legal rules applicable to the case.

Economic Rights

Although not the most spectacular line of decisions, perhaps the court's greatest contribution to liberalization has been undermining the legacy

---

[74] See, for example, the papers in *Transitional Justice and the Rule of Law in New Democracies* (A. James McAdams, ed., 1997) and the materials in *Transitional Justice: How Emerging Democracies Reckon with Former Regimes* (Neil Kritz, ed., 1995).

[75] West, *supra* note 64, at n.181.

of government controls over the economic system. In the *Kukje* case in 1993, the court considered the Chun regime's dissolution of one of Korea's *chaebol* industrial conglomerates, allegedly because of its failure to make donations to the ruling party. The court held that the government's action toward the private firms was an unconstitutional taking of private property and that the former owner could retake control of the firms through the ordinary judicial process.[76] In a country where the state has always had tremendous power over the economy, this decision struck a blow at state interference and marked a qualitative difference in the new era. The court has also invalidated tax legislation and provisions of property law that provided special privileges for state-owned firms.[77] Such mechanisms previously allowed Korean state capitalism to blur the distinction between the state and private economic activity.[78] In striking these rules, the court has bolstered the private-public distinction, a core principle of modern liberalism.

Social Issues

The court has also been active in articulating new norms for the highly traditional Korean social order, in particular by striking at features of the law that reflect Confucian paternalism. In doing so, the court has responded to demands of women's groups, who have used constitutional litigation as a strategy for pursuing social change.

In July 1997, the court struck an article in the civil code that prohibited intermarriage of Koreans with the same family name and regional origin.[79] This provision reflected a law originally written in 1308, when clan-based social structure prevailed.[80] This provision had the effect of denying thousands of persons the full freedom of marriage.[81] The decision

---

[76] "South Korean High Court Rules Chaebol Dissolution Unconstitutional," *AFP*, July 29, 1993, available in NEXIS, NEWS Library, NON-US File.

[77] Ahn, *supra* note 6, at 104–5.

[78] Peter Evans, *Embedded Autonomy: States and Industrial Transformation* (1995).

[79] Article 809, section 1.

[80] Its enactment corresponded with the founding of the Yi dynasty. In my view, the probable rationale behind the law was the need for a centralizing state to undercut traditional clan-based restrictions on marrying outside the group. By encouraging intermarriage among clans, the law broke down the chief source of resistance to central authority.

[81] Ahn, *supra* note 6, at 106. Technically, the court merely found the law to be nonconforming with the constitution, requiring amendment by the National Assembly. However, the assembly has not yet amended the law, allegedly because of intense

had immediate effects on an estimated 60,000 couples who lived together but whose clan names had prevented them from legally marrying. Again, the decision was welcomed by women's groups, but opponents staged a protest outside the halls of the court building, reflecting the judicialization of politics.[82]

Another interesting case concerned the legal regulation of adultery. Reflecting Confucian values, adultery was punishable by up to two years' imprisonment under Article 241 of the Criminal Code. This law was challenged as a violation of the constitutional right to pursue happiness, but an odd alliance of traditionalists, women's groups, and the bar association supported the law. The court refused to strike the law, but the Ministry of Justice, responding to dissenting opinions in the court decision, announced that it would initiate amending legislation to strike the controversial provisions. However, it ultimately failed to do so in the wake of protests by social activists. This decision illustrates the myriad ways a constitutional decision can shape social change: Although the court appears to speak for traditional values, it also reflects active interest group politics. The interest of advocacy groups in the constitutional litigation process shows that the court is an increasingly important political arena; furthermore, the role of these groups reflects the strengthening of civil society vis-à-vis the formerly dominant state apparatus.[83] Law and society are now playing symbiotic roles at the expense of state power.

Labor Issues

In December 1996, the government forced through the Assembly several controversial labor laws designed to make the Korean economy more globally competitive. The laws made it easier to fire workers, effectively ending Korea's famous system of lifetime employment, and penalize striking workers. The laws also continued to ban unions from political activities. Knowing the laws would be controversial, the government passed

lobbying by Confucian traditionalists. Despite this, the Supreme Court routinely accepts petitions for marriages from persons of the same family name and origin. Technically, this is an instance of noncompliance by the National Assembly, though in fact, the Constitutional Court succeeded in effecting its desired outcome.

[82] On the concept of judicialization, see *The Global Expansion of Judicial Power* (Neal Tate and Thorsten Vallinder, eds., 1995).

[83] See Gordon White, "Civil Society, Democratization and Development," 2 *Democratization* (1993).

them in a sneak six-o'clock-in-the-morning session of the Assembly with no opposition party members present. This ensured that the laws could not be debated. Labor groups responded with a series of violent demonstrations, shutting down key industries.[84] Several lower courts refused to apply the law to arrest striking workers and referred the law to the Constitutional Court.

In its decision, the court found that the passage of the laws violated Article 49 of the constitution, which provides that National Assembly members have a right to debate and vote. This right was infringed by the sneak session. The court found that these procedural defects did not require it to hold the statute itself unconstitutional. Clearly, the Assembly could have passed the laws quite easily in an ordinary session, but chose not to because the ruling party was afraid of the consequences of open debate. In this decision, the court speaks for a notion of deliberative democracy, in which outcomes are less important than process. The labor unrest and the court's rejection of the government tactics were a major embarrassment to President Kim Young Sam, but the court used a procedural flaw to avoid challenging the regime on substance.

According to one observer, the court remains more conservative on labor issues than on others.[85] For example, the court has upheld statutes that prohibit teachers from engaging in union activities.[86] It has, however, struck a blanket prohibition on strikes by government workers in the Labor Arbitration Act as nonconforming with the constitution. Its performance on labor issues can thus be characterized as mixed.

One decision widely viewed as antilabor came in August 1997, when the court held that it would be unconstitutional to require companies to pay an "unlimited amount" of retirement benefits before any other claims in a liquidation proceeding. The Labor Standard Law requires that companies being liquidated must pay the final three months of employee wages and "all accrued retirement benefits" before it pays secured and unsecured claims.[87] The court held that this specific clause was incompatible with the policy goal of the collateralization of assets, which it characterized as the very foundation of the nation's credit system, and called on the

---

[84] Shim Jae-hon and Charles S. Lee, "Test of Wills," *Far E. Econ. Rev.*, January 23, 1997, at 14–15.

[85] Ahn, *supra* note 6.

[86] See Holland, *supra* note 33, at 154.

[87] Seong C. Gweon, "Hope I Die Before I Get Old," *Korea Herald*, September 24, 1997.

legislature to amend the law. The court, as it frequently does, invoked foreign practice and noted that in the United States wages and salaries are paid before secured loans, but not without limit.[88]

The National Security Act Cases and Military Secrets

The court has been especially visible in dealing with the legacies of the authoritarian regime, particularly the National Security Act (NSA) and the Anti-Communist Act. These laws were used to suppress independent political organizations by providing draconian sanctions against dissenters and loosely defined illegal associations. The laws were therefore a target of human rights activists and regime opponents. The two laws operated by carving out exceptions to normal requirements of criminal procedure. For example, Article 19 of the National Security Act of 1980 allowed longer pretrial detention for those accused of particular crimes and this article was struck by the Constitutional Court in 1992.[89] The provisions in question extended pretrial detention for up to fifty days, an exception from the normal period of forty-eight hours allowed under the Code of Criminal Procedure.[90] The court held that the extended period constituted an excessive limitation on the basic right to a speedy trial.

Even more important was the court's limitation of offenses defined under the act. Article 7(1) of the NSA penalized any person who "praises, encourages, or sympathizes with the activities of an anti-state organization or its members, or any person who receives orders therefrom; and any person who by any means whatever benefits an anti-state organization."[91] This provision was held to be vague and overbroad and to threaten constitutional guarantees of freedom of the press and speech,[92] freedom of academic study,[93] and freedom of conscience.[94] Noting the continuing confrontation with North Korea, the court did not actually strike the law, but ruled that the provisions only be applied in the case of danger of actual

---

[88] In the United States, such benefits are limited to $2,000 per claimant, only including benefits earned within ninety days before the filing of the bankruptcy petition.

[89] Decision of April 14, 1992, 90 HonMa 82, 4 KCCR 194.

[90] Cho Kuk, "Tension between the National Security Law and Constitutionalism in South Korea: Security for What?," 15 *B.U. Int'l L. J.* 125, 161 (1997). Cho criticizes the decision for not going far enough by failing to declare the law definitively unconstitutional.

[91] National Security Act, as quoted in *A Brief Look, supra* note 34, at 16.

[92] Article 21(1).

[93] Article 22(1).

[94] Article 19; Decision of April 2, 1990, 89 HomKa 3.

security risks. The court restricted interpretations of the law and asked lower courts to balance the proximity of danger with the constitutional position of freedom of expression. In particular, the court held that the law could only be used to punish activities posing a substantive danger, so merely "encouraging" or "sympathizing" without a showing of substantive danger could not be prosecuted. However, a dissenting opinion called for the court to require a higher standard of "clear and present danger" before a prosecution could be upheld in an NSA case.[95]

The next year, the National Assembly amended the law to apply only where the person charged had *knowledge* that his actions might endanger the existence or security of the state or the "fundamental order of liberal democracy."[96] Once again, a court decision led the legislature to substantially narrow its definition of an offense, introducing the element of specific knowledge to limit the application of a law that had been subject to serious abuse.

In 1994, the court struck a provision of the Private School Act requiring that any teacher prosecuted in a criminal case would lose her job.[97] In the case at issue, a teacher was prosecuted under the NSA and immediately fired. The court found that this rule violated the presumption of innocence. This group of decisions had the effect of domesticating the administration of the National Security Act, the single most egregious law associated with military rule by bringing the act into conformity with the dictates of ordinary procedural law.

The Military Secrets Protection Act of 1972 that prohibited the collection or dissemination of military secrets led to another politically charged case for the court. The act had been interpreted quite broadly and was used to prevent any media coverage of military matters whatsoever. The court found that the constitutional freedom of expression encompassed a public right to information and that this could not be infringed by a broad application of the law.[98] The Assembly subsequently revised the bill, narrowing

---

[95] In characterizing the majority test as one of "bad tendency," Justice Byon Chong-soo self-consciously modeled his decision on the opinion of U.S. Supreme Court Justice Holmes in *Schenk v. U.S.*, 249 U.S. 47 (1919). His phrasing subsequently influenced a Supreme Court NSA case on May 31, 1992, where the minority argued that the threat must be a "concrete and possible danger" for prosecution, under Korea's "liberal democratic basic order." Cho, *supra* note 90, at 169.

[96] See *A Brief Look*, *supra* note 34, at 17; Cho, *supra* note 90, argues that the revision has not had much impact.

[97] *A Brief Look*, *supra* note 34, at 30. July 29, 1994, 6-2 KCCR 1.

[98] See Youm, *supra* note 2.

the interpretation of military secrets, so the decision had a direct impact on broadening freedom of expression. In another freedom of expression case the court struck a thirty-four-year-old law on censorship of films.[99]

Political Questions?

Perhaps the greatest political controversy the court has been forced to confront was the constitutional crisis following the election of Kim Dae-jung in 1997. This first handover of power to an opposition figure was a moment of triumph for Korean democracy, but was also accompanied by the conflict that has plagued Korean political culture.[100] Because Kim Dae-jung's support was especially drawn from the southwest part of the country, Kim had formed an unlikely electoral alliance with Kim Jong-pil, the conservative founder of the Korean Central Intelligence Agency. The bargain was that Kim Jong-pil would deliver support from his region and thus provide Dae-jung with a plurality; in return, Kim Dae-jung promised Kim Jong-pil the post of prime minister. However, the opposition Grand National Party (successor to the Democratic Liberal Party of Roh and Kim Young-sam) had control of the National Assembly, so Kim Dae-jung was unable to ensure Kim Jong-pil's confirmation as prime minister. During a confirmation vote in the Assembly, it became apparent that Kim Jong-pil would not obtain approval, but the vote was interrupted by a scuffle that broke out in the Assembly.

To avoid a parliamentary vote he was sure to lose, Kim Dae-jung appointed Kim Jong-pil "acting" prime minister.[101] Members of the Grand National Party brought suit in the Constitutional Court to declare the "acting" appointment unconstitutional and to enjoin it.[102] This put the court in a difficult position. The court had not developed a doctrine of

---

[99] "Government Censorship of Movies Ruled Unconstitutional," *AP*, October 4, 1996, available in NEXIS, NEWS Library, NON-US File.

[100] As reflected in the title of David I. Steinberg, "Korea: Triumph amid Turmoil," *supra* note 1, at 76.

[101] President Lee Teng-hui of Taiwan had used a similar technique to ensure the appointment of his favored candidate for prime minister following his own reelection in 1997. See Chapter 5, *supra*.

[102] They first took the unusual step of suing the speaker of parliament, himself a senior member of the Grand National Party, for failure to complete the vote. Some interpreted this suit as a tactic to frame the more important issue of whether the appointment as acting prime minister was acceptable. Shin Yong-bae, "Opposition Party Files Lawsuit against Speaker," *Korea Herald*, March 27, 1998, available in NEXIS, NEWS Library, NON-US File.

nonjusticiable political questions; nor was there any question that the dispute was justiciable under the Constitutional Court Act. The court dismissed the case on standing grounds, saying that only the Assembly as a whole, not individual lawmakers, had the right to bring a case to the court on the powers of the Assembly. This argument, while effective in dismissing the suit, was not certain to keep the case out of the court for long since constitutional petition and referral by ordinary court remained viable options. Dismissal did, however, signal the court's reluctance to become involved and forced the two parties to continue to negotiate to resolve the issue. In mid-August, Kim Jong-pil was finally confirmed after a compromise gave six of thirteen committee chairmanships to the Grand National Party. This incident illustrates the tendency for political issues to become constitutionalized, particularly in situations of divided government when opposing forces control the parliament and the executive. In this case, the court deepened democracy by failing to resolve an issue, for it forced continual negotiation that eventually produced a compromise.

RELATIONS WITH THE SUPREME COURT

In all systems with designated constitutional courts, relations between the constitutional review body and the top ordinary tribunals can be complex. This is particularly true in Korea, where the Supreme Court has been assigned the explicit power to adjudicate the constitutionality of administrative regulations in accordance with postwar Korean tradition.[103] Indeed, the past few years have witnessed a battle over jurisdiction between the two top courts.

The two courts are clearly separate but equal bodies in formal terms, each described in a separate constitutional article as an organ of state power. Ideally, the two courts have mutually independent jurisdictions while retaining equally high status. In fact, of course, cases do not neatly fit into one or the other's purview, and each court seeks to assert its dominance. The distinction between administrative and legislative interpretation is not as clear or straightforward as might be imagined. The question of the constitutionality of an administrative regulation frequently requires interpretation of the relevant statutory text. A restrictive interpretation of a statute will tend to void on constitutional grounds any administrative actions taken under it when those actions rely on a broad reading of the statute. So the Constitutional Court is able to shape Supreme Court

---

[103] Constitution, Article 107(2).

constitutional interpretations where the Constitutional Court is able to issue a prior decision on the statute underlying administrative action.

In 1990, the Constitutional Court unilaterally decided that it had implied jurisdiction over administrative regulations issued pursuant to statutes and that the assignment of administrative review in Article 107(2) to the ordinary courts was not exclusive.[104] The case was especially controversial because it concerned the administrative action of the Supreme Court itself in its role as the licensing authority for lower-level judicial officials known as judicial scriveners. The petitioner had charged that scriveners' licenses were given disproportionately to those with experience in courts and prosecutors' offices, without justification. The Constitutional Court found that, by failing to administer examinations, the Supreme Court had not followed its own administrative regulations under the Judicial Scriveners Act. In response to the decision, the Supreme Court issued a statement to all ordinary judges condemning the Constitutional Court decision and stating that it had "gone beyond its domain."[105]

The problem is caused in part by the design flaw that ordinary court decisions are not explicitly included within the jurisdiction of the Constitutional Court.[106] At the same time, the law provides that rulings of the court on unconstitutionality are to be respected by ordinary courts, other state agencies, and local government bodies.[107] This means that while ordinary courts must abide by Constitutional Court decisions, they are themselves the sole determiners of what those decisions require. Ordinary courts cannot be corrected by the Constitutional Court for failure to apply its decision correctly. Rather, the Supreme Court is the sole body able to overrule lower-court decisions. Therefore, much is at stake on the question of whether Supreme Court decisions can be appealed to the Constitutional Court. On the one hand, the maintenance of the constitution as the highest normative level of the legal system would seem to require reviewability of Supreme Court decisions. On the other hand, if Supreme Court decisions can be appealed, that means they are not final.

In keeping with its efforts to expand access to constitutional justice, the Constitutional Court has sought to extend its jurisdiction to cover

---

[104] Ahn, *supra* note 6, at 139. October 15, 1990, 89 HonMa 178, 2 KCCR 365. Article 107(2) reads, "[T]he Supreme Court shall have the power to make a final review of the constitutionality or legality of administrative decrees, regulations or dispositions, when their constitutionality or legality is a prerequisite to a trial."

[105] West and Yoon, *supra* note 30, at 103.

[106] Constitution, Article 111(1).

[107] CCA, Article 47(1).

ordinary court decisions. In 1995, the court declared a tax law partially unconstitutional and dictated that it could only be applied if given a particular narrow interpretation by ordinary courts. The Supreme Court responded in April 1996, saying that because the Constitutional Court had no authority over ordinary court judgments its decision could only be taken as an expression of opinion regarding constitutionality and had no binding force over ordinary courts. The ordinary courts then proceeded to apply the controversial tax law in the manner that the Constitutional Court had criticized. In December 1997, the original petitioner again sought relief from the Constitutional Court and the court obliged by annulling the Supreme Court judgment, even though it had no explicit power to do so in the Constitutional Court Act. The court also voided that portion of the Constitutional Court Act that excluded ordinary court decisions from constitutional review, saying that Constitutional Court decisions must be binding on all. The Supreme Court responded by holding a press conference asserting that it would reply through a judgment.[108] Subsequently, the Constitutional Court continued to consider ordinary court judgments in certain cases, and it now appears that the theory of the Constitutional Court has been accepted.

Ultimately, the conflict may be about competing ideas of the role of courts and the meaning of judicial independence. The Constitutional Court sees itself as the embodiment of a new constitutional order, a vehicle for making a bold break from the past. The Supreme Court sees itself as the inheritor of Korean legal tradition, a tradition that sought to preserve professional autonomy under difficult conditions of authoritarian rule. As such, the Supreme Court has always sought to insulate itself from other institutions intent on interfering with its position at the apex of the legal hierarchy.

Foreign influence is crucial in shaping these institutional self-conceptions, and each court draws on foreign models to support its position. Although American influence on Korean politics has been paramount, continental ideas of predominantly German and French origin are dominant in the legal community by virtue of the Japanese colonial transmission. While the Supreme Court appears to follow its notoriously

---

[108] This high-profile conflict led the *Korea Herald* to call for legislative resolution of the problem: "This complicated and subtle conflict between the two supreme juridical bodies calls for an intervention of the President and the National Assembly which can exercise their legislative prerogatives toward illuminating the balance of power and division of labor between the two highest courts." *Korea Herald*, December 30, 1997, available in NEXIS, NEWS Library, CURNWS File.

conservative Japanese counterpart, the Constitutional Court appears to model itself on its activist counterparts in Germany and the United States. American jurisprudence is particularly important in civil rights cases, and scholars have begun to make explicit comparisons.[109]

While the Supreme Court tends to be fairly conservative, an increasing number of lower-court judges have been utilizing the constitutional referral mechanism to undermine the judicial hierarchy.[110] The more independent stance of lower-court judges has been particularly apparent in cases involving the National Security Act, where lower courts have been denying arrest warrants sought by prosecutors.[111] We see a kind of alliance between lower-court judges and constitutional courts against the ordinary civil law structure.[112]

One final comment concerns the Constitutional Court's relations with prosecutors who are trained with judges. Prosecutorial supremacy was another area in which authoritarian tradition was clear prior to the 1987 reforms. Prosecutorial supremacy was reflected in the criminal procedure code – for example, in provisions that a decision of a court to grant bail could be automatically stayed by prosecutorial appeal.[113] Other provisions required that lower-court records be channeled through the prosecutor's office on their way to higher courts of appeal.[114] The Constitutional Court has explicitly declared that Korean criminal procedure is now based in the adversary system with the obvious implication that the court sits above the prosecution. This is another sign of a shift caused by the constitutional revolution of 1987.

CONCLUSION

In terms of the framework of this book, the Korean Constitutional Court is exercising high equilibrium judicial review and has since its birth. The court is deciding an increasing number of cases and is clearly a forum for groups seeking to advance social change as well as for individual disputes.

[109] Ahn, *supra* note 6; Cho, *supra* note 90.
[110] Ahn, *supra* note 6, at 81; Cho, *supra* note 90, at 173.
[111] Cho, *supra* note 90, at 169.
[112] This alliance is facilitated in the NSA cases by the assistance of a minority of Supreme Court judges.
[113] Article 97(3) of the Code of Criminal Procedure, struck by the court December 23, 1993, 93 HonKa 2, 5-2 KCCR 578. Ahn, *supra* note 6, at n.255.
[114] Article 361(1), (2), struck by the court November 30, 1995, 92 HonMa 44, 7-2 KCCR 651, 657. Ahn, *supra* note 6, at 113–14.

The court frequently strikes legislative action and also regularly overturns prosecutorial decisions. The court has demonstrated its independence in politically charged cases, such as in the retroactive justice case where it embarrassed the ruling party. The court has participated in the subjugation of both state and military to civilian political control, transforming the character of state-society relations.[115] At the same time, the court has avoided decisions that might provoke exit or counterattack by prominent political forces. The court has thereby contributed to the consolidation of Korean democracy in the sense that the process has become fundamentally irreversible, barring external shock.[116]

What explains this early and unexpected success? Some insight into the factors leading to active judicial review can be gained by comparing Korea with our other two cases. In terms of background conditions, Korea presents an equally inhospitable environment for the exercise of judicial power as do Taiwan and Mongolia. The Korean legal tradition was highly state oriented, norms of professional autonomy were not highly developed, and early systems of judicial review had not been effective at constraining state power.

Nevertheless, the Korean court has been arguably the most successful of our three courts. Its decisions have been nearly universally complied with. Politicians' attempts at restricting the role of the court have been deflected by a buffer of supportive public opinion. One important factor has been the court's formation as a new and distinct body with the express mission of protecting the 1987 Constitution. The court's position as designated protector of the constitutional bargain has given it a sense of institutional mission, identified closely with a broad notion of democratic values.

A second important factor is the extent to which the design reflected insurance needs. The 1987 constitutional design reflected the deep political uncertainty faced by three political forces of roughly equal strength. No party could confidently predict it would win power and the institutions of the 1987 Constitution reflected this, both in the single-term presidency and the Constitutional Court. A system of constitutional review served the interests of all parties under such uncertain conditions, and the design of the court provided it with institutional resources to expand its power.

A third factor in high-equilibrium judicial review is the support structure of activist claimants. Korean judicial review has been facilitated by a combination of an open-access regime and an expanding legal profession,

[115] See, generally, *State and Society in Contemporary Korea* (Hagen Koo, ed., 1993).
[116] Most obviously the threat of war with North Korea.

particularly an active civil rights bar.[117] In the late 1980s, civil rights lawyers took advantage of the more liberal climate to organize a group called "Lawyers' Group for the Achievement of Democracy," described as one of the most effective pressure groups in Korea today.[118] The court itself has helped to expand public access through its liberal readings on issues of justiciability and standing and by seeking to include Supreme Court judgments within its jurisdiction. For example, although the Constitutional Court Act requires that other legal remedies be exhausted before a petition is accepted,[119] the court has at least twice taken cases that did not meet this requirement.[120] In contrast with its Japanese brethren, the court has included informal "administrative guidance" in its definition of state action.[121] In these ways, the court has taken an aggressive stance toward constitutional protection while encouraging a steady stream of cases to its doorstep. The increasing number of petitions presented in Figure 7.1 (page 225), illustrates the effectiveness of this strategy.

A final factor in high-equilibrium judicial review is the party system after the constitutional scheme is in operation. Whereas both Mongolia and Taiwan have democratized under a dominant party associated with the old regime, Korean parties continue to be notoriously underdeveloped and reflect highly hierarchical personalistic structures. Scholars have identified several reasons for the weakness of the party system, including the strength and autonomy of the state bureaucracy, the authoritarian legacy that allowed no opportunities for policy innovation, and factionalized personality-based politics.[122] Whatever the sources, Korean parties remain weak and unstable, and attempts to stabilize the system, have failed. Self-consciously emulating Japan, three major groups attempted to merge in 1990 to form a dominant party, the so-called Democratic Liberal Party.

---

[117] Ahn, *supra* note 6, at 81–82. Ahn notes that increasing attention to international norms was also important beginning with the 1988 Summer Olympics, entry into the United Nations in 1991, and ratification of the International Covenants on Economic, Social and Cultural Rights and Civil and Political Rights.

[118] Ahn Kyong-whan, "The Growth of the Bar and the Changes in the Lawyer's Role: Korea's Dilemma," in *Law and Technology in the Pacific Community* 127 (Phillip S. C. Lewis, ed., 1994).

[119] CCA, Article 111.

[120] Ahn, *supra* note 6, at n.120.

[121] *Ibid.* at 92–93; Michael K. Young, "Judicial Review of Administrative Guidance: Governmentally Encouraged Consensual Dispute Resolution in Japan," 84 *Colum. L. Rev.* 935 (1984); Lorenz Kodderitsch, "Japan's New Administrative Procedures Law: Reasons for Its Enactment and Likely Implications," 24 *Law in Japan* 105 (1994).

[122] Han, *supra* note 20.

The experiment failed, and the system seems likely to continue to be based on shifting coalitions around dominant personalities.

Weak parties enhance judicial power in several ways. First, weak parties lack organized mechanisms to influence court composition and structure. With only loose organization, there is not necessarily a cadre of persons associated with the party who can be nominated for Constitutional Court positions and engage in constitutional politics from "the inside." Korean parties have heretofore had few policy differences, so there is little possibility of building party-based jurisprudential positions.

Second, weak parties that are unable to cooperate are unlikely to overrule or punish a court through legislative action. This expands the "tolerance zone" of the legislature and expands the policy space in which judges can work. More divergence and less party discipline lead to a greater range of possible judicial interpretations for the reviewing court. In contrast, a dominant party can pass legislation and hence can correct a court quite easily.

Weak parties can provide opportunities for judicial power in a third indirect way because they are less able to control the bureaucracy. A lone autocrat cannot effectively discipline the whole bureaucracy and needs a hierarchical structure such as a political party to mobilize support and monitor bureaucratic performance. Without such a hierarchical mechanism, politicians may have to turn to an alternative mechanism for monitoring bureaucratic agents. In many societies, courts perform this monitoring function effectively through constitutional review of administrative action. From the politicians' perspective, courts have the additional advantages of being reactive and having few tools of enforcement, therefore providing little threat to political power.

The tendency of Korean parties to coalesce into two groups of roughly equal strength enhances the court's power, particularly as the possibility of alternating power becomes real.[123] Alternating parties have a strong interest in safeguarding the court as an independent adjudicator. Conversely, where a dominant party holds sway it has little incentive to empower courts, as the party can rely on its more direct control of the enforcement machinery of the state to protect its adopted policies.

All this bodes well for the expansion of judicial power in Korea. The concentration of power in the presidency leads to a kind of zero-sum

---

[123] Park Chan-wook, "Partisan Conflict and Immobilisme in the Korean National Assembly: Conditions Processes, and Outcomes," in *Democracy in Korea: Its Ideals and Realities* 295 (Choi Sang-yong, ed., 1997).

politics and reinforces an aversion to compromise that has long been identified as part of Korean political culture. The powers of the presidency are such that there has been continuous discussion of limiting them and strengthening the role of the prime minister and cabinet, a move that would have suited the factional structure of the DLP. However, public support for the proposal has been minimal in a political culture where strong figures have been important.[124] Any weakening of the presidency may empower the courts further as competing power centers emerge.

The proposal to amend the constitution to provide for a cabinet form of government has been a continuous campaign promise of presidential hopefuls, including Kim Young-sam and most recently Kim Dae-jung. However, everyone elected to the presidency manages to find the office quite comfortable and constitutional modification falls by the wayside. Like previous presidents who pushed constitutional revisions to expand their power, democratic leaders have pursued self-interest in the politics of institutional design.

Strong presidentialism in Korea may have positive effects on the expansion of judicial power, especially if parties remain weak. This is particularly clear when there is a divided government as there was during the Kim Dae-jung administration, where disputes between executive and legislature were common. Losing parties can challenge decisions in court and thereby force a more deliberative, slower, and less aggressive form of politics. The Constitutional Court therefore has great potential to transform the nature of Korean politics away from personalism and conflict and toward institutionalized deliberation. Whether it will fulfill this promise bears close watching in coming years.

[124] Bedeski, *supra* note 1, at 44.

8

Conclusion

Comparing Constitutional Courts

An old proverb says that when elephants fight, the grass gets trampled. So it is with political conflict and democracy. When political conflict becomes too severe, democracy can be trampled by political institutions run amok. By transforming political conflicts into constitutional dialogues, courts can reduce the threat to democracy and allow it to grow. To play this important role of contributing to democratic stability and deliberation, courts must develop their own power over time.

Constitutional courts play games of power in legal arenas. Courts are empowered by constitutional designers and given tools to protect the constitutional bargain. But the subsequent choices courts make as they play their games can supplement or deplete their arsenals. Courts can challenge others or can seek powerful allies. They can cautiously accumulate policy gains in an incremental fashion or boldly battle for large pieces of territory. They can choose their battles carefully, limiting conflicts to those they can win and thus making future threats credible; or they can blunder badly and provoke crippling counterattacks.

This chapter draws some comparative conclusions from the three case studies of courts in new democracies. These cases, though unusual in the sense that they have been heretofore understudied, illustrate the universal political logic of judicial review and present a range of outcomes that can serve as the basis for broader theory.

THE DESIGN OF SYSTEM: JUDICIAL REVIEW AS INSURANCE

Chapter 1 analogized the decision to adopt judicial review to the decision to purchase insurance in uncertain contracting environments. Because at the time of constitutional design in a new democracy no party can predict with confidence that it will be able to maintain power indefinitely, it makes sense for all parties to adopt judicial review as an alternative forum in which to challenge government policy, as long as they perceive that there is some probability that a court will side against electoral winners. This lowers the risk of constitution making and helps conclude bargains that otherwise might not be made.

The optimal configuration of the insurance scheme, however, depends on the particular political circumstances of constitutional drafters. In situations where one party controls the drafting process and foresees that it is likely to maintain power, courts are likely to be granted a more limited scope of authority and be more difficult to access. This is because, from the perspective of the dominant party, the agency costs of judicial review are severe. By setting up a weak court, the dominant party may gain some marginal benefits in legitimacy without sacrificing policy flexibility. In contrast, where two or three parties of roughly equal strength are engaged in constitutional design, all parties are more uncertain about their ability to secure an electoral victory. They therefore may prefer a system of judicial review where a court has extensive formal powers and is easily accessible to maximize the possibility of constraining the majority.

There are other types of insurance needs that may be of particular importance in individual cases. For example, a geographically concentrated ethnic minority may need to be assured that it will be given fair treatment and the availability of a constitutional court provides a minoritarian guarantee. From the perspective of the majority, this can be seen as insurance against rebellion or secession. Similarly, constitutional protection of property rights, with a strong court as guarantor, may help prevent capital flight by private investors in situations where the old regime had capitalism but not democracy.

Does the evidence from the case studies support the theory? Korea, Taiwan, and Mongolia present a range of constitutional environments in which to test the proposition. Korea provides a particularly clear example of a constitution that involved negotiation among political forces in roughly equal balance. When constitutional reforms were initiated in June 1987, it was clear that the military was going to give up power in favor of civilian authorities. The civilian political parties, however, were divided into three roughly equal forces: those associated with dissidents Kim Young-sam and Kim Dae-jung and that associated with former general

Roh Tae-woo. Had the two parties led by dissidents combined forces, they could have easily assured themselves an electoral victory. But barriers to negotiation were high, suggesting that each party distrusted the other. Regional and personality differences divided the two leaders. In situations of such uncertainty, all parties had an incentive to set up a strong, accessible constitutional court, and the drafters adopted the German model. In the bargain, the ruling party preferred the designated court with limited access, while oppositionists preferred open access through decentralized review. In the compromise that followed, a designated court was set up, accessible not only to governmental bodies but to ordinary citizens through the petition process.

In Taiwan, the Council of Grand Justices was set up under the nationalist government on the mainland, essentially a one-party system once the possibility of compromise with the Communists disintegrated. As long as the issue of institutional design was open to bipartisan negotiation with the Communists, the KMT agreed to adopt the American model of a relatively powerful and accessible court. This open, strong model made sense in a situation of bipartisan uncertainty. The KMT valued judicial review as an element of modernity, but once the Communists exited constitutional negotiations, the KMT had little incentive to set up an independent constitutional monitor. It then rejected the American model of judicial review that would have given any court the power to strike legislation for unconstitutionality. Instead, a designated Council of Grand Justices was set up with limited access to the public, appointment power concentrated in the president, and capable of engaging only in abstract review. As the insurance theory predicts, a dominant party designed a relatively weak constitutional court. Over time, that court was able to expand its power through a series of incremental decisions to widen jurisdiction as the KMT's power declined, but the logic of constitutional design appears to conform with the theory set out in Chapter 2.

In Mongolia, like Taiwan, a dominant Leninist Party played a strong role in constitutional design, but it was constrained by newly formed opposition parties to a greater degree than was the KMT on Taiwan. Mongolia appears to present an environment somewhere in between those of Korea and Taiwan in terms of political diffusion during the constitutional design process. The design of judicial review also reflects a kind of intermediate outcome. Like its Korean counterpart, the Constitutional Court was accessible to anyone through the mechanism of citizen petition; but it was relatively restricted in terms of its power because of the requirement that decisions of unconstitutionality be confirmed by the legislature. This design served the interests of the dominant MPRP who have twice since won overwhelming legislative majorities while satisfying opposition demands for a court that was accessible to the public.

We can array the three cases ordinally in terms of the relative dominance of a political party in the constitutional design process. In Taiwan, the constitution was drafted by a single dominant party with a single figure clearly at the center of it in the person of Chiang Kai-shek. In Mongolia, the former Communist Party was in a strong position, but unable to dictate outcomes unilaterally because of a newly emergent set of opposition parties. Finally, the Korean situation reflected political deadlock between three parties of roughly equal strength, so outcomes were even more uncertain. It therefore made sense for all parties to demand a strong form of judicial review as a form of political insurance against likely electoral loss.

The Korean case suggests the superiority of the insurance theory of judicial review over the "commitment" theory discussed in Chapter 1. The commitment theory suggests that judicial review is a device of self-binding by powerful parties to get other parties to accede to the constitutional scheme. But in a design situation like Korea, no party would view itself as needing to provide such commitments because no party could confidently predict victory. Yet judicial review as designed by constitutional founders in Korea was stronger than in Taiwan or Mongolia. The origin of the demand for judicial review is unclear in the commitment theory.

The appointment mechanisms similarly reflect the prospective position of political parties in the political system. The most dominant party in our three cases, the KMT, reserved to the president all appointments to the Council of Grand Justices, allowing much tighter control of the membership of the constitutional court. In Korea and Mongolia, by contrast, three institutions each nominate one-third of the members. In Korea, three are nominated by the National Assembly, three are nominated by the chief justice, and three may be appointed by the president. In Mongolia, three are nominated by a vote of the Supreme Court, three by the parliament, and three by the president. Accountability to the political process is wider in these latter two cases than in the Taiwan case, again conforming to the predictions of the theory. Concentrated authority seeks to control appointments to the Constitutional Court.

The three case studies thus provide empirical support for the insurance theory of judicial review and for the more specific proposition that the design of judicial review reflects the prospective political positions of those involved in the constitutional bargain. This evidence from three cases also allows us to cast doubt on certain alternative hypotheses discussed as follows.

THE PERFORMANCE OF THE SYSTEM

We have used the constructs of high- and low-equilibrium judicial review to distinguish the performance of courts in the early years of new democracy. Low-equilibrium judicial review was characterized by relatively few decisions of little importance. High-equilibrium judicial review was characterized by a high number of important decisions that elicit compliance from political authorities.

As a variable to capture this concept, each case study examined statistics concerning the constitutional court's caseload over time. For a variety of reasons, it is inadvisable to make cross-national comparisons of caseload and disposal rates. Institutional structure is not always commensurable, and small variations in the institutional configuration can produce large variations in such indicators as strike rates, filings, and other variables.

This does not mean that comparison is impossible, however. We can examine the trajectory of each court's caseload over time and can use the concepts of high- and low-equilibrium review to characterize a court's development. Essentially, this strategy involves comparing each court with itself at different points in time and then comparing the overall pattern of development with that of other courts. This avoids the problems of incommensurable institutional design that would be faced by simply comparing caseloads.

Let us consider each of our case studies in turn. The Korean Constitutional Court emerged as part of the new 1987 constitutional order and was active from the very beginning, reflecting its favorable institutional design and a divided political environment. If we model the trajectory of its exercise of power, it would begin at a high equilibrium and remain there. The Mongolian Constitutional Court was constrained somewhat during the early years of the new constitutional order, but became more active after the handover of power from the MPRP, the former Communist Party, in 1996. However, the subsequent confrontation with the legislature led to severe disillusionment with the court. Its power trajectory would be rising toward a high equilibrium, then declining as confrontation inhibited effective compliance. Finally, the history of the Council of Grand Justices on Taiwan reflects more complex interaction with political forces.

Its initial institutional design was less compatible than the others with the exercise of high-equilibrium judicial review because it was limited to abstract review and had no jurisdiction over ordinary court decisions. Nevertheless, an incremental series of decisions has expanded the council's power and jurisdiction. But when it overreached in 1958, the council provoked political backlash in the form of the Council Law and became a compliant institution for decades. Only with renewed political liberalization in 1986 did the council take tentative steps to play a more prominent role in the society, and it has done so in a modest way. The pattern has been one of continual testing and gradual expansion with the particular equilibrium level of judicial review affected by the interaction of the council with its political environment. An incremental series of decisions has expanded the council's power, and it now appears to be at a high equilibrium.

Judicial power results from the interaction of three different components: the *independent* input of the court in producing *politically significant* outcomes that are *complied with* by other actors. In order to assert that judicial review was playing an important role in new democracies, we must identify specific instances of the court constraining current government policy in a politically salient case. How did the three case studies measure up in this regard?

The important independent variable here is not the position of political forces at the time of constitutional drafting; plausibly, that could only affect the institutional design of judicial review in the text of the constitution. Rather, the salient variable is the evolving political party system as it emerges in the early years of new democracies. Where a single party retains its dominant position, we would expect that constitutional courts are less able to exercise judicial power as defined previously, even holding institutional design constant. This is because dominant parties have collateral means of constraining courts so that courts are less likely to exercise independent input into politically salient decisions. In contrast, where the party system fragments, the tolerance zones of institutions that might discipline the court expand and with them the possibilities of exercising judicial power.

The party system in Korea has continued to evolve since 1987, but it retains the fragmented character that led to the adoption of an open system of judicial review at the outset. Indeed, each of the three major figures involved in the 1987 constitutional amendments has now served as president of the country, showing that perceptions of future electoral uncertainty were accurate at the time. In contrast, in Taiwan the KMT retained control of the important institutions of the country until the election of Democratic Progressive Party leader Chen Shui-bian as president in early 2000. During most of the period under this study, Taiwan was a classic dominant-party setting. Finally, Mongolia has witnessed the alternation of political power, including periods of divided government as well as a current phase of one-party dominance. Altogether, it appears at present more to resemble the dominant-party setting of Taiwan until 2000.

These three settings allow us to predict an ordinal ranking of the three courts in terms of the exercise of judicial power. Judicial power should be greatest in Korea, followed by Mongolia, and finally lowest in Taiwan. Do the case studies provide evidence in support of this ranking? This requires consideration of the level of *independent* input of each court in producing politically significant outcomes that are complied with. Despite the difficulty of making cross-national comparisons of power, the case study approach used a detailed analysis of court decisions in each country that allows us to draw some comparative conclusions.

The Constitutional Court of Korea has indeed been the most active of our three courts. It frequently strikes legislative action and also regularly overturns prosecutorial decisions that, in the Korean context, reflect core interests of the national executive. It has demonstrated its independence in politically charged cases, as in the labor law disputes and the attempts to modify the statute of limitations to facilitate prosecution of former military rulers. Both examples found the court on the opposite side of an issue from the governing party, and the court caused significant embarrassment to the administration of President Kim Young-sam. Most importantly, the court has made its decisions stick.

The Mongolian Constitutional Court has also been involved in politically important decisions constraining the government of the day. Early on, these were complied with, but not without struggle. In particular, the decision separating the government and parliament provoked a constitutional crisis and led to widespread dissatisfaction with the court. On balance, the Mongolian court appears to be less powerful than its Korean counterpart because it has faced more public criticism of its actions and received less compliance. Although it appeared to have a fairly high capacity to exercise power, its poor strategic choices have led to attacks. In the end, one must conclude that it failed to effectively exercise its power though it clearly took an independent stance.

The Council of Grand Justices on Taiwan has rendered a number of politically important decisions supporting the liberalization of the political system, most notably Interpretation No. 261 forcing the retirement of the

"old thieves" from active political life. Yet this decision and others striking various administrative rules associated with the authoritarian regime
should not be viewed as anti-KMT decisions. Rather, they appear to reflect what was an evolving consensus within the KMT as it struggled to
renew itself as the dominant party for a new generation of Taiwanese.
Most notably, this study was unable to identify a single decision wherein
the council sided against the interests of the mainstream KMT faction
headed by President Lee Teng-hui. This is not surprising given that the
president controls appointments to the council. Although the council has
constrained the state, its *independent* input into policy during the democratization period is unclear.

As political change continues, so will the role of the constitutional
courts. The election of Chen Shui-bian in Taiwan initiated a period of
divided government, and the experience of many countries suggests that
such environments can be fertile ground for the judicialization of political
conflict in constitutional courts. The council's careful decision in the 2001
nuclear power case appears to reflect this role. A key issue is whether
future presidential control over appointments will lead the Council of
Grand Justices to favor Chen or whether the council will seek to establish
a rough balance of institutional power to maximize its own freedom of
action.

Similarly, the weakening position of the president in Korea, vis-à-vis
the legislature, promises that institutional conflicts will be more likely in
the future. The Constitutional Court will no doubt be called on to arbitrate these conflicts. Whether this leads to comparatively less emphasis
on individual rights cases remains to be seen. The creation of alternative mechanisms for protecting citizens' rights from state interference (in
the form of a new administrative court and an Administrative Appeals
Commission under the prime minister) suggests that there may be less of
a need for constitutionalization of rights issues.

The situation in Mongolia is not altogether clear. Judicial review was
relatively uncontroversial until the "separation decision." Since that time,
public and elite dissatisfaction with the court has been on the rise. Some
have called publicly for amending the constitution and disbanding the
court, transferring the judicial review function to the Supreme Court. On
the other hand, broader concerns about the justice system may alleviate
pressure on the court to the extent that the Supreme Court is itself unpopular. A major effort to restructure and improve the justice system, now
under way with the support of foreign donors, could lead to systemic
reforms that will affect the Constitutional Court.

THE JUDICIALIZATION OF POLITICS

One inevitable implication of the successful development of a constitutional court is that political questions will tend to become judicialized and courts will find themselves playing roles that are really quite far afield from the conventional image of courts as engaged in rights protection. For example, all three of the constitutional courts have been involved in issues related to the composition of government. In Taiwan and Korea, the issue concerned interim appointments of the prime minister by a president in a split executive system. The Mongolian Constitutional Court was called on to determine the fundamental character of the political regime as parliamentary or presidential. In all these cases, the transfer of political struggle from the streets to the courtroom is a significant step. Regardless of the outcome, the fact that political forces have an alternative place to resolve core questions may facilitate democratic consolidation and illustrates that the insurance function can successfully constrain majority power.

These types of disputes, however, place constitutional courts in difficult positions in that they are called on to wield expertise that they may not have and may have to substitute for more-democratic processes. One need only consider the reaction to the United States Supreme Court's system in *Bush v. Gore* to understand the perils associated with these kinds of decisions. Arguably, the Korean and Taiwanese courts took the best approach by ducking the issue and letting the political process decide the outcome. In contrast, the Mongolian court derailed the entire constitutional system by refusing to allow the newly elected majority to form a government of its choosing. This led to a severe conflict with the political branches and the depletion of the court's authority. The lesson then is one of caution on core issues of the political process for courts in new democracies. This leaves attention to fundamental rights and constraint of state authority as the real roles the courts can play. Here the courts of Korea and Taiwan have been active in introducing international norms into new contexts, with both courts forcing significant reforms in criminal procedure. The Mongolian court also played such a role at least early in the postsocialist period.

INTERCOURT CONFLICT

In all three case studies, jurisdictional conflicts emerged between the constitutional court and the supreme court. Our theory does not predict how these conflicts will be resolved, only that they will occur as courts pursue their important goal of expanding institutional power. In Mongolia, the Supreme and Constitutional Courts appear to have reached an agreement on their division of labor, but it is one that leaves significant gaps in constitutional protections of individual rights. In Taiwan and Korea, in contrast, the top courts have engaged in struggles for jurisdiction. While the grand justices in Taiwan were able to secure the position of the constitution as the highest normative authority over a series of decisions, the Korean Constitutional Court's struggle with the Supreme Court over issues of supremacy and jurisdiction was less conclusive, though at the time of this writing the Constitutional Court seems to enjoy *de facto* supremacy.

EXPLAINING VARIATION: ALTERNATIVE HYPOTHESES

The evidence from the case studies is consistent with the insurance theory of constitutional court design and the diffusion theory of constitutional court performance. Political uncertainty leads to the adoption of judicial review as a form of insurance to protect the constitutional bargain. Political diffusion after the bargain is concluded allows courts to exercise greater power. By increasing uncertainty, democratization leads to greater demand for judicial review; the extent of political diffusion determines how successful courts can be in asserting power.

There are a number of alternative hypotheses that might affect the development of judicial review in new democracies. *Cultural traditions* are sometimes seen to provide important supporting conditions for the exercise of legal authority.[1] From this perspective, judicial review is the ultimate expression of a tradition of autonomous law associated with the modern West. This study has focused on three environments with no cultural tradition of autonomous law, including two heavily influenced by Confucianism. The robust exercise of judicial power in all three settings helps to confirm that cultural factors are not insurmountable obstacles to judicial review. Those who argue that "Asian values" are incompatible with liberal democracy will have trouble understanding the jurisprudence of the courts described herein.

Cultures are dynamic, of course, and change over time. One factor that might be called cultural concerns the *receptivity* of the society to foreign ideas, a factor particularly important in an era of "globalization." All

---

[1] See, for example, Roberto M. Unger, *Law in Modern Society: Toward a Criticism of Social Theory* (1976).

three of our case studies are drawn from small countries in the shadow of a great power, namely China. Such small countries may be particularly open to influence from the modern West because of their fear of cultural and political domination by the more proximate large state. Judicial review from this point of view is one element of a package of modernizing reforms that are adopted because of their very western-ness as part of a complex security strategy. "Westernization" gives the West a stake in the society and hence may deter the large neighbor from expansionism. Because all three of our case studies share this attribute of smallness, we cannot draw firm conclusions about the relevance of this factor for the adoption and development of judicial review. However, we can say that western influence did not determine institutional form. For Taiwan and Korea, the United States provided a reference society that influenced institutional and systemic changes during the long authoritarian period. Yet neither country has adopted the decentralized system of judicial review. Institutional design appears to be an issue where local, not international, forces are determinative.

One might expect that *prior history of judicial review* would provide an important source of support for constitutional judges in new democracies. After all, it is generally hypothesized that democratization has been easier in those countries where authoritarian regimes had displaced prior democracies. History, the argument runs, provides a source of inspiration as well as models of institutional design for new democracies.[2] In the Eastern European context, for example, the interwar history of democracy in Czechoslovakia and Hungary are thought to support the more rapid democratization of those countries than the ambivalent cases of Rumania and Bulgaria.

Yet prior experience can constrain as well as inspire. In particular, when an institution exists under authoritarianism, it may develop an institutional culture that favors restraint. Further, it is unlikely to be seen as legitimate in the very early years of democratization. In the cases of Taiwan and Korea, judicial review existed under authoritarian regimes and this may have hindered rather than supported the emergence of a more activist conception of judicial review. The Council of Grand Justices in Taiwan was quite cautious in building up its power, treading very carefully, in part because its legacy complicated the task of identifying core constituencies. The Korean Constitutional Court, as a new institution, had

---

[2] See *Institutional Design in Post-Communist Societies* 60–61 (Jon Elster et al., eds., 1998).

a bit more freedom to operate. This suggests that prior history is neither a
necessary nor sufficient condition for the successful operation of a particular institution.

Some scholars have attempted to tie the exercise of judicial power
to the *type of previous regime* with a peculiar threat posed by military
authoritarians.[3] Yet in some cases, military authorities may be more likely
to rely on judicial review as a means of protecting them once they return to
the barracks. The rule of law, institutionally embodied in a strong court,
promises an orderly transition without retroactive revision of the constitutional bargain. The case of Chile, where judicial review was secured by
an exiting autocrat, illustrates the role a constitutional court can play in
protecting former military rulers.

Our cases provide counterevidence to the assertion that military authoritarians hinder the development of judicial review. The Korean Constitutional Court has developed active judicial review in the shadow of
a departing military-authoritarian regime. Taiwan's grand justices have
also systematically dismantled the military-Leninist system of control of
civil society. It may be helpful that the only tool the military has to influence the court is to overturn the entire constitutional order, the political
equivalent of a nuclear warhead; civilian political parties and institutions
have more subtle ways of engaging with the court to communicate their
preferences and to encourage judicial modesty.

The *pace of transition*, in particular the timing of constitutional reform,
may affect the exercise of judicial review. A rapid transition following
constitutional reform would seem to favor an activist court as the old
forces attempt to challenge quick reforms and minorities seek insurance.
This hypothesis appears difficult to reject. Both Korea and Taiwan had
protracted democratic transitions, so pace of transition alone does not
appear to be the key factor. However, the two countries differed in the
pace of constitutional reform. In Korea, as well as Mongolia, constitutional reform was accomplished quickly at the outset of the transition
process. This provided the courts with an identifiable constitutional moment to invoke. Where constitutional reform is a gradual process, as in
Taiwan, the court must fear the real possibility of constitutional override
of any unpopular decisions and therefore will likely be more cautious.
Further research on other countries is necessary to evaluate this hypothesis, but our cases suggest that quick transition can support strong judicial
review.

---

[3] Bruce Ackerman, "The Rise of World Constitutionalism," 83 *Va. L. Rev.* 771 (1997).

Ackerman has suggested that *strong presidencies* were good for the exercise of judicial review.[4] Earlier, we cast doubt on his hypothesis, arguing that the party system was an important supervening variable, but also noted that the French-style split executive creates a need for independent courts to arbitrate institutional disputes. The case studies provide evidence in favor of our argument. All three case studies are semipresidential systems, but they vary in terms of presidential power. Korea and Taiwan were both strongly weighted toward presidential power in the period under review. Yet judicial power was most constrained in Taiwan, even more so than in the weak semipresidential system in Mongolia. In contrast, the Korean court was able to exercise a great deal of independent power under a strong presidency. The difference between Taiwan and Korea is best explained by the contrasting party systems. The president of the Republic of China has historically been at the center of a dominant party and hence more able to resolve intragovernmental conflicts before they become major constitutional issues. The Korean president operates in a weak party system and faces a hostile opposition that has often controlled the legislature. There are therefore more institutional conflicts that cannot be solved by negotiation, leading to greater constitutionalization of political issues. The party system is the crucial factor that determines how the institutions interact, not the mere fact of presidentialism. It is important to note here that the Council of Grand Justices appears to be playing a more minoritarian role in the current situation of divided government on Taiwan.

Certain other variables may affect demand for judicial review by creating incentives for plaintiffs to bring cases to courts. In particular, a *vigorous civil society* provides interest groups that may seek to challenge government action in courts.[5] Furthermore, an *unrestricted legal profession* may create incentives for individual lawyers to act as entrepreneurs by pursuing constitutional litigation. These two demand-side variables would support plaintiffs' propensity to bring constitutional cases. Charles Epp has argued that these are necessary underpinnings for a "rights revolution."[6]

On both of these scores, Korea provides counterevidence to the hypothesis. In contrast with Taiwan and Mongolia, associational life has

---

[4] *Ibid.*
[5] Stefan Voigt, "Making Constitutions Work – Conditions for Maintaining the Rule of Law," 18 *Cato J.* (1998).
[6] See Charles R. Epp, *The Rights Revolution: Lawyers, Activists and Supreme Courts in Comparative Perspective* (1998).

TABLE 8.1 *Alternative Explanatory Variables*

	Korea	Taiwan	Mongolia
Confucian Cultural Tradition	yes	yes, somewhat	no
Colonialism	Japanese	Japanese	Russian
Previous Judicial Review?	yes	yes	no
Previous Democracy?	yes	no	no
Type of Previous Regime	military	dominant Leninist Party	dominant Leninist Party
Type of Democratic Transition	gradual	gradual	quick
Type of Constitutional Transition	quick	gradual	quick
Governmental Structure	semipresidential	semipresidential	semipresidential
Divided Government?	yes	yes	no
Capitalist Economy?	yes	yes	no

been limited in Korea.[7] While certain types of private associations exist, for the most part these are not focused on public-interest issues of the type that would lead to greater demand for judicial review. If anything, the presence of an increasingly active system of judicial review has encouraged the formation of new interest groups, suggesting that the causal relationship runs in the opposite direction. Similarly, Korea and, to a lesser extent, Taiwan have historically placed significant restrictions on the practice of law, limiting entry into the profession. This should dampen demand for judicial review. But Korea's activist system of judicial review existed prior to recent efforts to liberalize the profession. The broader point, consistent with the general approach of this study, is that demand-side variables, while important, are insufficient on their own to explain variation in the performance of judicial review. We need to take into account supply-side constraints on the ability of courts to render decisions against important political interests.

In sum, many of the alternative hypotheses appear to be less plausible in explaining the exercise of judicial power than the political configuration. Table 8.1 summarizes the various factors discussed here. The obvious

[7] On Taiwan, see Linda Chao and Ramon Myers, *The First Chinese Democracy: Political Life in the Republic of China on Taiwan* (1998); on Korea, see *State and Society in Contemporary Korea* (Hagen Koo, ed., 1993); see also Tadashi Yamamoto, *Emerging Civil Society in the Asia-Pacific Region* (1995).

conclusion is that constitutional courts can emerge and thrive in a variety of environments and that neither culture nor history is as important as structure in determining outcomes.

CONCLUSION

In recent decades, judicial review has expanded around the globe from the United States, Western Europe, and Japan to become a regular feature of constitutional design in Africa and Asia. Constitutional courts have exercised review to challenge political authorities when conflicts arise among government institutions or they impinge on individual rights. Although the formal power to exercise judicial review is now nearly universal in democratic states, courts have varied in the extent to which they are willing to exercise this power in practice.

This study has examined the spread of judicial review to three "third-wave" democracies in order to try to answer two questions: (1) why the institutional design for judicial review varies across different countries; and (2) why some courts are more willing to exercise the power of judicial review than others, both across different countries and over time. It has provided a single answer to both questions – namely, that *political diffusion matters*. Dominant parties are less likely to design open and powerful systems of judicial review and are less likely to tolerate powerful courts exercising independent power once the constitution enters into force. In contrast, constitutional design in a situation of political deadlock is more likely to produce a strong, accessible system of judicial review as politicians seek political insurance. Political diffusion creates more disputes for courts to resolve and hinders authorities from overruling or counter-attacking courts. In sum, political diffusion is good for judicial power.

By providing alternative power centers, democracy creates incentives to take disputes to court. It also reduces constraints on political discourse and allows those out of power to challenge government action. Inevitably accompanying democratization, then, is a certain degree of "judicialization" of politics. But the extent of this judicialization will be determined by the particular configuration of political forces and the receptiveness of courts to accepting controversial disputes. The exercise of judicial power at any given moment is at least in part endogenously determined, but over time we should expect to see some instances of courts challenging political authorities when there are no political constraints preventing them from doing so.

Judicial review, then, is to a large degree a product of democratization. Without democracy, judicial review makes little sense from the point of view of political authorities. Whereas most legal scholarship emphasizes the countermajoritarian nature of judicial review of legislation, this study has shown that judicial review and democracy can and do develop together. Judicial power is both an expression of political diffusion and a force for preventing excessive centralization of power.

Is judicial review a good thing for democracy? The case studies presented here have suggested that on balance the answer is yes. Judicial review can deepen the constitutional order and contribute to the consolidation of the democratic system. By providing a nonpartisan forum that issues authoritative pronouncements drawn from the fundamental text, judicial review encourages losers in the legislative process to bring their disputes to court, increasing the likelihood that they will remain loyal to the constitutional order. Judicial review provides an alternative channel for those out of power, be they aspiring Democrats or erstwhile authoritarians.

Furthermore, judicial review can *express* fundamental values for the democracy and mark a break with the authoritarian past. By binding new leaders in ways that the old leaders were not bound, judicial review expresses and constitutes new notions of justice and law. Judicial review can transform political tension into legal constraint.

For example, the Korean court's willingness to overturn labor legislation passed by the legislature's "sneak" session may have helped to reduce tensions over the issue that remained the main source of political violence in that country a decade after democratization. By using law to constrain the government, the court has helped to redefine the notion of law in Korean society. The Council of Grand Justices has played an important role in striking, one by one, many of the tools of mainlander dominance and has thus helped shape an evolving Taiwanese identity even as the KMT continues to be an important political force. This may have served to legitimate the reform process in the eyes of many Taiwanese, allowing the eventual electoral victory of the DPP. The Mongolian court has similarly become enmeshed in major political controversies, although it has been less successful at defusing them.

The case studies from Asia have suggested that constitutional courts have for the most part acted with caution and prudence, challenging authorities but securing compliance. With the exception of the Mongolian decision separating the legislature from the government, the institution of judicial review has not been particularly controversial in these three new democracies. There appear to be mechanisms of signal and countersignal over time that moderate the countermajoritarian role of courts, but at the same time, the institutional pressures to expand judicial power help courts continue to push authorities. Over time, incremental decisions can expand the freedom of action available to the court and expand the protection of substantive rights associated with internationally derived notions of the rule of law. In this way, constitutional courts can develop constitutions and deepen democracy at the same time.

Bibliography

Aba-Namay, Rashed. "The Recent Constitutional Reforms in Saudi Arabia." *International and Comparative Law Quarterly* 42, no. 3 (1993): 295–331.

Abe, Masaki. "Internal Control of a Bureaucratic Judiciary: The Case of Japan." *International Journal of the Sociology of Law* 23 (1995): 303–20.

Abel, Richard, and Philip Lewis. *Lawyers in Society.* 3 vols. Berkeley: University of California Press, 1988.

Ackerman, Bruce. *We the People: Foundations.* Cambridge, MA: Belknap, 1993.

Ackerman, Bruce. "The Rise of World Constitutionalism." *Virginia Law Review* 83, no. 4 (1997): 771–97.

Ackerman, Bruce. *We the People: Tranformations.* Cambridge, MA: Harvard University Press, 1998.

Ahdieh, Robert. *Russia's Constitutional Revolution.* University Park: Pennsylvania State University Press, 1997.

Ahn, Kyong-whan. "The Growth of the Bar and the Changes in the Lawyer's Role: Korea's Dilemma." In *Law and Technology in the Pacific Community,* edited by Philip S. C. Lewis, 119–34. Boulder, CO: Westview Press, 1994.

Ahn, Kyong-whan. "The Influence of American Constitutionalism on South Korea." *Southern Illinois Law Journal* 27 (1998): 71.

Ainsworth, Janet E. "Categories and Culture: On the 'Rectification of Names' in Comparative Law." *Cornell Law Review* 82 (1996): 19–42.

Akande, Dapo. "The International Court of Justice and the Security Council: Is There Room for Judicial Control of Decisions of the Political Organs of the United Nations?" *International and Comparative Law Quarterly* 46, no. 2 (1997): 309–43.

Alexander, Larry, and Frederick Schauer. "On Extrajudicial Constitutional Interpretation." *Harvard Law Review* 110, no. 7 (1997): 1359–87.

Alvarez, Jose. "Judging the Security Council." *American Journal of International Law* 90 (1996): 1.

Aman, Alfred. *Administrative Law in a Global Era.* Ithaca, NY: Cornell University Press, 1992.

Amsden, Alice. *Asia's Next Giant.* Oxford: Oxford University Press, 1989.

Anand, Adarsh Sein. "Protection of Human Rights through Judicial Review in India." In *Judicial Review in International Perspective: Liber Amicorum Lord Slynn,* edited by Mats Andenas, 381–93. The Hague: Kluwer Law International, 2000.

Arnold, Bruce, and Fiona May. "Social Capital, Violations of Trust and the Vulnerability of Isolates: The Social Organization of Law Practice and Professional Self-Regulation." Paper presented at the Meetings of the Law and Society Association, Toronto, Canada, 1995.

Bailey, William Somers. "Reducing Malapportionment in Japan's Electoral Districts: The Supreme Court Must Act." *Pacific Rim Law and Policy Journal* 6, no. 1 (1997): 169.

Bainbridge, Stephen M. "Why a Board? Group Decisionmaking in Corporate Governance." *Vanderbilt Law Review* 55 (2002): 1–34.

Batbayar, Ts. "Mongolia in 1993." *Asian Survey* 34 (1994): 41–45.

Batbayar, Ts. *Collected Essays.* Ulaanbaatar: Mongolian Academy of Sciences, 1997.

Batchelor, Stephen. *The Awakening of the West.* Berkeley, CA: Parallax Press, 1994.

Bauer, Joanne R., and Daniel Bell, eds. *The East Asian Challenge for Human Rights.* New York: Cambridge University Press, 1999.

Baum Julian. "Under My Thumb." *Far Eastern Economic Review* (Feb. 26, 1998): 26–27.

Baum, Lawrence. *The Puzzle of Judicial Behavior.* Ann Arbor: University of Michigan Press, 1997.

Bawden, Charles R. *A Modern History of Mongolia,* 2d ed. London: Kegan Paul, 1989.

Bayar, S. "Mongolia's National Security Challenges." San Francisco: Center for Asian Pacific Affairs, Report No. 16, Sept. 1994.

Beatty, David. *Constitutional Law in Theory and in Practice.* Toronto: University of Toronto Press, 1995.

Bedeski, Robert E. *The Transformation of South Korea: Reform and Reconstitution in the Sixth Republic under Roh Tae Woo, 1987–1992.* New York: Routledge, 1994.

Bell, Daniel. *East Meets West: Human Rights and Democracy in East Asia.* Princeton, NJ: Princeton University Press, 2000.

Bell, Daniel, David Brown, Kanishika Jayasuriya, and David Martin Jones. *Towards Illiberal Democracy in Pacific Asia.* New York: St. Martins Press, 1995.

Berman, Harold. *Justice in the USSR.* Cambridge, MA: Harvard University Press, 1963.

Berman, Harold. *Law and Revolution.* Cambridge, MA: Harvard University Press, 1985.

Bickel, Alexander. *The Least Dangerous Branch: The Supreme Court at the Bar of American Politics,* 2d ed. New Haven, CT: Yale University Press, 1986.

Black, Charles L. *A New Birth of Freedom: Human Rights, Named and Unnamed.* New York: Grosset/Putnam, 1998.

Bodde, Derk, and Clarence Morris. *Law in Imperial China.* Cambridge, MA: Harvard University Press, 1967.

Brzezinski, Mark. *The Struggle for Constitutionalism in Poland.* New York: St. Martins Press, 1998.

Buchanan, James, *The Limits of Liberty.* Chicago: University of Chicago Press, 1975.

Burley, Anne Marie, and Walter Mattli. "Europe Before the Court." *International Organization* 47 (1993): 41–76.

Butler, W. E. *The Mongolian Legal System.* Boston, MA: Kluwer, 1982.

Cappelletti, Mauro. *Judicial Review in the Contemporary World.* New York: Bobbs-Merrill, 1971.

Cappelletti, Mauro. *The Judicial Process in Comparative Perspective.* Oxford: Clarendon Press, 1989.

Carothers, Thomas. "The Rule of Law Revival." *Foreign Affairs* 35 (1997): 23.

Carrasco, Enrique. "Rhetoric, Race and the Asian Crisis." *Los Angeles Times,* Jan. 1, 1998.

Carrasco, Enrique. "Tough Sanctions: The Asian Crisis and the New Colonialism." *Chicago Tribune,* Jan. 3, 1998.

Central News Agency. "Party Screening Committee Puts off DPP Independence Case." Feb. 20, 1992.

Chang, Wen-chen. *Transition to Democracy, Constitutionalism and Judicial Activism: Taiwan in Comparative Constitutional Perspective.* Unpublished J.S.D. dissertation, Yale Law School, June 2001.

Chang, Yook-Seok. "Prosecutor's Discretionary Power in the Republic of Korea." UNAFEI Resource Material Series 49 (1997): 69–78.

Chao, Linda, and Ramon Myers. *The First Chinese Democracy: Political Life in the Republic of China on Taiwan.* Baltimore, MD: Johns Hopkins University Press, 1998.

Chen, Paul Heng-cha. *Chinese Legal Tradition under the Mongols.* Princeton, NJ: Princeton University Press, 1979.

Cheng, Tun-jen. "Democratizing the Quasi-Leninist Regime in Taiwan." *World Politics* 41 (1987): 471–99.

Cheng, Tun-jen, and Stephen Haggard, eds. *Political Change in Taiwan.* Boulder, CD: Lynne Reiner, 1992.

Cheng, Tun-jen, and Yi-shing Lao. "Taiwan in 1997: An Embattled Government in Search of New Opportunities." *Asian Survey* 38, no. 1 (1998): 53–63.

Chiu, Hungdah. "Constitutional Development and Reform in the Republic of China on Taiwan." *Issues and Studies* 29 (1993): 1–38.

Chiu, Hungdah, and Jyh-Pin Fa. "Taiwan's Legal System and Legal Profession." In *Taiwan Trade and Investment Law,* edited by Mitchell Silk, 21–42. New York: Oxford University Press, 1994.

Cho, Kuk. "Tension Between the National Security Law and Constitutionalism in South Korea: Security for What?" *Boston University International Law Journal* 15 (1997): 125.

Choi, Dae-kwon. "Informal Ways vs. the Formal Law in Korea." Paper presented at the Research Committee on the Sociology of Law Meeting, Tokyo, Japan, July 1995.

Choi, Sang-yong, ed. *Democracy in Korea: Its Ideals and Realities.* Seoul: Korean Political Science Association, 1997.

Chu, Lawrence. "Legislators Pass Amendments to Hooligan Control Act." *Central News Agency*, Dec. 30, 1996.

Chu, Yun-han. "Taiwan's Unique Challenges." *Journal of Democracy* 7, no. 3 (1997): 69–82.

Clark, Cal, and K.C. Roy. *Comparing Development Patterns in Asia*. Boulder, CO: Lynne Reiner, 1997.

Clark, Donald, ed. *The Kwangju Uprising: Shadows over the Regime in South Korea*. Boulder, CO: Westview Press, 1988.

Clinton, Robert Lowry. *Marbury v. Madison and Judicial Review*. Lawrence: University Press of Kansas, 1989.

Clinton, Robert Lowry. "Game Theory, Legal History and the Origins of Judicial Review: A Revisionist Analysis of *Marbury v. Madison*." *American Journal of Political Science* 38, no. 2 (1994): 285–302.

Constitutional Court of Korea. *Constitutional Justice in Korea*. Seoul, 1993.

Constitutional Court of Korea. *The Constitutional Court*. Seoul, 1997.

Constitutional Court of Korea. *The First Ten Years of the Korean Constitutional Court*. Seoul, 2001.

Cooney, Sean. "The New Taiwan and Its Old Labour Law: Authoritarian Legislation in a Democratised Society." *Comparative Labor Law Journal* 18, no. 1 (1996): 1–61.

Cooney, Sean. "Taiwan's Emerging Liberal Democracy and the New Constitutional Review." In *Asian Laws Through Australian Eyes*, edited by Veronica Taylor, Sydney, 141–60. LBC Information Systems, 1997.

Cooney, Sean. "Why Taiwan Is Not Hong Kong: A Review of the PRC's 'One Country Two Systems' Model for Reunification with Taiwan." *Pacific Rim Law and Policy Journal* 6 (1997): 497.

Cooney, Sean. "A Community Changes: Taiwan's Council of Grand Justices and Liberal Democratic Reform." In *Law, Capitalism and Power in East Asia*, edited by Kanishka Jayasuriya, 253–81. New York: Routledge, 1999.

Cooter, Robert. *The Strategic Constitution*. Princeton, NJ: Princeton University Press, 2000.

Cooter, Robert, and Tom Ginsburg. "Comparative Judicial Discretion – An Empirical Test of Economic Models." *International Review of Law and Economics* 16 (1996): 295–313.

Dadomo, Christian, and Susan Farran. *French Substantive Law*. London: Sweet and Maxwell, 1997.

Dahl, Robert. "Decision-making in a Democracy: The Supreme Court as a National Policy-maker." *Journal of Public Law* 6 (1957): 279.

Dahl, Robert. *Democracy and Its Critics*. New Haven, CT: Yale University Press, 1989.

Dahl, Robert. "Thinking About Democratic Constitutions: Conclusions from Democratic Experience." In *Nomos XXXVIII: Political Order*, edited by Ian Shapiro and Russell Hardin, 175–206. New York: New York University Press, 1996.

Dashpurev, D., and S. Soni. *Reign of Terror in Mongolia*. Absecon Highlands, NJ: South Asian Publishers, 1992.

Davis, Michael, ed. *Human Rights and Chinese Values*. New York: Oxford University Press, 1995.

Davis, Michael. "Constitutionalism and Political Culture: The Debate over Human Rights and Asian Values." *Harvard Human Rights Journal* 11 (1998): 109.

Davis, Michael. "The Price of Rights: Constitutionalism and East Asian Economic Development." *Human Rights Quarterly* 20 (1998): 303.

De Bary, William Theodore. *The Liberal Tradition in China*. New York: Columbia University Press (1983).

De Bary, William Theodore. "The 'Constitutional Tradition' in China." *Journal of Asian Law* 9, no. 1 (1995): 7–34.

De Bary, William Theodore. *Asian Values and Human Rights*. Cambridge: Harvard University Press, 1998.

Devins, Neal. *Shaping Constitutional Values: Elected Government, the Supreme Court, and the Abortion Debate*. Baltimore, MD: Johns Hopkins University Press, 1996.

Devins, Neal, and Louis Fisher. "Judicial Exclusivity and Political Instability." *Virginia Law Review* 84 (1998): 83.

Diamond, Larry. "Is the Third Wave Over?" *Journal of Democracy* 7 (1996): 20.

Dicey, Albert V. *Introduction to the Study of the Law of the Constitution*, 8th ed. London: Macmillan, 1915.

Drexl, Josef. "Was Sir Francis Drake a Dutchman? – British Supremacy of Parliament after *Factortame*." *American Journal of Comparative Law* 41 (1993): 551–71.

Dreyer, June Teufel. Testimony Before Asian Affairs Subcommittee, U.S. House of Representatives, Hearings on Taiwan, Sept. 24, 1991.

Elman, Benjamin A. "Confucianism and Modernization: A Reevaluation." In *Confucianism and Modernization: A Symposium*, edited by Joseph P. L. Jiang, 1–19. Taipei: Freedom Council, 1987.

Elster, Jon. "Forces and Mechanisms in the Constitution-Making Process." *Duke Law Journal* 45 (1995): 364–96.

Elster, Jon. "Limiting Majority Rule: Alternatives to Judicial Review in the Revolutionary Epoch." In *Constitutional Justice under Old Constitutions*, edited by Eivind Smith, 3–22. The Hague: Kluwer Law International, 1995.

Elster, Jon. "Introduction." In *The Roundtable Talks and the Breakdown of Communism*, edited by Jon Elster, 1–20. Chicago, IL: University of Chicago Press, 1996.

Elster, Jon, ed. *Ulysses Unbound*. New York: Cambridge University Press, 2000.

Elster, Jon, Claus Offe, and Ulrich K. Preuss. *Institutional Design in Post-Communist Societies*. New York: Cambridge University Press, 1998.

Ely, John Hart. *Democracy and Distrust*. Cambridge, MA: Harvard University Press, 1980.

Emery, C. T., and B. Smythe. *Judicial Review*. London: Sweet and Maxwell, 1986.

Epp, Charles R. *The Rights Revolution: Lawyers, Activists and Supreme Courts in Comparative Perspective*. Chicago, IL: University of Chicago Press, 1998.

Epstein, Lee, and Jack Knight. *The Choices Justices Make*. Washington, DC: Congressional Quarterly Press, 1998.

Eskridge, William. "The Judicial Review Game." *Northwestern University Law Review* 88 (1993): 382.

Eskridge, William. *Dynamic Statutory Interpretation.* Cambridge, MA: Harvard University Press, 1994.

Eskridge, William, and John Ferejohn. "Politics, Interpretation, and the Rule of Law." In *Nomos XXXVI: The Rule of Law,* edited by Ian Shapiro, 265–94. New York: New York University Press, 1994.

Evans, Peter. *Embedded Autonomy: States and Industrial Transformation.* Princeton, NJ: Princeton University Press, 1995.

Fa, Jyh-pin. *A Comparative Study of Judicial Review under Nationalist Chinese and American Constitutional Law.* Asian Studies Occasional Reprints Series No. 3. Baltimore: University of Maryland School of Law, 1980.

Fa, Jyh-pin. "Constitutional Developments in Taiwan: The Role of the Council of Grand Justices." *International and Comparative Law Quarterly* 40 (1991): 198–209.

Faundez, Julio, ed. *Good Government and Law: Legal and Institutional Reform in Developing Countries.* New York: St. Martins Press, 1997.

Feldman, David. "Parliamentary Scrutiny of Legislation and Human Rights." *Public Law* (summer 2002): 323–48.

Feldman, Harvey J., ed. *Constitutional Reform and the Future of the Republic of China.* Armonk, NY: M. E. Sharpe, 1991.

Finkel, Jodi S. "The Implementation of Judicial Reform in Peru in the 1990s." Paper presented at the American Political Science Association Meetings, San Francisco, CA, Aug. 2001.

Fish, M. Steven. *Democracy from Scratch: Opposition and Regime in the New Russian Revolution.* Princeton, NJ: Princeton University Press, 1995.

Fish, M. Steven. "The Perils of Russian Superpresidentialism." *Current History* 96, no. 612 (1997): 326–30.

Fisher, Louis. *Constitutional Dialogues.* Princeton, NJ: Princeton University Press, 1988.

Fiss, Owen. "The Right Degree of Independence." In *Transitions to Democracy in Latin America: The Role of the Judiciary,* edited by Irwin P. Stotzky, 55–72. Boulder, CO: Westview Press, 1993.

Folsom, Ralph, John Minan, and Lee Ann Otto. *Law and Politics in the People's Republic of China.* St. Paul, MN: West Publishing, 1992.

Fox, Gregory H., and Georg Nolte. "Intolerant Democracies." *Harvard International Law Journal* 36, no. 1 (1995): 1–70.

Fox, Russell A. "Confucian and Communitarian Responses to Liberal Democracy." *Review of Politics* 59 (1997): 561–92.

Freedom House. *Freedom in the World.* Washington, DC: 1986–99.

Friedman, Barry. "Dialogue and Judicial Review." *Michigan Law Review* 91 (1993): 577.

Friedman, Barry. "A History of the Countermajoritarian Difficulty, Part One: The Road to Judicial Supremacy." *N.Y.U. Law Review* 73 (1998): 333.

Fuller, Lon. *The Morality of Law.* New Haven, CT: Yale University Press, 1964.

Gadbois, George H., Jr. "The Institutionalization of the Supreme Court of India." In *Comparative Judicial Systems: Challenging Frontiers in Conceptual and Empirical*

Analysis, edited by John Schmidhauser, 111–42. Boston, MA: Butterworths, 1987.

Ganzorig, Gombosurengin. "The Relationship between the Constitutional and Supreme Court of Mongolia," *Journal of East European Law* 7, nos. 3–4 (2000): 667–94.

Garrett, Geoffrey. "From the Luxembourg Compromise to Codecision: Decision Making in the European Union." *Electoral Studies* 14 (1995): 289–308.

Garrett, Geoffrey. "The Politics of Legal Integration in the European Union." *International Organization* 49 (1995): 175–81.

Garrett, Geoffrey, and George Tsebelis. "An Institutional Critique of Intergovernmentalism." *International Organization* 50 (1996): 269–99.

Geertz, Clifford. *The Interpretation of Cultures*. New York: Basic Books, 1973.

Gely, Rafael, and Pablo Spiller. "The Political Economy of Supreme Court Constitutional Decisions: The Case of Roosevelt's Court-Packing Plan." *International Review of Law and Economics* 12 (1992): 45–67.

Ginsburg, Tom. "The Transformation of Legal Institutions in Mongolia, 1990–1993." *Issues and Studies* 12 (1994): 77–113.

Ginsburg, Tom. "Between Russia and China: Political Reform in Mongolia." *Asian Survey* 35 (1995): 459–71.

Ginsburg, Tom. "Deepening Democracy: Mongolia in 1997." *Asian Survey* 38 (1998): 64–68.

Ginsburg, Tom. "Confucian Constitutionalism? The Emergence of Judicial Review in Korea and Taiwan." *Law and Social Inquiry* 27 (2002): 763–99.

Ginsburg, Tom. "Economic Analysis and the Design of Constitutional Courts." *Theoretical Inquiries in Law* 3 (2002): 49–85.

Ginsburg, Tom, and G. Ganzorig. "Constitutionalism and Human Rights in Mongolia." In *Mongolia in Transition*, edited by Ole Bruun and Ole Odgaard, 147–64. London: Curzon Press/Nordic Institute of Asian Studies, 1996.

Ginsburgs, George. "The Constitutional Courts of Eastern Europe." *Review of Central and Eastern European Law* 18 (1992): 6.

Glendon, Mary Ann. *Abortion and Divorce in Western Law*. Cambridge, MA: Belknap Press, 1987.

Glenn, H. Patrick. *Legal Traditions of the World*. New York: Oxford Univeristy Press, 2000.

Gold, Thomas. *State and Society in the Taiwan Miracle*. Armonk, NY: M. E. Sharpe, 1986.

Gold, Thomas. "Factors in Taiwan's Democratic Transition." Paper presented at the conference Consolidating the Third Wave Democracies, Institute of National Policy Research, Taipei, Taiwan, Aug. 27–30, 1995.

Goldsworthy, Jeffrey. *The Sovereignty of Parliament: History and Philosophy*. New York: Oxford University Press, 1999.

Goodman, John B. *Monetary Sovereignty: The Politics of Central Banking in Western Europe*. Ithaca: Cornell University Press, 1992.

Griffin, Stephen. *American Constitutionalism: From Theory to Politics*. Princeton, NJ: Princeton University Press, 1996.

Gutmann, Amy, and Dennis Thompson. *Democracy and Disagreement*. Cambridge, MA: Belknap, 1996.

Habermas, Jurgen. *Between Facts and Norms: Contributions to a Discourse Theory of Law and Democracy.* Cambridge, MA: MIT Press, 1996.

Haggard, Stephen, and Robert Kaufmann. *The Political Economy of Democratic Transitions.* Princeton, NJ: Princeton University Press, 1995.

Hahm, Pyong-choon. *The Korean Political Tradition and Law.* Seoul: Royal Asiatic Society, 1987.

Hahm, Sung-deuk, and L. Christopher Plein. *After Development: The Transformation of the Korean Presidency and Bureaucracy.* Washington, DC: Georgetown University Press, 1997.

Halmai, Gabor, and Kim Lane Scheppele. "Living Well Is the Best Revenge: The Hungarian Approach to Judging the Past." In *Transitional Justice and the Rule of Law in New Democracies*, edited by James McAdams, 155–84. Notre Dame, IN: Notre Dame University Press, 1997.

Hamilton, Gary, and Cheng-shu Kao. "Max Weber and the Analysis of the Asian Industrialization." University of California at Davis, Research Program in East Asian Culture and Development, Working Paper No. 2, 1986.

Han, Sung-joo. "South Korea: Politics in Transition." In *Democracy in Korea: Its Ideals and Realities*, edited by Sang-yong Choi, 21–47. Seoul: Korean Political Science Association, 1997.

Heaton, William. "Mongolia in 1990." *Asian Survey* 31 (1991): 1.

Henderson, Gregory. *Korea: Politics of the Vortex.* Cambridge, MA: Harvard University Press, 1968.

Henkin, Louis. *The Age of Rights.* New York: Columbia University Press, 1996.

Hirschman, Albert O. *Exit, Voice and Loyalty: Responses to Decline in Firms, Organizations and States.* Cambridge, MA: Harvard University Press, 1972.

Hofnung, Menachem. "The Unintended Consequences of Unplanned Constitutional Reform: Constitutional Politics in Israel." *American Journal of Comparative Law* 44, no. 4 (1996): 585–604.

Holland, Peter. "Towards Constitutionalism: The First Term of the Constitutional Court of South Korea." In *Asian Laws Through Australian Eyes*, edited by Veronica Taylor. Sydney: LBC Information Systems, 1997.

Holmes, Stephen. "Precommitment and the Paradox of Democracy." In *Constitutionalism and Democracy*, edited by Jon Elster and Rune Slagstad, 175–240. Cambridge: Cambridge University Press, 1988.

Hood, Steven J. *The Kuomintang and the Democratization of Taiwan.* Boulder, CO: Westview Press, 1997.

Hulan, H. "Mongolia's New Constitutional Regime: Institutional Tensions and Political Consequences." *Mongolian Journal of International Affairs* 3 (1996): 42.

Huntington, Samuel. *The Clash of Civilizations and the Remaking of World Order.* New York: Simon & Schuster, 1996.

Huntington, Samuel. "After Twenty Years: The Future of the Third Wave." *Journal of Democracy* 8, no. 4 (1997): 3–12.

Ishiyama, John, and Matthew Velten. "Presidential Power and Democratic Development in Post-Communist Politics." *Communist and Post-Communist Studies* 31 (1998): 217–34.

Jennings, Jeremy. "From 'Imperial State to l'Etat de Droit': Benjamin Constant, Blandine Kriegel and the Reform of the French Constitution." In *Constitutionalism in Transformation: European and Theoretical Perspectives*, edited by Richard Bellamy and Dario Castiglione, 76–92. London: Blackwell, 1996.

Judicial Yuan of the Republic of China. *The Grand Justices and Constitutional Court of the Republic of China.* Taipei: 1995.

Kahn, Paul W. *The Reign of Law: Marbury v. Madison and the Construction of America.* New Haven, CT: Yale University Press, 1997.

Kelsen, Hans. "La garantie jurisdictionnel de la constitution." *Revue de droit public* 44 (1928): 197–257.

Kenney, Sally J., William M. Reisinger, and John C. Reitz, eds. *Constitutional Dialogues in Comparative Perspective.* New York: St. Martin's Press, 1999.

King, Ambrose Y. C. "State Confucianism and Its Transformation in Taiwan." In *Confucian Traditions in East Asian Modernity: Moral Education and Economic Culture in Japan and the Four Mini-Dragons*, edited by Wei-ming Tu, 228–43. Cambridge, MA: Harvard University Press, 1996.

Klarman, Michael J. "How Great Were the 'Great' Marshall Court Decisions?" *Virginia Law Review* 87 (2001): 1111–84.

Klingsberg, Ethan. "Judicial Review and Hungary's Transition from Communism to Democracy: The Constitutional Court, the Continuity of Law and the Redefinition of Property Rights." *B.Y.U. Law Review* (1992): 41–144.

Klug, Heinz. *Constituting Democracy: Law, Globalism and South Africa's Political Reconstruction.* New York: Cambridge University Press, 2000.

Kodderitsch, Lorenz. "Japan's New Administrative Procedures Law: Reasons for Its Enactment and Likely Implications." *Law in Japan* 24 (1994): 105.

Kommers, Donald. *The Constitutional Jurisprudence of the Federal Republic of Germany*, 2d ed. Durham, NC: Duke University Press, 1997.

Kommers, Donald. "Building Democracy: Judicial Review and the German Rechtstaat." In *The Postwar Transformation of Germany: Democracy, Prosperity and Nationhood*, edited by John Brady, Beverly Crawford, and Sarah E. Wiliarty, 94–121. Ann Arbor: University of Michigan Press, 1999.

Koo, Hagen, ed. *State and Society in Contemporary Korea.* Ithaca, NY: Cornell University Press, 1993.

Koopmans, T. "Comparative Law and the Courts." *American Journal of Comparative Law* 45 (1996): 545–56.

Kritz, Neil, ed. *Transitional Justice: How Emerging Democracies Reckon with Former Regimes*, 3 vols. Washington, DC: U.S. Institute for Peace, 1995.

Krug, Peter. "Departure from the Centralized Model: The Russian Supreme Court and Constitutional Control of Legislation." *Virginia Journal of International Law* 37 (1997): 725–87.

Kuo, Deborah. "Grand Justices Say Conscription Regulation Unconstitutional." China News Agency, Dec. 26, 1997.

Kyvig, David. "The Road Not Taken." *Political Science Quarterly* 104 (1989): 473.

Laakso, Markku, and Rein Taagepera. "Effective Number of Parties: A Measure with Application to Western Europe." *Comparative Political Studies* 12 (1979): 3–27.

Landes, William, and Richard Posner. "The Independent Judiciary in an Interest-Group Perspective." *Journal of Law and Economics* 18 (1975): 875.

Larkin, Christopher. "Judicial Independence and Democratization: A Theoretical and Conceptual Analysis." *American Journal of Comparative Law* 44, no. 4 (1996): 605–26.

Lattimore, Owen. *Nationalism and Revolution in Mongolia*. New York: Oxford University Press, 1955.

Lattimore, Owen. *Studies in Frontier History*. New York: Oxford University Press, 1962.

Lawyers Committee for Human Rights. *Halfway to Reform: The World Bank and the Venezuelan Justice System*. New York: Lawyers Committee for Human Rights/Provena, 1996.

Lee, Teng-hui. "Chinese Culture and Political Renewal." *Journal of Democracy* 6, no. 4 (1995): 3–8.

Leigh, Ian. "Taking Rights Proportionately: Judicial Review, the Human Rights Act and Strasbourg." *Public Law* (2002): 265–87.

Lessig, Lawrence. "Introduction: Roundtable on Redesigning the Russian Court" *East European Constitutional Review* 3, no. 3–4 (1994): 72–74.

Li, Nigel T., and Joyce C. Fan. "An Uncommon Case of Bigamy: An Uncommon Constitutional Interpretation." *Journal of Chinese Law* 4, no. 3 (1990): 69–81.

Li, Nigel T. "The Less-Restrictive-Means Principle – A More or Less Restrictive Methodology?" Paper presented at Conference on the Evolving U.S. Constitution, 1787–1987, Institute of American Culture, Academica Sinica, Taipei, Taiwan, June 2–4, 1988.

Lijphart, Arend. *Democracies: Patterns of Majoritarian and Consensus Government in Twenty-One Countries*. New Haven, CT: Yale University Press, 1984.

Lim, C. W. "Student Clash with Riot Police over Kwangju Massacre." Agence France Presse, Nov. 27, 1995.

Lim, Jibong, "The Pursuit of Happiness Clause in the Korean Constitution." *Journal of Korean Law* 1 (2001): 71–103.

Linebarger, Paul. *The Political Doctrines of Sun Yat-sen*. Baltimore, MD: Johns Hopkins University Press, 1937.

Linz, Juan, and Alfred Stepan. *Problems of Democratic Transition and Consolidation*. Baltimore, MD: Johns Hopkins University Press, 1996.

Liu, Lawrence Shao-liang. "Judicial Review and the Constitution: A Tale of Two Institutions." Paper presented at Conference on the Evolving U.S. Constitution, 1787–1987, Institute of American Culture, Academica Sinica, Taipei, Taiwan, June 2–4, 1988.

Liu, Lawrence Shao-liang. "Judicial Review and Emerging Constitutionalism: The Uneasy Case of the Republic of China on Taiwan." *American Journal of Comparative Law* 39 (1991): 509.

Lubman, Stanley, ed. *China's Legal Reforms*. New York: Oxford University Press, 1996.

Ludwikowski, Rett R. "Constitution Making in the Countries of Former Soviet Dominance: Current Developments." *Georgia Journal of International and Comparative Law* 23 (1993): 155.

Ludwikowski, Rett R. *Constitution Making in the Countries of Former Soviet Dominance*. Durham, NC: Duke University Press, 1996.

Lutz, Donald. "Toward a Theory of Constitutional Amendment." *American Political Science Review* 88, no. 2 (1994): 355–70.

Ma, Herbert Han-pao, "The Rule of Law in a Contemporary Confucian Society: A Reinterpretation." Presentation to Harvard Law School, East Asian Legal Studies Program, spring 1998.

Mahbubani, Kishore. *Can Asians Think?* Singapore: Time Editions, 1998.

Marino-Blanco, Elena. *The Spanish Legal System*. London: Sweet and Maxwell, 1996.

McAdams, A. James, ed. *Transitional Justice and the Rule of Law in New Democracies*. Notre Dame, IN: Notre Dame University Press, 1997.

McAdams, Richard. "A Focal Point Theory of Expressive Law." *Virginia Law Review* 86 (2000): 1649–1729.

McCann, Michael. *Rights at Work: Pay Equity Reform and the Politics of Legal Mobilization*. Chicago, IL: University of Chicago Press, 1994.

McCloskey, Robert, and Sanford Levinson. *The American Supreme Court*. Chicago: IL: University of Chicago Press, 1994.

Mendel, F. Fraser. "Judicial Power and Illusion: The Republic of China's Council of Grand Justices and Constitutional Interpretation." *Pacific Rim Law and Policy Journal* 2, no. 1 (1993): 157–89.

Meyer, John W., John Boli, George M. Thomas, and Francisco O. Ramirez. "World Society and the Nation State." *American Journal of Sociology* 103 (1997): 144–81.

Montesquieu, Charles de Secondat. *The Spirit of the Laws*. Translated and edited by Anne M. Cohler, Basia Miller, and Harold Stone. New York: Cambridge University Press, 1989.

Mueller, Dennis. *Constitutional Democracy*. New York: Oxford University Press, 1996.

Mueller, Dennis, "Fundamental Issues in Constitutional Reform: With Special Reference to Latin America and the United States." *Constitutional Political Economy* 10, no. 2 (1999): 119–48.

Mukhopadhaya, Kaushik. "Jury Size and the Free Rider Problem." Forthcoming, *Journal of Law, Economics, and Organization* 19 (2003).

Murphy, Walter. "Constitutions, Constitutionalism and Democracy." In *Constitutionalism and Democracy: Transitions in the Contemporary World*, edited by Douglas Greenberg, Stanley N. Katz, Melanie Beth Oliviero, and Steven C. Wheatley, 3–25. New York: Oxford University Press, 1993.

Nathan, Andrew. *Chinese Democracy*. Berkeley: University of California Press, 1985.

Nino, Carlos Santos. *The Constitution of Deliberative Democracy*. New Haven, CT: Yale University Press, 1995.

O'Donnell, Guillermo. "Horizontal Accountability in New Democracies." *Journal of Democracy* 9 (1998): 112–26.

Oh, John Kie-chang. *Korean Politics*. Ithaca, NY: Cornell University Press, 1999.

Park, Chan-wook. "Partisan Conflict and *Immobilisme* in the Korean National Assembly: Conditions, Processes, and Outcomes." In *Democracy in Korea: Its Ideals and Realities*, edited by Sang-yong Choi, 295–327. Seoul: Korean Political Science Association, 1997.

Pashin, Sergy. "A Second Edition of the Constitutional Court." *East European Constitutional Review* 3, nos. 3–4 (1994): 82.

Peerenboom, Randall. "Answering the Bell: Round Two of the Asian Values Debate." *Korea Journal* 42, no. 2 (2002): 194–240.

Posner, Richard. *Overcoming Law*. Cambridge, MA: Harvard University Press, 1995.

Posner, Richard. "Is the Ninth Circuit Too Large? A Statistical Study of Judicial Quality." *Journal of Legal Studies* 29 (2000): 711–18.

Post, Robert. "Theories of Constitutional Interpretation." In *Law and the Order of Culture*, edited by Robert Post, 13–42. Berkeley: University of California Press, 1991.

Power, Timothy J., and Mark J. Gasiorowski. "Institutional Design and Democratic Consolidation in the Third World." *Comparative Political Studies* 30, no. 2 (1997): 123–55.

Prosser, Tony. "Understanding the British Constitution." In *Constitutionalism in Transformation: European and Theoretical Perspectives*, edited by Richard Bellamy and Dario Castiglione, 61–75. London: Blackwell, 1996.

Pye, Lucien. *Asian Power and Politics: The Cultural Dimensions of Authority*. Cambridge, MA: Harvard University Press, 1985.

Rakove, Jack. "The Origins of Judicial Review: A Plea for New Contexts." *Stanford Law Review* 49 (1997): 1031–64.

Ramseyer, J. Mark. "The Puzzling (In)Dependence of Courts: A Comparative Approach." *Journal of Legal Studies* 23 (1994): 721.

Ramseyer, J. Mark, and Eric B. Rasmusen. "Judicial Independence in a Civil Law Regime: The Evidence from Japan." *Journal of Law, Economics and Organization* 13, no. 2 (1997): 259–86.

Ramseyer, J. Mark, and Eric B. Rasmusen. *Measuring Judicial Independence: The Political Economy of Judging in Japan*. Chicago: University of Chicago Press, 2003.

Rawls, John. *A Theory of Justice*. Cambridge: Harvard University Press, 1972.

Riasonovsky, V. A. *Customary Law of the Mongol Tribes*. Harbin, China: 1929.

Riasonovsky, V. A. *Fundamental Principles of Mongol Law*. Tientsin, China: 1937.

Root, Hilton. *Small Countries, Big Lessons: Governance and the Rise of East Asia*. New York: Oxford University Press/Asian Development Bank, 1996.

Rosenberg, Gerald N. *The Hollow Hope*. Chicago, IL: University of Chicago Press, 1991.

Rubenfeld, Jed. *Freedom and Time: A Theory of Constitutional Self-Government*. New Haven, CT: Yale University Press, 2001.

Rupen, Robert. *Mongols of the Twentieth Century*. Bloomington: Indiana University Press, 1964.

Sandag, Shagdariin, and Harry Kendall. *The Stalin-Choibalsan Massacres in Mongolia 1921–1941: Forging the Second Communist State*. Boulder, CO: Westview Press, 2000.

Sanders, Alan J. K. "Mongolia's New Constitution." *Asian Survey* 32, no. 6 (1992) 506–21.

Sartori, Giovanni. *Comparative Constitutional Engineering: An Inquiry into Structures, Incentives and Outcomes*, 2d ed. New York: New York University Press, 1996.

Schedler, Andreas, Larry Diamond, and Marc F. Plattner, eds. *The Self-Restraining State: Power and Accountability in New Democracies*. Boulder, CO: Lynne Reiner, 1999.

Schelling, Thomas C. *The Strategy of Conflict*. Cambridge: Cambridge University Press, 1960.

Schmidhauser, John R., ed. *Comparative Judicial Systems: Challenging Frontiers in Conceptual and Empirical Analysis*. Boston, MA: Butterworths, 1987.

Schram, Stuart, ed. *Foundations and Limits of State Power in China*. Hong Kong: Chinese University Press, 1987.

Schwartz, Herman. "The New Courts: An Overview." *East European Constitutional Review* 2, no. 2 (1993): 28–32.

Schwartz, Warren, and C. Frederick Beckner III. "Toward a Theory of the 'Meritorious Case': Legal Uncertainty as a Social Choice Problem." *George Mason Law Review* 6 (1998): 801–20.

Searl, Alan. "Legislature Debates Need for Soldiers on College Campuses." *China Times*, Apr. 4, 1998.

Segal, Jeffrey A., and Harold J. Spaeth. *The Supreme Court and the Attitudinal Model*. New York: Cambridge University Press, 1993.

Seong, C. Gweon. "Hope I Die Before I Get Old." *Korea Herald*, Sept. 24, 1997.

Shapiro, Martin. *Law and Politics in the Supreme Court*. New York: Free Press, 1964.

Shapiro, Martin. *Courts: A Comparative and Political Analysis*. Chicago, IL: University of Chicago Press, 1981.

Shapiro, Martin. "Lawyers, Corporations and Knowledge." *American Journal of Comparative Law* 38 (1990): 683.

Shapiro, Martin. "Coments on the Draft Constitution of Mongolia." Unpublished ms., San Francisco: Asia Foundation, 1991.

Shapiro, Martin. "Federalism, the Race to the Bottom, and the Regulation-Averse Entrepreneur." In *North American Federalism in Comparative Perspective*, edited by Harry Scheiber, 47–56. Berkeley, CA: Institute of Governmental Studies, 1992.

Shetreet, Shimon, and Jules Deschênes. *Judicial Independence: The Contemporary Debate*. Boston, MA: Martinus Nijhoff, 1985.

Shih, Chih-yu. "The Style of Chinese Constitutional Development: China and Taiwan." *International Journal of the Sociology of Law* 23 (1995): 371–93.

Shim Jae-hon and Charles S. Lee. "Test of Wills." *Far Eastern Economic Review*, Jan. 23, 1997: 14–15.

Shin Yong-bae. "Opposition Party Files Lawsuit Against Speaker." *Korea Herald*, Mar. 27, 1998.

Slaughter, Anne-Marie. "The Real New World Order." *Foreign Affairs* 76, no. 5 (1997): 183–97.

Slaughter, Anne-Marie, Joseph Weiler, and Alec Stone Sweet, eds. *The European Court and National Courts, Doctrine and Jurisprudence: Legal Change in Its Social Context*. Oxford: Hart Publishing, 1998.

Smith, Eivind, ed. *Constitutional Justice under Old Constitutions*. The Hague: Kluwer Law International, 1995.

Snell, James G., and Frederick Vaughan. *The Supreme Court of Canada: History of the Institution.* Toronto: Osgoode Society, 1985.

Sólyom, László, and Georg Brunner. *Constitutional Judiciary in a New Democracy: The Hungarian Constitutional Court.* Ann Arbor: University of Michigan Press, 2000.

Spitz, Richard, with Matthew Chaskalon. *The Politics of Transition: A Hidden History of South Africa's Negotiated Settlement.* Oxford: Hart Publishing, 2000.

Steamer, Robert J. *The Supreme Court in Crisis.* Amherst: University of Massachusetts Press, 1971.

Stearns, Maxwell. *Constitutional Process: A Social Choice Analysis of Supreme Court Decision Making.* Ann Arbor: University of Michigan Press, 2000.

Steinberg, David I. *The Republic of Korea: Economic Transformation and Social Change.* Boulder, CO: Westview Press, 1989.

Steinberg, David I. "The Republic of Korea: Pluralizing Politics." In *Politics in Developing Countries: Comparing Experiences with Democracy*, edited by Larry Diamond, Juan J. Linz, and Seymour Martin Lipset, 369–416. Boulder, CO: Lynne Reiner, 1995.

Steinberg, David I. "Korea: Triumph Amid Turmoil." *Journal of Democracy* 9, no. 2 (1998): 76–90.

Sterett, Susan. *Creating Constitutionalism? The Politics of Legal Expertise and Administrative Law in England and Wales.* Ann Arbor: University of Michigan Press, 1997.

Stone, Alec. *The Birth of Judicial Politics in France.* New York: Oxford University Press, 1992.

Stone, Alec, and James Caporaso. "From Free Trade to Supranational Polity: The European Court and Integration." Berkeley: Center for German and European Studies Working Paper, University of California, 1996.

Stotzky, Irwin P., ed. *Transitions to Democracy in Latin America: The Role of the Judiciary.* Boulder, CO: Westview Press, 1993.

Su, Yong-chin. "Summary of Interpretations by the Council of Grand Justices." In *Zhonghua Minguo Xing Hsien Wu Shi Nien (Fifty Years of the ROC Constitution).* Taipei: National Assembly, 1997.

Sun, Yat-sen. *The Teachings of Sun Yat-sen: Selections from His Writings.* London: Sylvan Press, 1945.

Sunstein, Cass. *Designing Democracy: What Constitutions Do.* New York: Oxford University Press, 2001.

Sutil, Jorge Correa. "The Judiciary and the Political System in Chile: The Dilemmas of Judicial Independence during the Transition to Democracy." In *Transitions to Democracy in Latin America: The Role of the Judiciary*, edited by Irwin P. Stotzky, 89–105. Boulder, CO: Westview Press, 1993.

Taagepera, Rein, and Matthew Soberg Shugart. *Seats and Votes: The Effects and Determinants of Electoral Systems.* New Haven: Yale University Press, 1989.

Tate, C. Neal. "Book Review of Paula Newberg, Judging the State: Courts and Constitutional Politics in Pakistan." *Law and Politics Book Review* 6, no. 7 (1996): 109–12.

Tate, Neal, and Thorsten Vallinder, eds. *The Global Expansion of Judicial Power.* New York: New York University Press, 1995.

Teik, Khoo Boo. "Between Law and Politics: The Malaysian Judiciary Since Independence." In *Law, Capitalism and Power in East Asia*, edited by Kanishka Jayasuriya, 205–32. New York: Routledge, 1999.

Thurow, Lester. "Asia: The Collapse and the Cure." *New York Review of Books*, Feb. 5, 1998: 22–28.

Tien, Hung-mao. *The Great Transition: Political and Social Change in the Republic of China*. Stanford, CA: Hoover Institution Press, 1989.

Tien, Hung-mao, ed. *Taiwan's Electoral Politics and Democratic Transition: Riding the Third Wave*. Armonk, NY: M. E. Sharpe, 1995.

Tollefson, Edwin. "Compliance of the Mongolian Criminal Code and Criminal Procedure Code with International Norms of Human Rights." Ulaanbaatar: United Nations Center for Human Rights, 1996.

Tseng, Osman. "Legislature Grants No Honeymoon to President." *Business Taiwan*, June 24, 1996.

Tu, Wei-ming, ed. *Confucian Traditions in East Asian Modernity: Moral Education and Economic Culture in Japan and the Four Mini-Dragons*. Cambridge: Harvard University Press, 1996.

U.S. Department of State. "Korea Report on Human Rights Practices." Washington, DC: 1991–2001.

U.S. Department of State. "Mongolia Report on Human Rights Practices." Washington, DC: 1993–2001.

U.S. Department of State. "Taiwan Report on Human Rights Practices." Washington, DC: 1993–2001.

Unger, Roberto Mangaeira. *Law in Modern Society: Toward a Criticism of Social Theory*. New York: Free Press, 1976.

van Maarseven, Henc, and Ger van der Tang. *Written Constitutions*. Dobbs Ferry, NY: Oceana Publications, 1978.

Voigt, Stefan. "Positive Constitutional Economics: A Survey." *Public Choice* 90 (1997): 11–53.

Voigt, Stefan. "Making Constitutions Work – Conditions for Maintaining the Rule of Law." *Cato Journal* 18, no. 2 (1998): 275–86.

Volcansek, Mary, and Jacqueline Lucienne Lafon. *Judicial Selection*. New York: Greenwood Press, 1987.

Volcansek, Mary. "Political Power and Judicial Review in Italy." *Comparative Political Studies* 26, no. 4 (1994): 492–509.

Waltman, Jerold L. "Judicial Activism in England." In *Judicial Activism in Comparative Perspective*, edited by Kenneth Holland, 33–52. New York: St. Martin's Press, 1991.

West, James, and Dae-kyu Yoon. "The Constitutional Court of the Republic of Korea: Transforming the Jursiprudence of the Vortex." *American Journal of Comparative Law* 40 (1992): 73–119.

West, James M. "Martial Lawlessness: The Legal Aftermath of Kwangju." *Pacific Rim Law and Policy Journal* 6, no. 1 (1997): 85–168.

West, James M., and Edward J. Baker "The 1987 Constitutional Reforms in South Korea: Electoral Processes and Judicial Independence." *Harvard Human Rights Yearbook* 1 (1988): 135–76.

White, G. Edward. "The 'Constitutional Revolution' as a Crisis in Adaptivity." *Hastings Law Journal* 48 (1997): 867.

White, Gordon. "Civil Society, Democratization, and Development." *Democratization* 1, no. 2 (1994): 379–94.

Whittington, Keith E. "Legislative Sanctions and the Strategic Environment of Judicial Review." *I-CON International Journal of Constitutional Law* 1 (2003).

Winn, Jane Kaufmann, and Tang-chi Yeh. "Advocating Democracy: The Role of Lawyers in Taiwan's Political Transformation." *Law and Social Inquiry* 20, no. 2 (1995): 561.

Worden, Robert, and Andrea Marles. *Mongolia: A Country Study*, 2d ed. Washington, DC: Congressional Research Service, 1991.

Yamamoto, Tadashi. *Emerging Civil Society in the Asia-Pacific Region*. Singapore: Institute of Southeast Asian Studies, 1995.

Yang, Kun. "Judicial Review and Social Change in the Korean Democratizing Process." *American Journal of Comparative Law* 41 (1993): 1–8.

Yeh, Jiunn-rong. "Changing Forces of Constitutional and Regulatory Reform in Taiwan." *Journal of Chinese Law* 4 (1990): 83–100.

Yeh, Jiunn-rong. "An Analysis of Council of Grand Justices Interpretations Imposing Compliance Deadlines." *Proceedings of the National Science Council* 6, no. 1 (1996): 1.

Yoon, Dae-kyu. *Law and Political Authority in South Korea*. Boulder, CO: Westview Press, 1990.

Yoon, Dae-kyu. "New Developments in Korean Constitutionalism: Changes and Prospects." *Pacific Rim Law and Policy Journal* 4, no. 2 (1995): 395–417.

Youm, Kyu-ho. "Press Freedom and Judicial Review in South Korea." *Stanford Journal of International Law* 30 (1994): 1.

Young, Michael K. "Judicial Review of Administrative Guidance: Governmentally Encouraged Consensual Dispute Resolution in Japan." *Columbia Law Review* 84 (1984): 935.

Zakaria, Fareed. "The Rise of Illiberal Democracy." *Foreign Affairs* (Nov./Dec. 1997): 22–43.

Zhao, Suisheng. *Power by Design: Constitution-Making in Nationalist China*. Honolulu: University of Hawaii Press, 1996.

Index

CPSIA information can be obtained at www.ICGtesting.com
Printed in the USA

270144BV00002B/1/A